LORD CHATHAM

LORD CHATHAM

O. A. SHERRARD

———

Lord Chatham

A WAR MINISTER IN THE MAKING

———

THE BODLEY HEAD

First published 1952

Printed in Great Britain by
THE GARDEN CITY PRESS LIMITED, LETCHWORTH, HERTS
for JOHN LANE THE BODLEY HEAD LIMITED,
28 Little Russell St., London, W.C.1

Contents

Contents

List of Illustrations

Preface

Among my earliest recollections is one of my father taking me to visit two spinster great-aunts at West Wickham in Kent—in those days a tiny village. Their house—too large by modern standards, though then regarded as only of medium size—was full of charm and dignity, as I came subsequently to realise. But the charm and dignity of inanimate objects are qualities that make little appeal to boys, and on that occasion the two ladies loomed much more immediately on my horizon. The elder, whom I met first, seemed to me—and I believe was—extremely formidable, and her presence crushed me into a depressed silence. The younger, when she entered, proved to be of a very different cast. In her youth she had been dazzling and in old age still retained the gentleness of beauty without its arrogance. She noticed my gloom and suggested that I should be happier playing in the garden until it was time for tea, and as she pushed me through the door recommended Pitt's Walk as the ideal playground.

I have often puzzled over the reasons for her recommendation. At the time I was disposed to disagree. Pitt's Walk struck me as dark, dismal and dank. It was overhung by tall trees, it was shut in on each side by thick evergreens, and it ran with undeviating decision to nowhere in particular. There was, however, one quality which she may have had in mind—it was mysterious. There was a sense of adventure about it which drew me back to it time and again in spite of its unprepossessing appearance and the disappointment of its terminus. As for its name, I could make neither head nor tail of it. How should I know that the elder Pitt had laid it out for his friend Gilbert West or that he had spent his honeymoon in that very house where I was shortly to have my tea? The name meant nothing to me; nor did it seem significant that when I left Pitt's Walk I returned to Chatham, where my father happened to be stationed.

Yet at Chatham the mystery deepened. I discovered an old red

brick building which went by the name of Fort Pitt, and jumped
to the conclusion—erroneous of course—that it had belonged to
the owner of the Walk. From then onwards I was to find this
puzzling stranger crossing my path again and again—at Hayes,
at Bath, at Oxford, at Curry Rivel and Lyme Regis—until at last
a desire came over me to draw a picture of him in his own times
instead of in mine.

That was long ago and much has happened since—including
the war—to delay achievement, but the desire remains. When I
started I had no doubt that I was trying to write the biography of
England's greatest War Minister. Now I am not so sure, but the
doubt has been overlaid in part by the distressing realisation that
England is remarkably consistent in her treatment of her men of
genius. The elder Pitt may perhaps be no greater than the
Colossus of our own age, perhaps not even his equal, but
the parallel between their lives is striking and not a little
disturbing.

Pitt's life falls naturally into three unequal parts, each concerned with a separate interest, and each standing, so to speak, on
its own. The first part extends from his birth in 1708 to his
dismissal from office in 1755. They were years of struggle, not so
much for recognition of his powers, which he secured at an early
age, as for the opportunity to use them. That part forms the
subject of this volume, which I have called 'A War Minister in
the Making.' The second part covers the period of his triumphant
Ministry, and if ever written may fitly be called 'Pitt and the
Seven Years War'; it stands by itself—a monument of glory for
Pitt and England, with an undercurrent of shame for the faint-
hearts and intriguers. The third part deals essentially with Pitt
and the Empire, when the bunglers and the pettifoggers hemmed
in and suffocated the 'damned old fool' whose advice they did
not understand and were unable to follow. If fate is kind, it may
allow me to tell the remainder of the story.

No one can write a life of the elder Pitt without acknowledging
his great indebtedness to Professor Basil Williams, whose *Life of
William Pitt, Earl of Chatham* is a mine of learning and research.
If in the course of my own researches I have found a few facts
which have escaped his notice, I have borrowed more from him;
and if I have ventured to differ in my conclusions, I have done so
with trepidation. One last involuntary service I must beg of him.

His bibliography is very complete, and there seems no point in reprinting it, or the appropriate part of it, in this book. I would therefore refer those interested to his list. All I have done in my own bibliography is to set out the works from which I have actually quoted, and I have done this largely because the titles have occasionally been abbreviated in the footnotes.

I

BIRTH

The second half of 1708 was full of success for England. In July the Duke of Marlborough won the battle of Oudenarde and in December became master of Lille. In September a combined naval and military expedition captured Minorca. All these victories seemed of great moment, producing much jubilation in this country and many doubts and distractions on the Continent. Amid the hubbub—on the 15th of November, to be precise— Harriet Pitt, the amiable, pretty but rather colourless wife of a minor politician, gave birth to a son at her husband's house in Golden Square, Westminster. Just under a month later—on the 13th of December—and four days after the fall of Lille, the boy was christened at St. James's, Piccadilly, being given the common-place name of William. Compared with the news from the Continent, these domestic events seemed of no consequence. The boy, after all, was only a second son and the fourth child of a family which ultimately grew to be seven, while the victories were not only a source of national pride but also gave hopes of peace after a long war of which the country was tired. Time, however, was to reverse those values. The lustre of the victories was to dim as they were seen to be mere incidents in the sterile and never-ending quarrels of European ambitions, while the boy was to grow into the statesman of a new order, looking beyond Europe to the great world over the seas, and using the petty squabbles of the Continent as the means to mould the mightiest and the noblest of empires.

The boy came of little more than good yeoman stock. Here and there his family had crept beneath the shadow of great names, or at least great titles, but only by marriage or on the distaff side. His own mother, for instance, was the sister of an Irish earl and his grandmother a distant connection of a Scottish peer. More important, and rather nearer, his uncle by marriage came of a titled family and acquired for himself the English earldom of

Stanhope—a great step and one lending much vicarious lustre to the young William, though too late to bring him within the accepted circle. In a world much impressed by the patent of nobility, and in an age overshadowed by the Whig magnates, William Pitt lacked the authentic label. He was not true-blue vintage—and the fact coloured his whole life.

If he was not of the high patrician line, one would like to say that his forebears were at least of gentle birth. But even that is true only to a limited extent. His family was turbulent and coarse, seething with all the wanton vigour of the soil in that most earthy of counties, Dorset. They cultivated the land, buying and selling fields and farms; they owned provincial shops; they aspired to cut a figure in local administration, and one of them was Mayor of Dorchester. Only his great-grandfather had risen above the rough and tumble of country life and the squinthole of the parish pump, adding something of refinement as Rector of Blandford St. Mary.

The Rector had been a younger son, and in the Pitt family cadets had usually the lion's share of genius. So it was natural that Thomas, the third of the Rector's nine children, should have been the channel through which the Pitt blood flowed to its consummation. Thomas was to become notorious. Like many a parson's son, he grew weary of the 'integrity, probity, and simple faith' which in after years he ascribed to his father in a fit of filial piety and on a monument, and as soon as his father was dead, threw decency to the winds to become the nearest approach to a pirate that a shrewd discretion allowed. His trade was that of an 'interloper,' or illegal trespasser on the preserves of the East India Company. He had no vestige of right in law to carry on his interloping trade, but he took the law into his own hands, and was so successful that the company gave up their attempts to suppress him by force, and tried the more subtle method of smothering him with confidence. They appointed him Governor of their Fort St. George. There he ruled with an outstretched arm, till the company, sickening of his insubordination, deprived him of office. None the less he amassed one way or another a great fortune, chief ornament of which was the notorious 'Pitt' diamond,[1] and returned home to become one of the earliest of nabobs.

---

[1] Sold in 1717 to the Regent of France. At the marriage of Louis XV to Marie Leczinski in 1725 it formed the button of the young King's hat. See *Memoirs of a Royal Chaplain*, p. 96.

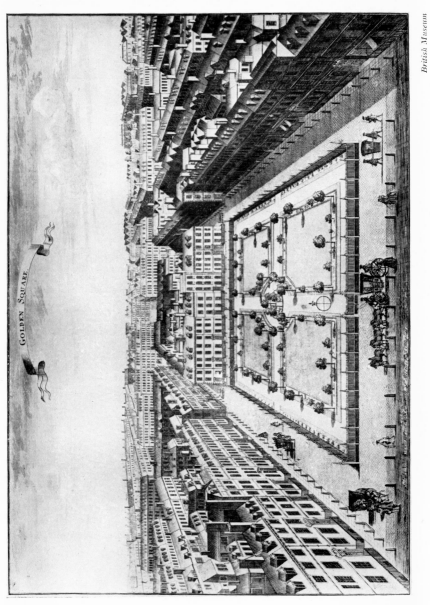

GOLDEN SQUARE AT THE TIME OF PITT'S BIRTH

It is usual to say that William took after his grandfather, and that in the tantrums of the Governor are to be traced the incalculable factors of William's character. But, as so often happens, the usual is incorrect. William differed from his grandfather, that 'roughling, immoral man,' in almost every particular, except sudden daring and high self-confidence. There is no comparison between the irascible freebooter cursing and swearing through life towards the goal of self-aggrandisement, and the high-minded patriot, building an empire in his prime, and toiling in old age to save his country from enemies abroad and at home.

But if there is little in common between the two, there is no doubt that the Governor exercised a profound influence on William's career, perhaps the more profound because it was unconscious. He had inherited to the full the lawless vigour of his stock, and had learnt in India the tricks of ostentation and command. On his return to England he meant to play a leading part in the great world, a part suited to his indomitable energy and in keeping with his experience and wealth. To achieve his end, he embarked on the sea of politics, using his money in the typical eighteenth-century game of borough-mongering. But in spite of money, influence, force of character and undoubted ability, he did not succeed in impressing the political world or making either a name or a party. The fact would be curious, if the reason were not obvious. The Governor was a self-made man, vulgar, ostentatious, loud and brawling, and the ruling classes were more exclusive, and more rightly exclusive, then than now. The early years of the eighteenth century were a period of wild vice and lawlessness. Indeed, the lack of amusements on Sunday was said to be the only sign that the English were a Christian people.[1] The whole age tended to be nasty and brutish, more particularly in the towns. The upper classes, though including many who were great and good, were largely given over to gambling and debauchery; the middle classes, with their essential gravity, must have been more numerous than appears, but so far as influence went were practically non-existent, while the lower classes were riddled with disease and permeated with violence. The laws were partial, winking at the peccadilloes of the great and breeding crimes of desperation among the rabble by their unconscionable harshness. This was the age of Jack Sheppard (executed November 1724) and Jonathan Wild (executed May 1725); this was the age

[1] London in 1710, from the Travels of von Uffenbach, p. 36.

when Hounslow Heath and Finchley Common were the haunts
of highwaymen and Blackheath was infested with footpads; this
was the age when robberies were everyday affairs in the streets of
London, when children were exposed to die in the gutter and
vagabonds were rampant and ruthless. And the age grew worse as
Gin Lane began to prosper in the seventeen-twenties. Fielding and
Hogarth were faithful artists depicting the age in all its filth and
folly. It could hardly get worse, and indeed the violence and villainy were beginning to die of their own excess. The spectacle of
human misery was soon to shock the conscience of a band of
reformers—Thomas Coram, John Wesley, John Howard, Robert
Raikes—whose efforts began the works of charity and human love
which have so changed the whole character of social life.

But for the moment the reformers were to seek, and the herd
remained cut off from the upper classes by something more than
either birth or wealth. The gulf fixed was the greater because it
consisted of an attitude of mind. For the great men of the earth
the mob did not exist when it was quiescent, and became a wild
beast to be shot down when it woke ravenously to life. Even the
large-hearted Henry Fielding could speak of 'wretches very little
removed, either in their sensations or understandings, from wild
beasts.'[1]

The Governor had heaved himself out of the rut, but the upper
ten still looked askance at him. He could flaunt his fine clothes and
broad acres, but the upper ten were in no mood to admit that they
were separated from the mob only by such mundane matters—
which for all their importance were won and lost every night at
Almack's without a thought or a sigh. It was not merely the
outward trappings that made their behaviour so tediously correct
above its inward scandal; that enabled them to carry their
drink like gentlemen, or, if they must be sots, to indulge their
whims behind closed doors; that if it urged them to gamble like
fools, taught them to lose without a wince, and if necessary to
shoot themselves with decency. They were of finer clay, and the
Governor for all his wealth was not of them. They distrusted him;
they accepted him only on sufferance; and the suspicion they
meted out to him, they meted out to his descendants—in lesser
degree, no doubt, but in some degree all the same.

The Governor, in a word, placed his family in a false position.
He would have done so in any event, by the mere fact of his

[1] Fielding. *A Clear State of the Case of Elizabeth Canning*, p. 14.

opulence; but he made assurance double sure by exuding the huckstering spirit of a tradesman wherever he went—even in the royal presence. George I was rash enough to give him an audience, and the old rascal seized the opportunity to extol the merits and cheapness of his diamond! But if the position was false, it also had potentialities. His children, had they possessed the genius, could have made a figure in history. But they had no genius, and after marrying into 'superior' families, came to disagreeable ends. This book is barely concerned with them.

The eldest, Robert, must be mentioned because he was the father of William Pitt, Earl of Chatham. Apart from this glory, which is stupendous, Robert was a colourless man, completely overshadowed by that outrageous buccaneer, the Governor. Robert was never able to assert himself. He disapproved of his father, perhaps was ashamed of him, and possibly for that reason, when he dabbled in politics, played the part of a mild Jacobite to his father's uncompromising Whig. But for all his disapproval, Robert lived on his father, a miserable querulous existence, exposed to the full blast of the Governor's temper, and not even comforted by a goodly inheritance. Robert outlived his father by a year, which was long enough to show that the Governor's wealth had been exaggerated, that some of it had been lost in the South Sea Bubble, and more had been squandered on Robert's thriftless younger brothers. Robert's patrimony was not large, and before the year was out became a subject of litigation among the Governor's children. Robert was a mere channel, and as such may be forgotten.

It was the Governor, not Robert, who produced the money, and so paved the way for William's education, and when the education was complete, it was through the Governor that William received a small competency of £100 per annum, and a pocket borough which gave him a seat in Parliament. William owed to his grandfather all his opportunities, and with them inherited the burden of suspicion and dislike for the parvenu, which is always with us, but in the early eighteenth century was far greater in volume and much deeper in intensity.

B

2

'COWED FOR LIFE'

The first effect of the Governor's money was an education at
Eton. How far this was a benefit must be a matter of speculation.
William himself looked back upon his schooldays with loathing,
and kept his own children at home. He told Shelburne many
years later that he preferred private to public education because
'he scarce observed a boy who was not cowed for life at Eton.'[1]
His biographers usually suggest that the remark, if applicable to
Pitt at all, is so only in the sense that his ill-health cut him off from
the sports and boyish games of his contemporaries and that consequently he was lonely and unpopular. There is not much evidence
—in fact none—that he was lonely and unpopular, nor much
reason for supposing that games held a high place in the school
life of those days, or that such twinges of gout as appeared kept
him from sharing in them. We know from his own letters that he
indulged in birdnesting at 'Eaton School.'[2] He could play cricket
'very well' at Stowe when he was twenty-six,[3] and later in life,
when the gout had made fearful ravages on his constitution, he
was a persistent and confirmed horseman, rising almost from his
sick-bed to canter over the countryside. It is unlikely that gout
was more than a spasmodic handicap to whatever sport William
pursued or wished to pursue at school. But if it is mere conjecture
that Pitt's remark sprang out of ill-health, it is a complete mis-
reading of his life to suppose that the remark is obviously untrue
of himself. There is a very real sense in which William Pitt was
cowed for life; he was driven in upon himself by the superior airs
of the nobility, and his whole life coloured by the resultant
snobbishness. To what extent Eton cowed Pitt can be seen in the
tergiversations of his policy in later life, in his secretiveness, in his

[1] Fitzmaurice. *Shelburne*, I, 72.
[2] To his wife, past seven (1757). Chatham Papers. Record Office.
[3] Letter to Ann, 14 Sept. 1735. Rosebery, p. 80.

inability to join wholeheartedly with others, in his sad depend-
ence on Earl Temple, in his violences, in his deplorable prostra-
tions before the throne, in the misery and degradation of his
nervous breakdown. None the less he is supposed to have made a
mark at school, on the strength partly of a tutor's letter and partly
of some fulsome verses written by his school friend Lyttelton.
But although the tutor was 'never concerned with a young gentleman of so good abilities,' and although Lyttelton thought that
good humour 'to Pitt's genius adds a brighter grace, and' (to
get rhyme if not reason) 'sweetens every charm in Coelia's face,'
the fact remains that at Eton Pitt's scholastic course did not rise
above the normal, and his social career was probably a failure.
His remark to Shelburne did not spring from the memory of
weary hours spent on the classics, but from the bitter taste of
frustration. Eton was a hotbed of young aristocrats, and Pitt's
good humour, which was not a characteristic of his manhood,
was the desperate desire of an outsider to please.

None the less, if Eton was from one point of view wholly and
irretrievably bad, from other points of view it had its uses. The
frustration itself had a positive side; it sharpened William's wits
and taught him how to fend for himself. His one weapon was his
tongue, and he trained it—in persuasion, in invective. At Eton,
too, he formed certain friendships which, like everything in his
life, were markedly various in their results. The Grenvilles and
Lytteltons were great families in the eighteenth century, but for
the future their main distinction must be that certain of their
offspring, chancing to be at Eton with William Pitt, introduced
him into the political world, and so helped to give England one of
her greatest statesmen. Here the Lytteltons' claim ceases, but the
Grenvilles may also take to their comfort that they gave William
his wife and through her the sacred and exquisite pleasures of a
perfect marriage. It was their last and greatest gift—and they
made haste to discount it by deserting him politically. It is not,
perhaps, without significance that the most notable of his school
friends failed or opposed him in Parliament. Fox was his perennial
enemy; Temple and George Grenville denied him one after the
other; Lyttelton was estranged; Charles Pratt proved a broken
reed. Indeed, Pitt's experience of Eton was not satisfying either at
the time or thereafter. Yet it was essential as the ladder to his
fame. The Governor probably had no education worth the name,
and certainly none which gave him the entree to the great world.

As a consequence he spent the greater part of his life acquiring a position, and had no time or opportunity to use it when acquired. Robert had been taught by a reformed Jesuit at Rotterdam, and the result was not encouraging. Eton and the Governor's wealth at least shortened the path, giving William the wider outlook of a rich family, grander connections, influential friends, and a position that was definite, if not very assured.

3

UNIVERSITIES—HOME AND FOREIGN

Pitt left school in the middle of 1726. On the 18th of February 1735 he became Member of Parliament for Old Sarum. Not much is known of the eight and a half intervening years and not much needs to be known. Whatever may be true of others, William Pitt was a prodigy neither as an infant nor as an adolescent. He served a long apprenticeship, and if he matured greatly, he matured slowly. It is however necessary to relate such facts as are known.

In January 1727 he entered Trinity College, Oxford, as a Gentleman-Commoner. But neither Trinity nor Oxford made anything of him. In little more than a year he left, without a degree and with nothing in particular to his credit but some Latin verses written on the death of George I, which still survive to no one's advantage. It is commonly said that his career was cut short by gout, but as he left for another university—Utrecht—the fact may be doubted. An equally plausible reason could be found in the condition of Oxford during the first half of the eighteenth century. That home of lost causes was still losing itself in the bog of Stuart charm, and poking pedantic gibes at the House of Hanover. Scholarship was adrift on a sea of port, and Learning walked unsteadily in the quadrangles. True, Salvation was round the corner, but it was coming in the doubtful guise of John Wesley, whose mixture of method and madness was too nearly akin to Pitt's own genius to attract him. Pitt could have found little that was admirable at his university, even in youth, and nothing that was likely to blossom into his maturity. In politics he was or became a 'Revolution Whig'; in religion he was or became a quiet and sincere Christian, disliking the flummery of Rome and suspecting the effervescence of Dissent. He was not likely to find spiritual comfort or political wisdom in the High Church antics of a Jacobite Oxford. What he may perhaps have picked up in that otherwise unprofitable year was a love of gardens. It is permissible for the son of a later and more reputable Oxford to fancy that William Pitt's soul was endued with grace in Addison's Water Walks, in Christ Church Meadows, in the intoxicating fragrance of the Lime Walk newly made by his own college, and that it was from them he learnt his true, if somewhat undisciplined, love of gardening.

Another and perhaps more potent reason for his departure from Oxford may have been his father's death in May 1727, and the consequent effect on the family income. As the estate was entailed, William's elder brother, Thomas, succeeded. The Pitts were never a united family, and Thomas celebrated his accession to whatever wealth litigation had left by absorbing the greater part of his mother's money—perhaps embezzling would be the truer word. The poor lady struggled for a while, and finding the contest unequal, retired to France, where she died a few years later. She was not in a position to pay for William's university career, and maybe William, who had started with highflown notions, pre-ferred to come down from Oxford before coming down in the world. He could hardly hope for success with his brother on the subject of extravagance, even if he approached him in the diplo-matic spirit in which he had approached his father. Thomas knew all about it; he lived in debt and died in something like destitution, and was not likely, whilst he was robbing his mother, to be very tender towards the flamboyancies of the younger members of the family. Yet, to give him his due, Thomas did contribute towards the expenses of Utrecht, and possibly chose it as cheaper than Oxford. After all, as he was paying the piper, he had the right of calling the tune, and there is no taskmaster like an elder brother.

Be that as it may, William undoubtedly left Oxford at the end of 1727 for Utrecht, and it may be some solace for the less gifted to know that he was abominably seasick on the journey. How long he stayed at his new university is not known for certain, but not more than a couple of years at most. What he learnt in the scholastic line, if anything, is not recorded, or even hinted at in his letters. In other directions he began to taste the world, and found it not unsucculent.

His career at both universities seems to have been merry and cheerful. Most of his biographers note approvingly that he had a bookseller's bill; they omit to note that it is unique and was con-tracted within the first few days of his arrival at Oxford, when the gilt of expansiveness was no doubt still on the gingerbread of good intentions. He may well have been studious at intervals, since in after years he discovered an amazing capacity for taking pains when his interest was engaged, but at no period of his life did he suffer scholarship to overlie wisdom and at all periods he was disposed to let his soaring imagination treat mountains as molehills. Certainly there were other less studious, and probably longer intervals, which were filled with the normal growing pains of 'varsity life. He bought clothes, as witness the bills—more than one—for various articles of apparel, indulging schoolboy dreams of a would-be beau with silken hose and buckled shoon and a regiment of ruffled shirts. He furnished his rooms, no doubt with taste but not without expense, and made a number of high-born friends, well qualified to lead him into trouble. One, his best and dearest, and incidentally a connection—Lord Villiers— was recalled from Utrecht in a hurry, to William's dismay, but not to his surprise; for 'if a little indiscretion arising from too much vivacity be a fault, my Lord is undeniably blameable.'[1] As in later life William was more renowned for vivacity than discretion, one might suppose it was all Lombard Street to a China orange that fortune rather than desert kept him on the Continent. There is no doubt his father had thought him extravagant at Oxford, which is typical of fathers, and seems to have been ingrained in the paternal elements of the Pitt family—William always excepted. But Mr. Pitt may have been justified, for William made no attempt to deny the charge; all he did was to plead that 'you would not attribute it to my extravagance, but to ye Custom of this Place, where we pay for most things too at a high rate'[2]— a plea which does credit to William's faith in his father's indulgence.

Whether the extravagance, such as it was, continued after Mr. Pitt's death cannot be said, but one may guess that it did, partly because his father's death doubled his own small income, raising it from £100 to £200 per annum, partly because he always was extravagant throughout his life—in money no less than in character, ambition and achievement—and partly because after returning from Utrecht he is next found in the early months of 1730 at the family seat of Boconnoc in Cornwall, undergoing a course of retrenchment, which made him inveigh bitterly at 'this cursed hiding place.' It was, naturally, sad to leave the delights of

[1] Rosebery, p. 41.   [2] *Ibid.*, p. 35.

the Continent and the company of 'vivacious' sprigs of nobility for Cornwall and the country clodhoppers.

For just a year he continued to kick his heels, and then on the 9th of February 1731 received a commission in the 1st Dragoon Guards. It is a date to be remembered, for it is the date on which he passed from tutelage to manhood. The great statesman had stepped into the world, and it is not without significance that he stepped into it as a Cornet of Horse. William had been destined for the Church—regarded in those days as a fitting occupation for younger sons—and if his oratory and burning enthusiasm had been poured into ecclesiastical moulds one may well believe that the religious revival of the eighteenth century would have been utterly different, and that spiritual life would have sprung again from the Established Church instead of from the roots of Methodism. William Pitt would never have allowed Wesley to be driven to Dissent—and perhaps the religious life of today would for that reason alone have been the poorer.

But the point is academic. William never entered the Church, nor apparently even wished to. He entered the army, and if ever genius and inclination joined hands in choosing a career, they did in the case of Pitt. His biographers note that he had a bent towards the profession of arms from an early age, and that his uncle Stanhope used to call him 'the young Marshal'; they even hint that his career as a subaltern may have been useful to the future War Minister. It may have been, but it sounds improbable. What is much more true is that Pitt had the heroic cast of mind which goes with the great conquerors of the world. He is known as a statesman, and stands beside Cecil, Walpole and Disraeli. He was, more truly, a general, and should stand beside Cæsar, Marlborough and Napoleon. It makes little difference that he stayed at home to be the brains of his campaigns, and left the actual fighting to others. The great conquerors are not the tacticians on the field, but the strategists, wherever they may happen to be—upon or behind the scenes—not the leaders of armies but the inspirers of men. In English history Pitt was the successor, not of Walpole, but of Marlborough, and he was greater than his predecessor precisely in so far as his strategy was wiser and wider. Marlborough won battles; Pitt conquered an empire.

4

'THIS TERRIBLE CORNET OF HORSE'

William had now joined the army, and was to remain in it for just five and a quarter years. It was a short career, but from some points of view remarkable. The army was not popular. During the reigns of William III and Anne it had been fully occupied abroad, winning honour for itself and renown for England. So long as it continued in those foreign parts, the people would tolerate, and perhaps admire it. They could also forget it, which was even more seductive. For the army was the only effective police force in England, and ever since the ferment of the Glorious Revolution it had been the people rather than the soldiery who were brutal and licentious. Dick Turpin stood higher in the ranks of popular heroes than the Great Duke, and the huzzas of the populace at Tyburn were reserved for Macheath in preference to the Guards who had hunted him down. There was a glamour about the highwayman, whose prey was not the penurious peasant but the bedizened lord, and whose robberies and riotous living brought some colour, however lurid, into the drab lives of the poor. The same could not be said of the soldiers who enforced discipline while they were in the ranks and when they were disbanded swelled the number of cut-throats and murderers beyond endurance. Either way the army was unpopular, and the Opposition challenged its very existence year by year in the House of Commons, protesting that a standing army was subversive of the liberties of England.

This aura of disfavour was still glowing, though perhaps more faintly, when Pitt received his commission. Perhaps he was not aware of the popular distaste; he was not yet, by many years, the Great Commoner. But, aware or not, he entered his profession with all the fervour of youth and genius. Later in life he told Shelburne that there was not a military book which he had not read during those five years.[1] He may have been exaggerating in

---

[1] Fitzmaurice. *Shelburne*, I, 73.

fact, but not in spirit. Pitt was enthusiastic. If he did not dream of
Alexander and Cæsar he may well have dreamt of Marlborough,
whose body had not yet been ten years in the grave and whose
Duchess was still jerking tempestuous if unconnected strings.
At least he must have hoped to emulate his uncle, Earl Stanhope,
or his colonel, Lord Cobham. He was full of his own peculiar
brand of startling ambition and confident ebullience when he
entered the profession of his heart's desire, and found—unutter-
able boredom.

The army was more than unpopular. In the long years of peace
it had become a sheltered trade, with nothing to do, and no
knowledge of life. Pitt found himself snatched away from the wit
and laughter of London to something even worse than Boconnoc.
Ennui descended upon him as he tried to fraternise with the stocks
and stones of the Northampton mess. He was sorry for himself,
as he sampled their tightly buttoned minds, and not much happier
as he tested the sluggish looseness of their living. What sustenance
was there for his genius or for his delectation? There was drink;
there was 'muzzy conversation'; there was Dolly, the barmaid,
'who young at the bar is just learning to score.' He was drearily
unhappy, and a little ashamed of himself as he tried to be an
inarticulate young subaltern imagining that he was draining life
to the dregs. 'What must I do?' he wrote to his favourite sister and
confidante, Ann, 'my head is not settled enough to study, nor my
heart light enough to find amusement in doing nothing.' He would
be glad enough to fall in love, if Dolly were not the only resource,
and he half bamboozled himself into thinking he had. 'I shall
every Post go near to waft a sigh from Quarters to the Bath,
which you shall rally me very prettyly upon, suppose me in Love,
laugh at my cruel fate a little, then bid me hope for a Fair wind
and better weather.' But it was all airy nonsense, with a touch of
self-pity. There was no Dulcinea as yet—only flirtations with the
giggling Dolly, and perhaps a faint half thought of Molly
Lyttelton, his friend's sister, a girl 'not quite despicable' with her
'gentle Impertinencies and sportly Sollicitations.' It was not much
and the ennui returned. 'My spirits flag.'[1]

But not his ambitions. The empty hours gave plenty of time
for thinking about the future. What Pitt thought must remain a
sealed book, but one or two hints survive, and the curious fact
is that the quality uppermost in his mind in these early years was

[1] Rosebery, p. 64.

prudence—the quality one might expect so long as the influence of Eton was strong upon him; the quality which tended to grow one-sidedly throughout his life, hampering and clogging his ardent spirit, so that his genius came only in swift flashes of glory through long nights of sad inhibition and sulky reluctance. There were none of the sudden heats of youth in Pitt, no impulsive snatching at rainbow dreams, no headstrong flouting of authority. Prudence and interest were his watchwords, both for himself and in his advice to his favourite sister, Ann—prudence in action, which is surprising in a young man, and prudence in love, which is intolerable in anyone. At Utrecht while still a mere boy he had jeered loftily at Lyttelton's infatuation for his eldest sister, Harriet—'Lyttelton prevented you in ye account of his own Madness'[1]—but now that he was a precocious young man 'prudence' was intervening, and when his sister Ann became a Maid of Honour in 1733 and rather tremulously asked her brother for advice, he told her, sagely enough, to dismiss from her mind the alarming popular conceptions of Court life for a more sane and balanced view, and then proceeded to lecture her on modesty and prudence, and the wisdom of placating the god of love, who was a power given to exacting vengeance. And when shortly afterwards he fell a victim himself to the charms of a French mademoiselle, the point which impressed itself insistently on his mind was her lack of birth. 'Elle n'a point de titre,' he wrote to Ann, 'ni de grand nom qui impose; et c'est là le diable.'[2] His prudence was unexceptionable, for as he soon came to realise, 'c'etoit de ces flammes passageres'; it also paid, for he was destined not only to marry very happily but very well. Only, it is a little depressing in a dashing Cornet of Horse!

It is impossible to say over what country his thoughts ranged, but judging after the event, such insistence on prudence, such harping on interest, could only spring from a mind so intensely ambitious that it was prepared even on the threshold of life to walk warily, to weigh measures, and to advance step by ordered step to the preordained goal—and incidentally a mind expecting more than a little opposition.

Patience seems to have been near snapping point after two years of Northampton, for in 1733 Pitt left England for a prolonged tour on the Continent lasting from May till the end of the year. It was in the course of this tour that he met the untitled lady of

---

[1] Rosebery, p. 42.   [2] *Ibid.*, p. 73.

France at Besançon and forgot her again at Luneville. Otherwise the tour was uneventful, though it had its uses many years later in the knowledge it had given him of the French tongue. If there was one part of his military career which was truly helpful to the future Minister it was this leisurely tour, which enabled the Secretary of State of later years to discard interpreters and to deal at first hand with the diplomats of France, deciding for himself the exact degree of their sincerity and the exact language in which to reply. The knowledge which made this possible was perfected at Paris, where he could do nothing but 'run up and down and see . . . the variety of fine sights which have engaged me'; at Besançon, famed city of Pitt's calf love; at Marseilles, where he realised that parting was such sweet sorrow; at Montpelier and Luneville, where he spent the winter forgetting his love; and then in the course of wanderings through Lyons, and Geneva, along the Rhine to Strasbourg and Lorraine. He returned home some time in 1734, and was stationed at Newbury.

By this time, and especially whilst the glow of foreign travel was upon him, he appears to have found the tedium of military life too great. At all events when next authentic light is turned upon him he is busily engaged in the preliminaries of a parliamentary career. Brother Thomas had not been idle in the last few years, and with the boroughs inherited from the Governor in his pocket, was becoming notorious, if not particularly famous. One of his boroughs, Old Sarum, was placed at William's disposal, and on the 18th of February 1735 he was duly elected.

5

THE POLITICAL BACKGROUND

Pitt entered Parliament barely forty-seven years after the Glorious Revolution. Time in those days was much slower of foot and memories much longer than they are today. Men had leisure to ponder over the past and recollection was still one of the quiet pleasures of human life. In such an age forty-seven years could not obliterate the overwhelming fact of the Revolution. It had been the beginning of a new epoch, a line of demarcation not merely between the old and the new, but almost between the impossible and the actual. In 1735 'pre-revolution' connoted something even more shadowy and unreal than 'pre-war' does today. The revolution had marked the end of one dynasty and the beginning of two new dynasties—both foreign. There had been, first, Dutch William, and then, after the brief interlude of Anne, there had been German George. Neither was, in any real sense of the word, popular, both depending for their crown in the last resort on the unpopularity of James II and a hatred of the Roman religion. This break with the past was kept continually before the public eye by a variety of factors. There were, in the first place, the incalculable activities of the two Pretenders, culminating in the '15 and the '45; there was the preoccupation of William with the Continent, which altered the whole trend of English politics; there was the hankering after Hanover felt by the first two Georges to the dismay of Ministers and the disgust of the people; and perhaps most important of all, there was the deliberate policy of Sir Robert Walpole.

Walpole was the incarnation of that Whig oligarchy which, making the most of Bolingbroke's hesitations at the end of Queen Anne's reign, had invited George I into England with much the same blandness of smile as that with which the spider invites the fly into its parlour. The Whig magnates saw with vivid clearness the possibilities of the situation—a dull German princeling, unable to speak English, reluctant to leave Hanover, distrusting

29

the Tories who appeared to be Jacobites, and wholly dependent on the Whigs who had rallied to his side and given him his crown. Here were the makings of an absolutism entirely after their own heart. The Revolution Settlement had done away with the Divine Right of Kings and in its place the Whig magnates proposed to set up their own Right. Their efforts, as it happened, led them into the disaster of the South Sea Bubble, which ought to have exploded them. But they survived, partly because the Tories were in no condition to seize their opportunity, partly because the Whigs had a genius amongst them capable of calming even the South Seas, for all the blots on his own reputation. Walpole picked up the broken bits and entrenched himself in power so successfully that he remained there for twenty-one years. But he continued the general scheme, merely narrowing the Whig oligarchy into himself. The other Whig magnates he brushed contemptuously aside, leaving them to fight among themselves in numberless small and shifting factions. With the Tories he took another line; he did not brush them aside; he did not leave them to fight among themselves; he damned them simply and effectively by calling them Jacobites—pre-revolutionary, archaic, antiquated; traitors to England's Crown, to England's Religion, to England's Destiny. It was not true, but they were lost in a maze and Walpole was determined that they should never get out of it. It was his deliberate and ruthless policy, wholly effectual from his own point of view, but not for the ultimate good of the country nor for the orderly growth of the constitution. Walpole made himself, by this simple expedient, a dictator not far removed from the modern type but much more cleverly disguised. Until Walpole, the King had been the head of the Government in more than a conventional sense. He had presided at the Council Meetings; he had determined policy; he had been his own Prime Minister, forming the nodal point of the Cabinet. The Ministers had been in every sense of the word the King's Servants, reporting to him, receiving their orders from him and carrying out his wishes in Parliament. They could of course give advice, and since the Glorious Revolution their moral position had been the stronger, since the King was no longer absolute, but constitutional, ruling at the request and under the ultimate authority of the people as represented in Parliament. But, if his powers had been circumscribed, they still existed. It was the King and not his Ministers who ruled. With the advent of George I the position altered. It was useless for a Hanoverian who knew no English to preside over the meetings of Ministers who knew no German. So the Council was left without a head, and Walpole would have been forced to take the lead, if he had not intended from the first to take a great deal more. He became automatically Prime Minister, and was doubtless chagrined to find that his courtesy title was twisted into Sole Minister, and became a reproach. Yet Sole Minister he most certainly was, and of his own deliberate policy. He brooked no rival among the Whig magnates, and one by one ousted all the Ministers who had a spark of ability—Carteret went in 1724, Townshend in 1730, Chesterfield was dismissed in 1733, Pulteney had long since been routed. His own Whig party was controlled by an admixture of bribery and execution—the mediocre were given sinecures and titles, the able were put down from their seats. As for the Tory Opposition, Walpole's methods were almost Chinese in their refined cruelty. The rank and file were stupefied by the label of Jacobite, and the leader, Bolingbroke, was hamstrung by having his attainder reversed, while still being debarred from the House of Lords. So long as he was out of Parliament, he could not be more than a shadow, striving to inspire subordinates who would *ipso facto* have ceased to be his mouthpiece if they had been able to speak for themselves with a tithe of his own brilliance and authority. It was a hopeless task, and Bolingbroke retired despairing to France in 1735. The consequence was that for the best part of the century there was no true Opposition, and its place was taken by a shifting quicksand of Whig malcontents, combining and dissolving without policy or principle, and finding themselves for ever frustrated by something which they could neither understand nor define, but which in fact was the absence of an official Opposition. They attempted blindly to rectify this lack, each in his own way. Pitt wanted to abolish 'faction' and set up a 'National Government'—a method which succeeded to admiration for a brief and enthralling period. Burke on the other hand boldly created an Opposition by inventing the King's Friends, thereby adding one more element to the confusion. Wilkes worked hard to turn the Scotch into a reach-me-down Opposition, and Grenville almost harder to use the colonies for the same ends. But of this more in its right place. In 1735 the mischief was not complete. At that time there appeared to be a real Opposition because Bolingbroke had managed to create a

temporary coalition between the Whig malcontents and the
Tories. Though neither element of the coalition was easy at the
marriage, both gained enormously from it. The Whig malcontents secured at least the broad semblance of genuine Opposition,
while the Tories obtained a status and a footing on something
less shaky than alleged high treason. Yet it was in keeping with
the topsy-turvy character of the age that fundamentally Walpole's
position became the less vulnerable as Bolingbroke's efforts
succeeded; for the sole binding element of the Opposition was
antagonism to the Minister, not the presentation of an alternative
policy or even of an alternative leader. There was nothing here
to shake the King's confidence in Walpole or to combat Walpole's
own system of bribery. On the contrary, the placemen and pensioners were more firmly wedded to their source of income; the
politically minded became hesitant and uncertain and the more
serious thinkers were discouraged and abashed. Had Walpole
when he brought forward his Excise scheme in 1733 been faced
by a homogeneous Opposition backed by some talent and headed
by a parliamentarian, he might well have been defeated before
Pitt entered the House; but in fact he was faced by a mixed and
suspicious Opposition backed by very little talent and led by the
echo of a voice, and so he survived.

But the constitutional aspect of his time and government
probably entered little, or not at all, into Walpole's mind. His
main preoccupation was to adapt his policy to the needs of the
age. He realised more profoundly than anyone else the actual
situation of the country. England had been utterly exhausted by
Marlborough's wars, and it was hardly satisfactory that her
stupendous efforts and resounding victories on the Continent
should have brought her precisely nothing except a promise from
France, not needed and never fulfilled, to destroy the fortifica-
tions of Dunkirk. There were, of course, other gains—Gibraltar,
Minorca, Newfoundland, Nova Scotia and a few settlements on
Hudson Bay—but some of these were captured early in the war
by other commanders than Marlborough, and all could have been
both captured and retained without undue exertion or expense
and without tramping the fields of Flanders. Still less satisfactory
perhaps was the thought that these small and scattered acquisitions
solved nothing, not even their eventual ownership, since their
recapture might easily be attempted overseas or their return
demanded as the outcome of a fresh continental struggle. The

Treaty of Utrecht (1713) had been necessary to end a meaningless war, but it had not been glorious. In making it England had deceived and deserted her allies, if she had not actually betrayed them—and all apparently for a few outlying rocks and the right— legal, not moral—to ship negro slaves to Spanish America and to send a single trade ship once a year to Portobello.

It was not surprising that Walpole, Whig though he was, looked askance at his own party's foreign policy, which had produced such poor returns for so stupendous an outlay. He would have nothing to do with continental entanglements, but would pursue peace so that England might have time to retrench and recuperate. And 'retrench' meant something very specific. The Treaty of Utrecht had been followed by the usual economic troubles of exploded wars. The disbanded heroes of a hundred battles had forgotten the arts of peace and almost of manhood; they had lived too long like children, fed and clothed by a paternal Government and marching to and fro in something not unlike schoolgirl crocodiles. Now the heyday of victorious campaigns was over; they had seen the world and they had tasted blood, but they had not acquired a competence or anything that could be called a trade. They ceased to be heroes or even soldiers and became problems when they did not become highwaymen. The sailors who had captured Gibraltar and Minorca and swept the enemy's trade off the seas were on another footing altogether. They had been pressed from the merchant vessels to the men-of- war, where they had continued their lawful calling, subject only to occasional fights. If they were paid, it was for sailing ships over the seas, as they had done before and would continue to do thereafter. It was easy for them, once they were discharged, to return to the merchant marine. But then they were not by any means so numerous as the soldiers. Meanwhile, what of the home front? What of the fortunes made and lost by contractors and purveyors and manufacturers? That too had its aftermath. The spirit of easy wealth infected all men; the restless itch conceived and gave birth to credulity till at last the monstrous South Sea Bubble spread its miasmic rainbow hues for one dazzling moment and burst. Chaos followed the Bubble, and Walpole followed chaos. There could be no cure but time and trade—time to wind up the bankruptcies, and trade to restore the broken treasuries.

There was a further reason for peace. The new dynasty was not yet firmly settled on the throne and the Pretenders, old and young,

C

were very visible across the Channel. So long as peace lasted, their menace was a mere gesture; to be crushed as easily as the '15, provided a strong Government were in the saddle. But if war came, their powers of mischief would increase a hundredfold. It was not the Pretenders nor yet the House of Stuart that distressed Walpole. Nor, one may guess, was this rough, loose-living, loud-mouthed, cynical country squire much concerned with matters of religion. He may have preferred the Protestant Succession—he certainly worked for it; he may have distrusted Rome as obnoxious to his robust common sense. But his rejection of the Pretenders had nothing, at bottom, to do with either Scottish ancestry or Romish faith. He would have accepted James III as readily as George I but for two considerations. The first was the position occupied by himself and the Whig party, whose downfall must follow the return of James. The second, and one may believe the more potent factor, was the inevitable war which must have preceded or followed a return of the old dynasty. The country as a whole did not want the Stuarts, who were dependent for their restoration on foreign, or at least Scottish, help. If they returned the Union might go; the Continental War might revive; there must be internal conflict; there could be no advantage. And Walpole determined to run no risk.

This ambition to avoid war made his path the more thorny. The first two Georges were by preference Electors of Hanover before they were Kings of England. It seems a curious preference even to the meek Englishman of today, but to the Englishman of the eighteenth century it must have been humiliating as well. They had offered this stout, stolid and somewhat stupid German what they secretly believed to be an incomparable gift, something which, if good manners and eighteenth-century good sense did not forbid, they could describe in Shakespeare's immoderate language as this other Eden, demi-paradise, and so on. And he had accepted it, without enthusiasm, more as a burdensome duty than as a distinguishing honour. Like Lot's wife the fellow was for ever looking back, though unlike her there was no attic salt about him. He seemed to be sighing after the fat fraus of Herren-hausen and the tinpot parades of Hanover. Almost he had put the gift into his breeches' pocket without looking at it—and England felt humiliated. But Walpole felt something more. For him the problem was not to salve his own feelings or England's pride, but to prevent the King from dragging England into continental politics. The Elector must have felt a well-nigh irresistible temptation to brandish his mighty royal sceptre in the face of wrangling princelings and petty potentates. His outlook was largely Hanoverian, and Walpole had to restrain him as best he could, incidentally jeopardising his own position in the process.

Whilst the King was one problem, the people were another. The more prosperous they grew the more they chafed at what seemed to be a tame policy, particularly as regards Spain. The Spanish-American colonies were a fruitful field for trade, and Walpole, fearful of going too far, did not adopt the forceful, imperious attitude demanded by the merchants. He could not secure all they claimed by negotiation, and he was not prepared to threaten war. All he could hope to do was to satisfy the public at large by a course which produced prosperity.

For twenty-one years he was successful, but looking back it is possible to see the weak spots in his system. In a sense the greatest blot was his thoroughness and consistency. Times change, and with them policies should change too. But Walpole never changed. From beginning to end he pursued his familiar methods in dealing with the Whigs; from beginning to end he proscribed the Tories; from beginning to end he held the Scotch at arm's length; from beginning to end he curbed the King's Hanoverian sympathies and maintained peace with France; from the beginning and until he was forced by the people into war, he continued endless and seemingly aimless negotiations with Spain; from beginning to end he played with the Dissenters, promising an eventual relief from disabilities which he never intended to give, and in the one sphere where he made an effort to secure a needed reform—the Excise scheme—he retreated from the field. Walpole's policy was as inflexible as it was essentially negative. Consistency is often and perhaps always a personal virtue, but there are times when it becomes a public disaster. There can be little doubt that in certain respects Walpole delayed the full recovery of the country by his inflexibility. This fact at once explains and justifies the slowly gathering opposition which finally threw him from power.

6

THE OPPOSITION

At the end of 1734 when Pitt first seriously thought of entering Parliament, Walpole had been in power for nearly fourteen years, and his position might well have seemed unassailable. It is true that only the previous year he had been forced to abandon his Excise scheme, but although the Bill was dropped, Walpole had weathered the storm, and had even felt strong enough to dismiss from their offices and regiments a number of nominal supporters who had helped to thwart him on this favourite point. In the general election of 1734 he had been returned with a majority nearly as big as before, and the Court showed no signs of withdrawing their confidence. It was the Opposition, not the Government, who from high hopes were dashed and dispirited; it was Bolingbroke, not Walpole, who was on the point of throwing up the sponge and departing for France. Such in broad outline was the state of the two parties when Pitt had to choose which camp he would join—the triumphant Minister or the dejected Opposition. He decided to oppose.

Bearing in mind the facts as they must have presented themselves to Pitt, and remembering his tendency to prudence and calculation, the choice seems strange. It is not made less so by the *ex post facto* knowledge that Walpole remained in power for a further seven years. And his biographers, relying on Lord Camelford (Pitt's nephew), add to the mystery by declaring that Pitt's abilities were so well known before he entered the House, and his political tendencies so notorious that Walpole offered Pitt's elder brother, Thomas, 'any terms not to bring him or his brother-in-law, Mr. Lyttelton, into Parliament.' Still more strange, Thomas Pitt, the eternal debtor, and the never-very-loving brother, rejected this blank cheque backed by the First Lord of the Treasury—presumably on principle, since he could not have done it for profit and does not seem to have done it for love. It sounds improbable. What then is the truth in this sea of doubt? Was our young Cornet of Horse nodding? And if not, what guided his choice?

It is better first to clear away the rubbish which obscures the view, and there can be little doubt that Lord Camelford's evidence is pure rubbish, in the form in which it is presented. Prime Ministers may possibly, though perhaps not probably, keep their eyes on brilliant schoolboys and undergraduates who are likely to enter the House. With so many pocket boroughs in the family there was at least a chance that Pitt would be returned—though not perhaps a good chance seeing that he was destined for the Church—but, as we have seen, there is no reason to suppose that he shone either at school or university, still less that he displayed strong political tendencies. When young men first pass into the world they are apt to be forgotten, however brilliant they may have been as boys. If Walpole, therefore, was unlikely to note William Pitt at Eton or Oxford, he was still more unlikely to note Cornet Pitt at Northampton or Newbury. Nor, if Walpole's eyes were glued upon him, is there reason to suppose that small garrison towns, well away from the capital, offer much scope for displaying parliamentary prowess. Even so, Pitt was abroad during 1733, falling in and out of love and learning French; the memory of his previous brilliance, if it had appeared, would have dimmed and died, and Walpole would have known little or nothing of his latest views. The fact is, of course, that Walpole neither knew nor cared what Pitt's abilities or tendencies were. What he or his henchman, the Duke of Newcastle, did know was that Thomas Pitt was proposing to fill the pocket boroughs at his disposal with his own relations, who might or might not be Government supporters, but were certainly young, unknown and untried. The 1734 election was important because of the trouble over the Excise Bill; no one could say for certain how it would go or what would happen, but at least Walpole and Newcastle were doing their best to fill the new House with trusted and steady friends. Of course they urged Thomas Pitt to let them have his spare seats. We know from William's own letters to his sister Ann that they nearly succeeded, and we get an interesting sidelight on Newcastle's electioneering methods. Someone sent Thomas Pitt a message through his sister Harriet suggesting that Harrison, who had been Member for Old Sarum in the previous House, should be re-elected on condition that he paid William Pitt a sum of money as compensation for his disappointment.

Thomas clearly turned the suggestion over in his mind, but did
not feel very strongly about it because the blank cheque of Lord
Camelford's imagination backed by the First Lord of the Treasury
was after all only a modest and hypothetical solatium from Mr.
Harrison to brother William. William himself was indignant,
not so much at the thought of losing the seat as at the meagreness
of the offer. 'I thought it indeed,' he wrote to Ann, 'so monstrous,
that ye best way of treating it was not to vouchsafe it any answer';
and again 'it appears to me, as it did at first, of no consequence,
and deserves being spoken of only for the Impertinence of it. I
am persuaded it is no more than an absurd sudden thought of ye
Coll's. . . . My Brother's Interest no doubt do's not persuade
him to such a bargain between Harrison and me. . . . I am very
much deceived if I hear anything more of it.'[1] He was not
deceived, and did not hear anything more—but the episode gave
him posthumously a reputation in 1734 which he certainly did not
enjoy at the time. What does emerge, quite unmistakably, is the
calculating spirit typical of Pitt at this period. He was fully aware
of the difference between the blank cheque in Thomas's pocket
and the solatium in his own, and he was quite capable of weighing
his chances.

If Pitt was not entering Parliament as an opponent whom
Walpole particularly feared, he was none the less entering as a
member of the Opposition, and, as will be seen, lost no time in
making his attitude clear. His reasons for opposing are not
known, but at least some of them may be guessed on general
principles, and others may be inferred from his actions. Youth is
a time of generous revolt; dreams come with such vivid reality,
and youth neither knows nor pauses to ask whether others have
seen the same visions and found them impracticable. There are
loyalties and friendships which still bear the marks of immortality
—not yet known to be painted in water colours and liable to run.
There are hopes and aspirations, big with a self-confidence as
touching in its hesitations as it is ingenuous in its arrogance. All
combine to flout authority, to blacken the ills we know of and to
brighten the mirages that we imagine. Pitt admitted in later years
that had he been in Parliament in 1733, when Walpole introduced
his Excise Bill, 'he would probably have been induced by the
general and groundless clamour to have joined with those that
opposed it.' He did in fact join with those who had opposed it

[1] Rosebery, pp. 74-6.

1ST VISCOUNT COBHAM 1675–1749

from the oil painting by J. B. VAN LOO

eighteen months earlier, and were now hoping to exploit the victory they had won. Perhaps he might have chosen differently if Walpole's defeat had been more crushing, or if the old Minister had not bared his teeth and snapped back at the crowd pressing round him. For amongst those whom Walpole had angrily dismissed were more than one of Pitt's friends. Most important of these martyrs was his colonel—Lord Cobham—important, not for his own merits, but for the influence which his dismissal was likely to have upon Pitt.

Richard Temple, Viscount Cobham, was an old soldier of Marlborough's wars, where, like Gilbert's House of Lords, he did nothing in particular and did it very well. A grateful country loaded him with wealth and honour, and he felt it incumbent on him to continue his life of exemplary uselessness. Peace offered the retired veteran two battlefields—the warfare of words and the strife of politics. He absorbed them both, becoming the Maecenas of the Augustan age of literature and a sturdy, if slightly muddle-headed, supporter of the Whigs. Unfortunately the two activities tended to clash, since Walpole, whose reading was mainly confined to his gamekeeper's reports, neither sought nor encouraged literary aspirants, so that one by one the great men of letters gathered to the Opposition, absorbing in their varying degrees the twisted venom of Swift and Pope. It was pleasant for them to take their ease in the stately halls and among the spacious gardens of Stowe, and they repaid their magnificent host with discreet flattery. Not that it amounted to much; even Pope could do no more than dub him 'brave Cobham,' a colourless description that no doubt covers an undeserved contempt. But the literary dripping must have helped to fry Walpole's goose, and by 1733 Cobham was sufficiently emancipated to oppose the Excise Bill. Walpole retaliated by depriving him of his colonelcy. Here was something which Cobham could understand. He had been wounded in his pride, if he was not touched in his honour, and the sword must be drawn. 'Brave' Cobham did not hesitate. All his wealth and influence were at once thrown into the scale of opposition, and since numbers count in politics as well as in war, his energies were turned to a recruiting campaign. He had in his own family and connections the makings of a respectable party. There were his five Grenville nephews, who were one day to succeed to his estates and titles—Richard, who was to become

Earl Temple; George, the budding author of American independence; James, who may perhaps be styled 'the Less'; Henry, who
was no greater; and Thomas, who served his country in the navy
far better than his brothers did in Parliament, and died in action
obscurely but none the less honourably in 1747. Then there were
the Lyttelton nephews and nieces, and through the Lytteltons a
connection with the Pitts, since Thomas Pitt had married
Christian Lyttelton. They were all roped in, and partly by their
position, partly by their merits, won a considerable notoriety,
being known by various nicknames, such as the Boy Patriots, the
Cobham Cubs, the Brotherhood, the Cousinhood, and so on.

Pitt's whole future was coloured by this sudden emergence of
a new party. He was bound to be attracted, for not only was youth
calling to youth, not only was friendship and even relationship
engaged, but the mainspring of action was something in the
nature of a crusade. It was notorious that Walpole ruled by
corruption, and now he had added coercion and cruelty. Officers,
and more particularly Pitt's own colonel, were being deprived of
their commissions, perhaps of their livelihood, not for military
sins, not for want of ability, but simply because of political votes.
It was the negation of the Glorious Revolution; it was the end of
freedom; it was the triumph of Prerogative. Pitt's soul was moved,
and he threw in his lot with his friends.

Not that he flung caution to the winds. There had been a time,
one may well believe, when Pitt would have acted differently.
There had been, and still was, some connection between his
family and the Court. His father Robert had been a minor Court
official; his sister Ann was a maid-in-waiting. William had
encouraged Ann to walk circumspectly at Court and make good
her footing, no doubt with the thought that she might be useful
to him. All that, however, had been two years ago, and the waters
had since been troubled. Ann had attached herself to Lady Suffolk,
a mistress of whom the King had lately grown a trifle weary, and
it was just at this point of time that Lady Suffolk retired from
the Court. 'I foresee,' the judicious William wrote to Ann, in
November 1734, 'a very disagreeable consequence to you from
this change, which is, that your Friendship with Her may be
charg'd upon you as a crime, and what was before a support may
now be a prejudice to you.'[1] If Ann was thus likely to prove a
broken reed at Court, Thomas had been currying favour with

[1] Rosebery, p. 76.

Frederick, Prince of Wales, the embryonic leader of the Opposition. Family interests, therefore, joined with the pull of friendship and military loyalties to decide Pitt's politics. He was bound to oppose; he was bound to join the party of youth and progress, ready to endure rebuffs for the moment in the expectation of honours and power when the Prince of Wales succeeded his elderly and by no means robust father.

7

THE BACKGROUND OF FOREIGN AFFAIRS

There was a further reason. How far it can be fairly ascribed to Pitt at this precise juncture must remain a matter of doubt, but beyond question it grew rapidly in importance. And it was this— Pitt was fundamentally opposed to Walpole's foreign policy; he was no less fundamentally opposed to the whole Whig conception of foreign politics, which in certain respects differed from Walpole's.

To appreciate the significance of this fact, it is essential to realise that politics in Pitt's days differed utterly from politics in this twentieth century. Even the terms employed today can hardly be applied to the eighteenth century without doing violence to the terms or injustice to the century. Nor is this difference to be found solely or mainly in the great constitutional points which were obviously agitating then and equally obviously have been settled since. The problem of the royal prerogative can be appreciated by a generation which has savoured the problem of the House of Lords; and the slow emergence of the Premier's authority presents no real difficulty for those who have seen the birth of a Minister for Co-ordination, or even have interested themselves in the Head of the Civil Service. The essential difference lies in the scope and emphasis of parliamentary affairs.

Today home affairs, and specially social legislation, have the pre-eminence. Foreign affairs are supposed to be above party, and except at crucial intervals are not only a sealed book, but a wearisome and uninteresting book. In the eighteenth century the position was reversed. Home affairs did not consist of social legislation. The country believed in individualism—a healthy, wholehearted individualism that gave full scope for talents to rise to the top—a strong and selective individualism that, having obtained power for itself, used that power to assist friends and relations. It was at bottom a preference for personal liberty over Government control which defeated Walpole's Excise scheme. The country did not understand his aim, but they were running no risk of a totalitarian state or the regimentation of eternal planning. They asked Government, if it must interfere, to give them the big prizes of a lottery, not the dead level of a forced and untrue equality. So it came about that home affairs took the form of bewildering and baffling manœuvres to secure power and extend patronage. The appointment to bishoprics and the distribution of sinecures were the eighteenth-century equivalent of social legislation, and the difference of principle between the parties—if it can be said to have existed—was simply the difference in the names placed on the lists for promotions, peerages and pensions. The results were not very pleasant, though perhaps no nastier than the abuses of the present day. It is undoubtedly repellent to find how speedily the news of illness spread. Let a dean, or a bishop, or even a minor canon, retire to bed, and an ugly host of clerical vultures crowded the doorstep of the dispenser of patronage; begging letters flowed in, unguarded promises were recalled, and the whole machinery of influencing the Powers that Be was put in motion. Not that the Church stood alone in this ambition for preferment. Yearning, not loving, hearts followed with deep interest the health of the owners of knightly ribbons. And the decease of any meagre placeman or obscure tide-waiter was known to a vast horde of applicants almost before it was known to the Angel of Death. So far-sighted is greed.

But if home affairs then tended to be no more than scrabbling in a bran tub, foreign affairs gave point and substance to the political instincts of the day. So far from being above or beyond party, they were the basis of party, the one unmistakable dividing line. Something of this eighteenth-century attitude towards politics can be inferred by those who feel strongly about the United Nations, or a policy of isolation, or even one of the numbered Internationales, if they will bear in mind that in the eighteenth century the problems of Lake Success would have swamped and ousted all the problems of unemployment, education, social reform and the like, and that those problems would have been not unlike the clash of twentieth-century ideologies! After all, the original cleavage between Whig and Tory sprang out of divergent views of foreign alliances, out of the question whether England should side with France or Austria. It was deepened by a wider divergence—the rival claims of a colonial or a continental policy. Governments rose and fell on these issues; they never rose or fell on matters which today would be called matters of domestic interest, because for all practical purposes there were no such matters. Even the few burning subjects such as religious toleration were tacked on to the wider—or narrower—question of the royal succession, which was rather more deeply involved in foreign affairs than any other question. 'We shall find,' Pitt said or was made to say by his reporter in March 1742, 'that our treasure has been exhausted, not to humble foreign enemies, or obviate domestic insurrections; not to support our allies, or suppress our factions; but for ends which no man, who feels the love of his country yet unextinguished, can name without horror —the purchase of alliances and the hire of votes, the corruption of the people and the exaltation of France.'[1]

Pitt was indicting Walpole's administration, and the indictment is not very interesting, but this summing up of the uses to which Walpole had put the revenues of the country expresses the general views of the times. Clearly Pitt thought, or was made to say, that public money should be spent on the army first and the police force next. In contradistinction to this ideal, Walpole had squandered the money on foreign subsidies and the purchase of constituencies. Whether Pitt actually used these words may be doubted—reporting had less of mechanical precision and more of fine art then than now, especially when the reporter was Dr. Johnson writing in his own room—but at least they could be ascribed to him without exciting wonder. It would be impossible today, or if possible would take some different form. The purchaser of constituencies for instance would descend from honest barter with a borough-monger to dishonest promises of a proletarian heaven.

Perhaps the most curious point is that foreign affairs should have so dominated an age when travel was slow and dangerous, when telephones and telegrams were non-existent, and newspapers were badly served and irregularly issued. One would have supposed that such conditions would have forced politicians to found their views on prejudice and intuition, and the public on rumour. Yet on the whole the country was amazingly well-informed, the general ideas were clear and the interest intense. True, the information as a rule was tantalisingly incomplete, but

[1] Speech, 9th March 1742, as reported by Dr. Johnson in the *Gentleman's Magazine*, May 1743.

generally it went to the heart of affairs, and was not distracted by too much police news or an excess of beauty queens.

Parliament's absorption in foreign affairs decided the nature of the House. It was far more of a debating society than a legislative body. One cannot easily pass Bills for regulating the country's relations with foreign states; and Parliament in the eighteenth century did not try to. It spent little time on what we now imagine to be its proper functions. A few Bills, mostly private, were introduced and passed without much noise or division. But the serious business of Parliament in the few weeks during which it sat was first to pass the Budget, which it did usually at the end of the session in a brief sitting or two, and for the rest of the time to debate motions. Whether the motions were carried or lost made little enough difference to the ordinary affairs of the ordinary man, but they gave ample scope for indulging in fine periods and for the interplay of wit. Hence the emphasis laid upon oratory. It is difficult to indulge in flights of rhetoric over the social legislation of today; it was almost more difficult to avoid them when politicians were mainly talking in the air. Certainly the system, such as it was, bred the finest of English orators, and not least among them, William Pitt.

If the nature of the eighteenth-century parliamentary affairs is borne in mind, it will be easier to understand both Walpole and the Opposition. The Whig conception of policy had been settled by William of Orange and confirmed by Marlborough's victories. It involved enmity with France, alliance with Holland and Austria, and an active participation in continental affairs. The accession of George I had not affected fundamentals, but had added the complication of Hanoverian interests. These, so far as they were outside the traditional Whig views, being mainly Germanic and rather trifling, were apt to be regarded with suspicion in England, the more so as England began to realise her King's preference for his Electorate. In contradistinction, the Tory conception of policy was colonial and maritime; it looked with disfavour on continental entanglements, turning its eyes and aspirations over the seas.

Walpole's policy fitted neither conception. Truth to tell he was not interested either in the Continent or the colonies. By nature and instinct he was an administrator rather than a statesman; his capacity shone best in the day-to-day performance of executive functions, whether they consisted in the activities of the Civil

Service, or the more disreputable 'management' of Members of
Parliament. In all these arts he was pre-eminent. No one in
England could vie with him. But in the realm of foreign affairs
there was a very different story to tell. There were several statesmen in England whose knowledge of the Continent was wider,
and whose skill in diplomacy was greater. Walpole's bluff cynicism
was no match for the astute finessing of continental cardinals, and
if he had been Minister in days when foreign affairs were insistent
he would not have stood so high in the ranks of England's
statesmen. It was his good fortune as well as England's that his
talents coincided with the necessity for them. England needed
peace; so did the Continent, and there were internal reasons
which induced the French to keep quiet. So it came about that
Walpole had something of a clear field for his new conceptions.
He became the forerunner of modern statesmen, turning his
attention to the quiet and orderly government of the country,
encouraging trade, promoting manufacture, strengthening
finances, and above all maintaining peace.

Yet there was an Achilles' heel. The people were ready to
applaud when Walpole resisted the lure of Hanover; they were
ready to acquiesce when he preserved peace with France; but they
grew steadily more restive at his attitude towards Spain. Here was
a country which could almost unite Whig and Tory. It was
continental; it was Bourbon; and in 1733, unknown to Walpole,
it bound itself to France by the Family Compact. For all these
reasons it might attract the enmity of the Whigs. It was equally
a colonial power, and both by its presence and its policy across
the Atlantic was distasteful to English merchants and a challenge
to English Tories. It gave many causes for offence, large and
small, and it received good measure from irate English traders.
Largely the rivalry was commercial, but there were deeper,
underlying causes. Spain was ruled at this time by Elizabeth
Farnese, whose untamed spirit and vaulting ambition were prepared to set the world alight if a universal conflagration offered
hope of gain or glory for her children. Her object was to overthrow the Treaty of Utrecht in just those provisions which
affected England and Austria on the Continent, and her restless
schemes were pursued with unabated energy. Here, if anywhere,
was the danger spot. Walpole toiled ceaselessly to preserve peace,
but the odds were increasingly against him. Spain was in a
truculent mood, and England was chafing. It was precisely over

this question that an Opposition might come not only to life but to success.

It cannot be claimed that at his entry into Parliament Pitt was much affected by the Spanish question, but the growing current of criticism was there, and later Pitt found that it chimed in with his deepest and most profound convictions. Spain was ultimately to undo him; it may well have been a factor in guiding his first steps.

8

THE MAIDEN SPEECH

Pitt's first year in Parliament has long been a baffling enigma. There is no rhyme or reason in the story that has come down to us, no glint of light in its dark absurdity, and the midnight oil that has been spent on it has shed no illumination. Pitt, so we are told, rode his passionate and impetuous tongue on so tight a curb that his maiden speech was not made till the 29th of April 1736—nearly a year and a quarter after his election. During all those months he did nothing but act as a teller in a minor division some few days after taking his seat. At long last, however, the maiden speech burst out when the House was debating a congratulatory address to the King on the occasion of the Prince of Wales's marriage. And what a speech! To his friends it was more enthralling than the highest flights of Demosthenes and Cicero— or so they said. To his enemies it was devastating. It surprised Walpole into uttering one of the better known *obiter dicta* of romantic history—'we must muzzle this terrible cornet of horse' —before depriving Pitt of his commission some three weeks later on the 18th of May. More amazing still, it cast its radiance in advance so that the reporters paid him the unique honour of recording the first twitterings of that eloquence which was afterwards to become so famous. Not that the speech which has come down to us lives up to its reputation. It is tiresome and dull, and though some of his biographers, trying to find a scintilla of merit, have suggested that it was an exceedingly bitter satire or a masterpiece of innuendo, at bottom all are agreed with Macaulay's verdict that 'it is just as empty and wordy as a maiden speech on such an occasion might be expected to be.' In short everything connected with the story is unlikely and incredible—and in fact untrue. Pitt was certainly cautious, but even caution does not demand and did not receive fifteen months of dumbness in the House of Commons. His friends were loyal, but not entirely

besotted, and their praise had a reason even if it had no foundation. Walpole made at least two mistakes, but he was not stung
into an egregious blunder at the mere sound of Pitt's voice. Nor
was Macaulay right in suggesting as explanation of the furore
that the 'fluency and the personal advantages of the young orator
instantly caught the eye and ear of his audience.' On any other
occasion he would have known that fluency which is empty and
wordy is more apt to provoke yawns than to catch ears. But
Macaulay, like the rest, was misled by John Almon, the publisher
and Pitt's earliest biographer, who states briefly but quite
erroneously that 'Mr. Pitt's first speech in parliament was on the
29th of April 1736.'[1] It would have saved a lot of trouble if his
biographers had followed probability rather than Almon. Nothing
was less likely than this prolonged silence, nothing more improbable than the story as it has come down to us. And in fact Pitt's
maiden speech was made within a few weeks of his taking his seat.
It created no stir, let alone sensation; it won no extravagant
praise and provoked no ministerial temper. There was no one to
record it, and the very fact would have been forgotten but for a
brief passage in Lord Egmont's *Diary*. He records that on the
22nd of April 1735 the Place Bill gave 'several young members
who never spoke before,' including 'Mr. William Pitt,' an opportunity of distinguishing themselves.[2] Pitt spoke for the Opposition, thus early making his attitude known. His friends no doubt
offered congratulations but they were not vociferous in their
praise, and Walpole, if he bothered to listen, fingered no thunderbolt. It was, in short, very ordinary, and very unexciting. On how
many other occasions Pitt spoke in this first year we cannot now
tell, but it is likely enough that he practised his one art, which was
also his one asset, as often as he could. Certainly he spoke once
more—on the 5th of April 1736—before his reputed maiden
speech. Again the reference is slight. 'Mr. Pitt' is a mere name
given by Lord Egmont in a list of speakers against the Mortmain
Bill. If there is any interest it lies not in Pitt's eloquence but in
this glimpse of his views. The Bill proposed to increase the
number of Church livings which the two universities might
purchase or accept, but the Opposition, so Lord Egmont says,
declared 'that the increase of power in the Church is dangerous,
and would render the clergy independent on the laity. That
numbers of livings in the University only made the Fellows lazy,

---

[1] Almon, I, 24. [2] H. M. C. Egmont MSS., II, 171.

D

whereas when pinched in their circumstances, and without prospect of College livings, they would study hard to go out into the world.'[1] Presumably Pitt followed this general line of argument, and one may thus note the first beginnings of that trust in the laity which ultimately made him the Great Commoner. Possibly one may also get a hint of the views which he brought down from the 'varsity—not unduly flattering to his pastors and masters. But this is a digression.

If one supposes, as one reasonably may, that Pitt not only broke silence at the first opportunity, but continued to take an active share in debate, it is easy to make sense of Walpole's actions. In later life Pitt told Shelburne that Walpole had offered him the troop which was afterwards given to Conway, so that had he remained in the army he would have stood high by seniority alone.[2] His biographers have been forced to suppose that this offer was made before Pitt was elected, and was an effort bred of fear to keep him out of the House. But there is no reason to suppose that Walpole grasped the stature of the young giant or feared his powers. The fact is that Walpole, like most Ministers, disliked opposition, and finding Pitt an opponent, did his best to seduce him by the method he found generally effective—bribery. The offer was almost certainly made after Pitt's election and merely proved Walpole's ignorance of his character. But it paved the way for Walpole's next step. By the time of the 'maiden speech' Walpole's patience had gone. The young man was taking too active a part in opposition, and would not apparently respond to kindness. Well, he was of no particular account—a mere gnat, buzzing and exasperating—and could easily be broken. So at the end of the session Walpole cashiered him. For the second time Walpole completely misread Pitt's character. He was not to be broken so easily, and he was not to be browbeaten at all. On the contrary he was to react immediately and skilfully. The bribe had merely been a test of his integrity; he could gain little credit by a refusal which he could scarcely make known. But the crack of the whip was another matter altogether. It gave him an opening which he was prompt to seize. Publicity was a natural gift with him, and Walpole's rash act gave him the opportunity of posing as a martyr. He flung himself into the part with zest, and his friends were delighted to rally round him, partly no doubt because of a genuine indignation, but also, beyond doubt, because of the

[1] H. M. C. Egmont MSS., II, 255-6.   [2] Fitzmaurice. *Shelburne*, I, 73.

advantages they were likely to secure for themselves and their party. It was now for the first time that their ears were caught by the fluency of the young orator; it was now that a speech they had forgotten these three weeks outscintillated the classics; it was now that the authors in their Grub Street attics began to report the periods they had never heard. And so the legend grew, and the great ladies of the land gossiped of the rising star—'a young man of no fortune, a very pretty speaker, one the Prince is particular to, and under the tuition of my Lord Cobham'—while their lords muttered that the 'Army is all alarmed at this, and 'tis said it will hurt the King more than his removing my Lord Stairs and Lord Cobham, since it is making the whole army dependent, by descending to resent a vote from the lowest commission.'[1] Here was a pretty state of affairs! No wonder Almon dated Pitt's maiden speech from that lucky day. Lucky perhaps in another respect. Now that Pitt had been cashiered from the army, he had no alternative to a political career, and no distraction from parliamentary duties. For all that a military career chimed in with his genius, the army did not. Northampton and Newbury and the numbskulls of the mess were no fitting soil for his abilities. He needed to sharpen his wits by interplay with the best brains of the country—Walpole, Carteret, Pulteney—he needed also perhaps that 'pinching in his circumstances' which would force him to study hard in order to rise in the world. Walpole did a vast deal more than he imagined—he thought he was cashiering a factious opponent; actually he was confirming his spiritual successor.

[1] Lady Irwin to Lord Carlisle, 20th May 1736. Historical Manuscripts Commission. Carlisle MSS., p. 172.

9

FREDERICK, PRINCE OF WALES

The next six years of Pitt's life (May 1736 to January 1742) are doubly interesting. They portray with the clearness of an etching the growth of a young statesman, and, as chance would have it, epitomise his life as a whole. He stepped rapidly up the ladder, confirmed the brightest expectations of his friends and gained a crushing victory over his opponent, but for all his brilliance and success he failed to secure the prize. There was never yet a career where success was so unsuccessful, where popularity was so forlorn, where the solid substance of achievement melted more completely into a wrack.

For the moment, however, all was clear. Walpole himself had marked out Pitt's course with minute precision. There was to be no further attempt at bribery; gone was the day of parleyings and gone too any lingering prospect that Pitt might pick up again the courtly threads fingered by his father and dropped by his sister. He was confirmed in opposition, and it remained for him to pass out of the stage of mere negation into the formulation of his own policies.

His immediate reaction had something of boyish defiance in it, but a defiance that was marked by action and stamped with finality. He made a parade of himself, ostentatiously driving about the country in a one-horse shay and without a servant, posing in fact as a poor man—and posing deliberately, since he had never been rich and had no need now to expose his sores. But the reception given him wherever he drove must have confirmed his innate tendency to appeal from the great and powerful to the common people. Besides, he must have enjoyed his popularity. It was a new and heady wine, which he rolled round the tongue tucked tightly in his cheek!

As a commentary on his catchpenny drives, he returned from them to Stowe, perhaps the stateliest of England's stately homes and certainly one of the most magnificent. Here Cobham received

his white-headed boy with open arms and open doors, lapping
Pitt in the twofold luxury of corporal ease and mental adulation.
His bribery was more subtle and infinitely more effective than
Walpole's, and Pitt found it so satisfying that he practically
adopted Stowe as his permanent residence. He had already been a
visitor since July 1735, and he seems to have remained there on
and off for the next three years. After all, here he was appreciated
by the wits and the beauties of the age; here he could hobnob with
Pope; here he could 'pun and talk nonsense with Mrs. Blount
most elegantly'; here he could play cricket or wander among the
groves and walks, flattered by the great and snuffing the incense
of their praise. Pitt enjoyed every minute of it, and while he fed
his innate snobbery, taught himself the profusion of one of the
richest palaces in England. It was for him a more penetrating
temptation than the grosser vices of Northampton and Newbury.
Others might win or lose fortunes in gambling or waste their time
flirting with barmaids; Pitt was of a different mould. In his soul he
believed in the legend of nobility—the patent of peerage was the
roll of honour. 'Noblesse oblige' was more than a French tag
from the age of chivalry; it was a profound truth from the Golden
Book. And somehow in the eighteenth century and in Pitt's eyes
nobility was not far removed from ostentation. Ribbons and stars
were outward and visible signs of an inward and spiritual grace—
or at least should be—and for Pitt very nearly were. His inward
and spiritual grace was undoubted, yet somehow it urged him to
an open and blatant ostentation, the seeds of which were sown in
the shady walks of Stowe.

Yet the influence of Stowe was not altogether worldly, nor yet
entirely bad. One must believe that even in these early days there
brushed lightly and unperceived over Pitt some touch of that
sweet affinity of souls which in due course united him to Hester
Grenville. She was a girl of fourteen when he first came to
Stowe, but before that long visit was over she was a woman—
young and vigorous and with a deep well of wise and tender love
waiting to be drawn upon. Pitt might be too lost in political
dreams and polite philanderings to notice the facts of flesh and
blood—but they were there.

But neither Calypso-Cobham nor the as yet immature Penelope-
Hester could hold Pitt for long. Cobham and Stowe were the
first rungs on the ladder, tremendously exciting at the time, but
destined to fall steadily flatter. Nothing but the highest could

content Pitt, and for the time being the highest was the uncrowned leader of the Opposition—no less a person than the Prince of Wales.

Frederick, Prince of Wales, was about Pitt's age, having been born in 1707. There the resemblance between the two ends abruptly. But not the connection. To Frederick belongs the glory of befriending Pitt when the King and Walpole had cast him down, and the glory is dimmed only by the fact that Frederick had no idea what manner of angel he was harbouring, and harboured him merely to spite his father. For Frederick was a typical product of a German principality. It seems to have been inevitable for Hanoverian princelings and their eldest sons to be at loggerheads. George I had hated George II, and now George II in his turn loathed Frederick. He had kept the boy in Hanover as long as he could, refusing to let the heir-apparent visit the kingdom till 1729, when he had come at least chronologically to man's estate. Frederick arrived in London, a pitiful figure of good intentions twisted awry and brains too small to be properly addled. His chief asset, as he very well knew, was a mathematical calculation—the twenty-four years that separated him from his father. He had no present, but the future seemed to be his, and when the family feud grew too strong, he began to hawk that future abroad. It was attractive, and the youth of the country tried to rally round him. Their difficulty lay in the fact that Frederick fulfilled to a marvel the definition of a point—position without substance. He had nothing to offer in himself but assiduity in seeking popular applause and an involuntary skill in stirring his parents to enmity. Beyond that lay emptiness which death was to confirm. As heir-apparent, however, he played at forming ministries; he peopled the future with make-believe statesmen, and he won the flattering attentions of all those politicians who noted that the King was old and not very well, and all those politicians who realised that Walpole was hale and hearty and nowise disposed to take them into partnership. In short he offered to perfection the one thing necessary—an opposition. What small merit he can claim springs out of this sole fact. He restored the vital ingredient in our constitution which Walpole was intent on scrapping, and by so doing, however little either he or Walpole or any other statesman realised it at the time, laid the foundations for the Pretender's final defeat and much of Pitt's military success. The Tories were given a hope of returning to power at a not too extravagant distance, the Jacobites an excuse for dropping a loyalty which had become ludicrous. Here was something which widened England beyond the exclusive circle of the Whig magnates and substituted Scotland and the colonies for Hanover and the Continent. In this alone there were all the makings of a policy if Frederick had possessed the brains, but he never succeeded in fashioning more out of it than a family feud, and instead of becoming a leader had to be content with the rôle of a figurehead. But, however unwittingly, he had sown the seeds, and Pitt was to reap the harvest.

He did one other thing by way of example. Having no official status in Parliament, and being at enmity with his father and his father's Government, he was forced back on the estate which offered some prospect of support—the common people. Like Pitt, his only weapon was popularity, and he tried to achieve it. To some extent he succeeded, but the brand which his character inevitably attracted was the half-pitying, half-patronising kind which might evoke sentimental tears in a cinema but could never form the proverbial plank for a party platform. Frederick offered Pitt an example at once 'awful' and encouraging, and when the time came Pitt knew how to profit by it.

For the moment, however, Pitt was too young and too little experienced to appreciate either Frederick's essential inanity or the possibilities which a mocking fate was holding out to him. For Pitt, Frederick was the next rung upon the ladder; he was the future—and not so very future—King; he was the rallying point of the Opposition; and he was disposed to take Pitt up. Pitt, therefore, with admirable if rather obvious prudence set himself to woo the Prince. He had already won very unexpected spurs by his speech on the Prince's marriage, and he followed up the chance opening. As Society had remarked, the Prince was particular to Pitt, which meant that the Prince was inclined to listen to his advice. The pity was that from the beginning to the end of his life Pitt's advice was never very sound. Or perhaps it would be truer to say that Pitt was the only man capable of profiting by it. It is a strange fact, and not to be forgotten, that this master of language, whose voice could sway multitudes and whose scorn could quell Parliament, found it nearly impossible to impart his thoughts to his colleagues. There was an inhibition constantly at work to check an honest interchange of ideas. Pitt was for ever holding something back, or at best flinging out hints which he expected others to interpret with his own fertile imagination. His difficulty in imparting his views sprang from both sides of his curiously intermingled character—his pride and his humility—the eternal conflict between his innate genius and his inferiority complex.

But of this, more anon. In these early days little enough is known of his advice. What is known are the two facts that Frederick consulted Pitt, and that he was sorely in need of guidance. Frederick was always floundering, for ever anxious to carve out his own career, but by the decree of a malignant fate, for ever following the paths marked out for him by others. Even in his love affairs he was not his own master. He is said—one may hope untruly—to have been content with his father's mistresses; but it is more than mere gossip that he became wildly enamoured of Wilhelmina, sister of the future Frederick the Great, and did his unsuccessful best to escape to her, though he had never seen the lady and had no knowledge of the reception she was likely to give him. No less harebrained—one can hardly call it romantic—was his equally unsuccessful effort to marry Lady Diana Spencer, granddaughter of the Duchess of Marlborough—a clandestine match, by which he was to sell himself to the formidable old Duchess for the substantial dowry of £100,000. But in spite of all these sudden shifts and starts, like the plungings of a foal, he finally accepted his father's choice and married the Princess Augusta of Saxe-Gotha, a small-minded and narrowly proper young woman whose obstinacy, as developed by her son, cost England the American colonies.

Frederick's marriage, however, did not solve the problems of his life. Domestically it made his position still more intolerable, since the newly wedded couple were expected to live with their in-laws, the King and Queen, and were given their allowance of £50,000 a year only at the King's pleasure. Frederick thought he should be given a bigger allowance and that it should be settled upon him absolutely. He had some justification. George I out of a smaller Civil List had settled £100,000 a year on his son, and there seemed no very good reason why that son, having now become King, should not allow Frederick at least as much as he had himself enjoyed. Anyhow Frederick needed money; he had a wife; he had his amusements; he had his popularity-hunting expenses; he had his ostentatious list of charities, and not least he had his debts. Applications to the King for money had no results, and so he applied to Pitt for advice.

From one point of view he could hardly have made a worse choice, since money was always an enigma to Pitt; but from another point of view he could hardly have done better. Pitt was young, energetic and fearless. Better still, he was searching for methods to attack the Government; and here was one very promising line of approach. Frederick had reason on his side, if not absolute right; he was a man with a legitimate grievance, and any comparison with his father would inevitably be to his advantage. The King was elderly and in bad health; he was not popular and his married life, though in many ways ideal, was also notorious for its scandals. As against this unedifying picture, Frederick represented youth and popularity, the glamour of the newly married and the irresistible appeal of oppressed royalty. Pitt must have felt that here was a hand containing all the trumps. At least it provided the ingredients for a parliamentary bout. Pitt advised the Prince to ignore the King and apply directly to Parliament. As tactics nothing could be better, but it may be doubted if as strategy the move was good. Walpole and the King were both placed in a difficult and invidious position, and there was even the prospect of a Government defeat. Yet the defeat, if it had come, would have achieved nothing, since Walpole could scarcely be expected to resign on such a question, and when it did not come, merely deepened the enmity between father and son. Pitt had been carried away by the prospect of a speedy victory without properly counting the cost, but the lesson was not lost on him. For the rest of his life he grew steadily more distrustful of captious opposition and more insistent upon the clash of principles.

Meanwhile the family feud grew more outrageous, and reached its culminating point a few months later. The Princess of Wales was pregnant, which may have been one of Frederick's reasons for demanding an increased allowance, though he deliberately concealed the reason from his parents. It was not until the 7th of July that he breathed a word of her condition. On the 31st of July she was seized with the pangs of childbirth, and Frederick at once lost his head. Urged on by one of the momentary spasms of violence which overtook him from time to time, and regardless of everything but the panic in his own mind, he hurried his wife away in the middle of the night from Hampton Court where the

royal family were in residence, to St. James's Palace, which was
wrapped in dust sheets. The King and Queen were ready enough
to be affronted by anything which Frederick did; in their eyes, if
their recorded language is to be believed, he was hardly a human
being. Not unnaturally, therefore, they regarded this sudden
flight for which no reason with the least shred of plausibility has
either then or since been offered, as a gross insult, and peremp-
torily denied him the Court. The breach was complete, and
Walpole saw to it that there should be no reconciliation.

All this childishness was of small moment in itself, but it had a
profound effect upon Pitt's future. The first and immediate result
of the breach was that Frederick set up an establishment of his
own at Norfolk House in St. James's Square, which from the
first became the headquarters of the Opposition and a sort of
rival Court. There was no traffic between the Square and the
Palace, and much agitated discussion amongst the rival courtiers
as to etiquette and propriety. Private friendships were at cross
purposes with public decorum and family feelings with royal
wishes. The Pitts were not exempt. Pitt himself, as a high-spirited
young man, half contemptuous of his social betters and wholly
delighted to play with fire, insisted on visiting his sister Ann at
Hampton Court. Ann, who shared fully in the quarrelsome genius
of her stock, flaunted his visits among the circle of her doubting
friends, but for all her bravado was a little nervous and sought
advice from the Duchess of Queensberry. 'You will hate me for
trifling with you,' the Duchess replied, 'but really I cannot decide
without knowing whether the servants of both Courts are forbid
visiting each other.' She was inclined to think Pitt's visit to his
sister could 'not be construed going to Court,' but on the other
hand she noted that 'Mr. Young declared the other day that he
should not visit his daughter at Norfolk Court, thinking it
improper as he belonged to the other Court.'[1] Pitt, in short, had
notice that he would be ostracised from royal favour if he persisted in his fidelity to the Prince, becoming, as the Duchess of
Queensberry described it, 'one of the Prince's family.' Others took
the hint and resigned their posts in the Prince's household, but
Pitt, having made his choice, moved unswervingly forward. So
far from deserting his leader, he gladly accepted one of the posts
made vacant by resignation, becoming a Groom of the

[1] Duchess of Queensberry to Ann Pitt, October 1737. H. M. C. Fortescue MSS.,
I, 101.

Bedchamber, while his friend, George Lyttelton, became Private Secretary. The salary of £400 helped to eke out his domestic finances at the moment, but, as events were to prove, it was a poor bargain, keeping Pitt from power and profit many a weary year. Undoubtedly Pitt's choice was wrong.

But it was wholehearted and had at least the effect of keeping him before the public eye. As the foremost amongst the younger set to champion the Prince he became the legitimate butt of Government scribblers. The *Gazetteer*, in true eighteenth-century style, ridiculed his long neck and his slender body, for which he was no doubt much to blame. It also told him, with as much truth and more pertinence, that he had an overbearing disposition and a weak judgment. Where the *Gazetteer* was neither truthful nor prescient was in declaring that Pitt was not a person of real consequence, but was raised by a party as a proper tool for their present purposes, and was destined to be pulled down as soon as those purposes were served. However, the *Gazetteer* must be pardoned, for it added to his fame and importance, incidentally stirring up its rival, the *Craftsman*, to the wildly ridiculous statement that Pitt 'in every situation, hath conducted himself in the nicest and discreetest manner.'

THE OPENING GAMBIT

Normally Pitt's duties as Groom of the Bedchamber should have been light, but they seem to have kept him fully occupied. At all events he once wrote to Lady Suffolk 'I shou'd have thank'd your ladyship for the honour of your note by the post of Tuesday, if the numberless arduous occupations of groom of the bed-chamber in waiting had allowed me time.'[1] This is the one reference in his letters still extant to his duties. It should not be taken as polite fibbing since Pitt was always punctilious and generally prompt in answering letters, and on this occasion not only was his correspondent a valued friend but the subject of the letter was the refutation of baseless scandals spread about Pitt's favourite sister, Ann. If he did not answer at once, it was because he could not.

The duties were, however, intermittent, and one may well believe included a great deal more than merely waiting on the Prince. Pitt had become a power in Norfolk House, and was recognised as such. As early as February 1737 Lord Egmont was hoping that the Prince 'would not be left in the hands of such young men as Littleton and Pitt.' Lord Winchilsea, to whom he was talking, comforted him with the fallacies of the *Gazetteer*, declaring that Pitt was merely the mouthpiece of 'more consider-able persons.'[2] Egmont, however, was nearer the mark than Winchilsea. 'More considerable persons' might perhaps imagine that they were using Pitt, but in fact they were using him only so far as he was ready and willing to be used. He was rapidly forming his own views, and the time was not far distant when he was to know himself superior to the Prince, and be prepared to break with him.

As the Prince's mentor, he was plunged into opposition up to the hilt. The main object was to oust Walpole, whose sins were twofold—support of the King and obstruction to the Prince. At the outset Pitt seems to have had little more in his mind than these

[1] Lady Suffolk's *Letters*, II, 189.   [2] Lord Egmont's *Diary*, II, 353.

two sins, and possibly, had he been of a different mould, he might have become as dejected as the remainder of the Opposition. They, as a body, were reluctant to take any definite steps in the House alleging, as Lord Marchmont told Montrose in May 1738, 'the want of right points to push,' and that 'points must arise from the other side.' Marchmont knew Walpole well enough to realise that he would give nothing away, and so 'in short, I look, as several others do, upon the Opposition as at an end.'[1] But Pitt was of a more fiery, if not more optimistic, temper. Points must be found, and if necessary snatched from under Walpole's very nose. And the interesting fact is that Pitt moved, however fortuitously, along the one road which must and did lead to the necessary points, which must and did bring Walpole toppling to the ground.

The strength of Walpole's position did not lie merely in the royal favour, but in the gifts which flowed from his policy. He offered a distracted country the two blessings of peace and trade. It would have been difficult, if not impossible, for the Opposition to formulate a more attractive programme. Hence their discouragement. But the great Minister had his Achilles' heel; his policy, however desirable in itself, was not uniformly consistent or successful. It was precisely at the weak spots that Pitt aimed his blows, with increasing weight and accuracy of aim, and it was precisely at those weak spots that the Opposition finally broke through.

The first line of attack was on the question of the standing army. It was not a new subject, but it was one which Pitt could approach with some semblance of authority both because he had served an apprenticeship in the Dragoons and because he had been unjustly cashiered. In 1737 and again in 1738 he supported the annual plea for a reduction in the size of the army, but only the speech on the latter occasion has survived.

As the Opposition was in those same years attacking Walpole's Spanish policy and urging a line of action which might easily lead to war, Pitt's biographers find his attitude towards the standing army inconsistent,[2] almost incredible[3] and even senseless.[4] One may well agree that Pitt, as a young parliamentarian eagerly engaged in overthrowing the Ministry, did not bother much about logic. Yet the charge of inconsistency is two-edged. If the

---

[1] Papers of the Earls of Marchmont. [2] Williams, I, 74.
[3] Rosebery, p. 164. [4] Von Ruville, I, 155.

Opposition were urging a smaller army with a warlike policy,
Walpole was demanding a larger army with a policy of peace. Why
maintain a huge army in idleness? Why burden the taxpayer
unnecessarily, especially when it was notorious that the cost of an
English soldier was far greater than the cost of a soldier on the
Continent? This was Pitt's line of argument. He anticipated his
biographers by a century or so and in effect accused Walpole of
inconsistency. It was not for him (Pitt) to assume that the Opposition's Spanish policy would necessarily prevail, and if it did, it
would surely be better for the Opposition to assume responsibility
and raise their own armies. Meanwhile he must face facts as they
were, not as he wished them to be. Walpole himself could find no
worthier enemy for the army to attack than the Pretender's friends,
the Tories and suspected Jacobites. Well, Pitt for one believed
'there are so few of either in the kingdom, that I am sure they can
give no man an occasion for being afraid of them.' Three-quarters
of Walpole's army 'never underwent any fatigue except that of a
review nor were ever exposed to any danger except in apprehend-
ing smugglers or dispersing mobs.' Year after year they had been
costing the country two to three hundred thousand pounds, and
so long as Walpole remained in power and pursued his present
policy, they would continue to be an unprofitable expense to the
country. Let the numbers be reduced.[1]

Apart from the merits of the case, Pitt had a further and very
practical excuse for his line of action in the parliamentary pro-
cedure of the times. Nowadays the introduction of the estimates
enables the Government to be attacked at many points and on
many subjects, but in the eighteenth century conditions were very
different. There were no Civil Service estimates other than the
Civil List, which was fixed once for all at the beginning of the
reign. The only estimates which came before the House were for
the army and the navy, and even so, the navy occupied a privi-
leged position. The Treasury had no voice in its expenditure,
which was settled by the Admiralty and presented to the House
by the First Lord.[2] True, the First Lord might have been attacked,
but in the eighteenth century with its lack of Cabinet responsibility this was not the same thing as attacking the Prime Minister.
Moreover, the Opposition could more justly have been charged
with inconsistency if they attacked the navy, since war with Spain

---

[1] Speech, 3rd February 1738. *Parliamentary History*, Vol. X.
[2] *Calendar of Treasury Books and Papers, 1742-1745*, p. xxxviii.

both in their view and in its nature must be more naval and colonial than military and continental. It may therefore be accepted that if Walpole was to be attacked on the estimates, it could only be in connection with the army, and Pitt and the Opposition had no alternative between 'inconsistency' and a tacit acquiescence in Walpole's proposed expenditure.

II

THE WAR OF JENKINS' EAR

If Walpole's advocacy of a large army appeared to be at variance with his professed policy of peace, equally his pacific attitude towards Spain clashed with his desire to encourage trade. Spain owned a large and rambling empire in the New World, where British merchants were anxious to find a market. The possibilities were great; there was no reluctance on the side of the Spanish colonists and no hanging back on the part of English traders. Everything was set for a flourishing commerce, and clearly it was in keeping with Government policy that it should be fostered. Unfortunately Spain herself was wholly and totally opposed. She was not prepared to allow anyone to trade with her colonies unless she were forced to do so. The last occasion on which she had been forced was at the Treaty of Utrecht in 1713. Under that treaty England had extorted the right to carry on a traffic in slaves and to send one ship annually with merchandise for the Spanish colonies. The fact that this concession had been wrested from her by force made Old Madrid the more reluctant to admit its existence and the more ready to invent obstacles and hindrances. And if Spain was sulky and obstructive, the English were restless and unsatisfied. One ship offered them little enough scope, especially when it was shackled by the red tape and thwarted by the malicious ingenuity of Spanish officialdom. They clamoured for more concessions to be obtained through diplomatic channels, and in the meantime they filched whatever advantage they could lay their hands on by less reputable means. Smuggling became rampant and was met by customs regulations and coastguard methods which steadily became more violent. Meanwhile Walpole was, both of inclination and of necessity, negotiating with Spain. His efforts were not successful, and would have been even less so had the Spanish Queen, Elizabeth Farnese, been less intent upon schemes for the aggrandisement of her sons. It was she who was the European irritant of this particular period, and as usual with absolute monarchs or dictators of an ambitious turn of mind, her schemes had their root in personal and family greed, not in Spanish necessity or even in Spanish good. In the earlier years of Walpole's ministry Spain had been fearful of the Anglo-French *entente*. She had therefore been prepared to dangle a carrot before Walpole's nose and for many years he had stumbled forward hoping to achieve a nibble. But Elizabeth, who in spite of her Italian blood had more than the traditional Spanish inflexibility, meant to give nothing; and her determination hardened as friction grew off the coast of America. Meanwhile as her European policy succeeded, the need to placate England waned, particularly after the signing of the Family Compact between France and Spain in 1733, and still more in 1735 when the conclusion of the War of the Polish Succession gave Elizabeth much of what she coveted. There was nothing now to prevent her from growing more and more intransigent, and in consequence nothing to wean the English merchants from their smuggling or stop the Spanish coastguards from bullying and bludgeoning. Affairs were bound to go from bad to worse and war was as nearly inevitable as anything human can be.

Walpole hoped to ward off the inevitable—perhaps thought it was not inevitable—and continued his feverish negotiations. Meanwhile the Opposition in general and Pitt in particular came more and more to the conclusion that the Gordian knot must be cut. However true it might be that war was bad for trade, conditions were becoming desperate. The merchants of Great Britain had a long and increasing list of grievances which demanded redress. It was intolerable that Spanish coastguards should claim and exercise the right of search, not only in Spanish territorial waters but even on the high seas, so that no innocent merchantman coming from the English West Indian Islands was safe. It was still more intolerable that cargoes should be confiscated as the result of this search and honest British tars thrown into Spanish prisons to face torture and death.

It is perhaps hardly necessary to add that the honest British tars were as often as not smugglers, and that the British merchants were as little regardful of Spanish rights and lives as the Spaniards were of British ships and sailors. That both sides were in the wrong on matters of detail is generally agreed. Modern historians are disposed to go further and admit that if Spain was savage in her retaliation, England was guilty of all the provocation by her

E

flagrant disregard of the law. So much may be allowed, but perhaps something may be said beyond the usual plea that Spain had claimed more territory in the New World than she could control or supply with European goods.[1] Certainly that was not Pitt's argument. He was not concerned with the extent of Spain's empire, or the inability of her colonial governors, or the volume of her exports. He was not in fact concerned with Spain at all. His views were at once narrower and wider—narrower in that he was thinking mainly of England's advantage; wider in that he was fighting for free trade in the sense of the right to trade. 'When trade,' he declared, 'is at stake it is your last entrenchment; you must defend it, or perish.'[2] The Spanish colonies were ready enough to trade with us or there would be no smugglers. It was not a question of tariffs or duties; the gravamen of his charge was that Old Spain was imposing an absolute and arbitrary prohibition on imperative and indispensable activities in the New World. It is quite true that all other countries, including England, kept trade with their colonies strictly in their own hands, and that England would certainly have adopted the same attitude had she been in Spain's shoes. It is more than possible that Pitt would have supported the adoption of that attitude, for when his patriotism was aroused his toleration if not his logic was apt to fail. But that means merely that England and Pitt were as short-sighted as other nations in their colonial policies, and one is bound to add that the effect of this short-sightedness was profound in determining the ultimate sovereignty of colonial lands. But if Pitt was blinded by patriotism on one side, he was clear-sighted enough on the other. It was essential that trade should flourish between England and the New World when both sides were willing and anxious to exchange goods and services. It was intolerable that Madrid should be able to crush this promising trade and stifle the benefits that flowed from it. It was still more intolerable that in order to crush trade and stifle benefits she should seek to distort the rules of international law and to limit the rights of British ships on the high seas.

In clamouring for pressure to be brought to bear on Spain the Opposition were undoubtedly voicing the wishes of the country. A spirit of exasperation had been steadily growing, and in 1738 it received a catchword that was also an inspiration. The story of

---

[1] Williams, I, 73.   [2] Speech, 8th March 1739, *Parliamentary History*, Vol. X.

Robert Jenkins was dragged to light and told at the bar of the House. Jenkins declared that the Spaniards had boarded his sloop when he was trading from Jamaica, and though they had found no proof of smuggling, had torn off his ear and flung it jeeringly in his face, bidding him carry it to his King. There was little in this to differentiate Jenkins' case from a score of others. Where he showed a bizarre and indeed gruesome touch of individuality was in taking the Spaniards at their word. He had wrapped the mutilated member, or something that purported to be it, in cotton wool and had carried it about with him ever since— doubtless to show to the King if the opportunity came his way. He displayed it now, some seven years after the event, at the bar of the House, and the dried and mummified piece of flesh exercised a compelling fascination. One can imagine the scene—the inquisitive faces dodging to and fro and peering over shoulders to get a glimpse of the dark and disgusting piece of corruption, the goggling eyes, the gaping mouths, the swaying throng, half shuddering at their own emotions and more than ready to succumb to mass hysteria. Someone in that heated atmosphere asked Jenkins what he had felt, and his answer is emblazoned in history: 'I recommended my soul to God and my cause to my country.' The words had the singing audacity of genius, something of that high-hearted simplicity which reverberates through the *Pilgrim's Progress*, and even to this day they give a lift to the heart in spite of their familiarity. When they first broke upon England's ear they rang and re-echoed like a trumpet throughout the length and breadth of the country. It was hardly necessary for the Opposition to act; it would have been gilding refined gold. Without their efforts, petitions poured in and the clamour for war grew daily.

Walpole found it increasingly difficult to resist. Even the King was growing lukewarm. He still believed in Walpole, and was still prepared to support him, but since the death of the Queen in the previous November (1737) his political bondage had automatically diminished, and he had been able to indulge his martial instincts, if only in secret. George II was a fiery and impetuous soul, with more than a hankering after war, and if he was not himself prepared to coerce Walpole, he none the less hoped that Walpole's hand would be forced. The King's attitude affected the whole Government, and it was now that the Duke of Newcastle, for all the haverings of his weak and easily frightened nature, first began to scheme against his chief and build up a war party in the Cabinet.

The clamour of the people, the assaults of the Opposition, the intrigues of the Cabinet and the predilections of the King, had their combined effect. Though Walpole tried to resist, he found himself borne along by a growing wave of popular determination. He found himself, surprisingly, dispatching a fleet to the Mediterranean, and taking tardy steps to protect the West Indies and to garrison the young colony of Georgia, which abutted on the Spanish possession of Florida. As usual, the sudden display of force after a long period of quiescence had its effect. Spain was frightened into a genuine effort at conciliation; she offered to treat with rather more appearance of sincerity and Walpole jumped at the offer. By January 1739 he had cobbled up the Convention of the Pardo. It was not a brilliant effort—Walpole was no match for the continental diplomatists at any time, least of all when he was striving to prevent war and knew that his only hope was to produce a settlement that was definite, whatever else it might be. What he did by the Convention was to set off the various claims made by the merchants on either side, and strike a balance in England's favour. It was not a large balance, some £200,000 all told, and when the figure had been agreed Spain began the delectable process of whittling it away. By the time the figure had been reduced to £95,000 the Spanish debt to England began to look ridiculously small and deplorably distant. As for other matters Walpole conveniently forgot them or left them muddily vague. Where neither course was possible, he shelved the problems on to commissions of enquiry. One way or another he secured his Convention and brought it back to the House.

It was, however, all in vain. His brother, Horatio, dutifully moved a vote of thanks, but the Opposition were not to be fobbed off, and the country at large was not to be fooled. The Convention was not what they wanted, and they said so in no uncertain voice. Very possibly it was not what Walpole wanted. At best it was an effort to establish a preliminary basis for a future more complete and satisfactory agreement. One may believe that Walpole's instinct would have been to continue negotiations until all points had been settled, but his hand was forced by the need to produce something. Hence his readiness to compromise on the monetary claims and to refer all harder questions to plenipotentiaries. What he failed to recognise was the impossibility of continuing his foreign policy. Facts had changed, and with them his policy must change also—at home and abroad. That was the gravamen of the Opposition's attack. Walpole's efforts could not succeed, and must bring dishonour on the country. 'This Convention,' Pitt thundered, 'I think from my soul is nothing but a stipulation for national ignominy'; it was 'an illusory expedient to baffle the resentment of the nation; a truce without a suspension of hostilities on the part of Spain; on the part of England, a suspension, as to Georgia, of the first law of nature, self-preservation and self-defence; a surrender of the rights and trade of England to the mercy of plenipotentiaries, and in this infinitely highest and sacred point, future security, not only inadequate, but directly repugnant to the resolutions of Parliament and the gracious promise from the Throne. The complaints of your despairing merchants and the voice of England have condemned it. Be the guilt of it upon the head of the adviser; God forbid that this Committee should share the guilt by approving it.'[1]

Pitt and the Opposition were as deeply interested in 'future security' as Walpole himself, but they differed from him as they differed from the old Whig policy. It was, in their eyes, useless to rely on the Anglo-French *entente*. Sooner or later England had to settle her account with France, and no doubt that would mean with the whole House of Bourbon. On the Continent nothing could be done, and consequently the Opposition had acquiesced in Walpole's policy during the War of the Polish Succession. But in America there was a different story to tell. Walpole might plead in favour of his Convention our 'low, unallied condition abroad'; he might point to the fact that the House of Bourbon was united, and ask 'who knows the consequence of a war?' When he asked that question, he implied a war on the Continent; no other war seems to have existed for him. But to Pitt the answer seemed simple, 'Sir,' he cried, 'Spain knows the consequence of a war *in America*; whoever gains, it must prove fatal to her.' And again he urged the same point when he asked 'Is this any longer a nation? Is this any longer an English Parliament, if with more ships in your harbours than in all the navies of Europe, with above two millions of people in your American colonies, you will bear to hear of the expediency of receiving from Spain an insecure, unsatisfactory, dishonourable Convention?'[2] In those

[1] Speech, 8th March 1739, *Parliamentary History*, Vol. X.
[2] Speech, 8th March 1739.

two brief sentences he summed up his own foreign policy and
adumbrated his famous Ministry. War was inevitable, but on the
seas and in America it must be successful.

In spite of all that the Opposition could do, Walpole secured
the assent of Parliament to his Convention, whereupon the
Opposition in a foolish fit of pique seceded in a body from the
House. Their action did not enhance their reputation either at the
time or with posterity, yet indirectly its effect was supremely
successful. Their absence gave Walpole a free hand; he could do
as he saw fit without the harassing necessity of placating or
defeating his opponents in the House. If in these circumstances
his policy should fail, the blame would be his alone. And his policy
did fail; he was unable to conciliate Spain; he was unable to soothe
the English merchants; he was unable to protect English ships;
he was unable to promote English trade. Affairs went from bad to
worse, and while the Opposition were silent of their own volition,
Walpole was forced to justify them by adopting their policy. He
declared war on Spain on the 19th of October 1739, with every
sign of agitated reluctance and genuine apprehension. He
expected nothing out of the war but stringency at the Exchequer
and rebellion in the Highlands. 'They may ring their bells now,'
he muttered bitterly, as the City broke into frenzied rejoicing,
'but they will soon be wringing their hands.' It was true enough,
but the very truth of the prophecy should have wrung his own
withers, for the disasters which were to follow were due to his
own sins, both those of omission and those of commission. He
had failed to read the signs of the times at home or abroad; he had
failed to notice the inevitable trend of European politics; he had
neglected the navy, even if he had kept up the army; and, greatest
sin of all, he had for nigh on twenty years kept the Jacobite cause
alive by his treatment of the Scotch, the Tories and the Opposition.
Now his sins were finding him out, and he added one final
blunder—he tried to conduct a war which he disliked and for
which he had no ability.

Meanwhile the Opposition returned to Parliament, and Pitt
came back as one of the marked men. His speech on the Convention of the Pardo had raised him above the common rank. The
praise which had been fortuitous and unreal when given to his
so-called 'maiden' speech, was now given in more sober and more
genuine guise. He had compelled attention; even Walpole had
made notes of his speech, and two of his lieutenants had been put

up to reply. In the renewal of the attack on the reigning Minister, Pitt took a foremost part. His importance was not due solely to his tongue. It was due to the intuitive feeling that he represented a new idea in politics, a new angle in statesmanship; that behind his hot-headed sallies, his impertinencies, his inexperience, lay something greater and grander than the Ministry could understand; something wiser and fuller than the Government could achieve. Pitt was groping after his own message, and the fact differentiated him from the hacks of party strife. He produced an atmosphere of expectation as well as a cloud of temporary excitement.

12

WALPOLE'S DECLINE

Meanwhile there was the war to conduct both at home and abroad. Walpole was likely enough to fumble since his whole conception was out of tune with the facts. Many years ago, in 1708, he had become Secretary at War at the comparatively early age of thirty-one, and had thriven and expanded in that office during the latter years of Marlborough's triumphs. It was, after all, easy to be a great War Minister when there was nothing to do but admire the general in the field and pay his accounts. But now everything had changed. Marlborough was gone and Walpole himself was twice as old. It was hard at his time of life to combine the routine of paymaster with the strategy of commander-in-chief, and not easier when he grudged the money, besides lacking the military skill. Even his previous experience was a hindrance, since it coloured his ideas with the faded light of a past age. He still looked at war primarily from Marlborough's angle, regarding it as an adventure of red coats on the Continent. When he escaped from the overpowering genius of Marlborough, it was merely to fall into the conceits of the Whigs and believe that war meant the appearance of the Pretender on the coast of Scotland, and the rising of the Highland clans. If, by chance, he shook off that fear also there was still the King at his elbow to descant on Hanoverian policy and the hiring of German mercenaries. Wherever he looked, war was a matter of soldiers—probably in England, certainly on the Continent, and not at all in America. This was the reason why he had so persistently kept up the strength of the army, and indirectly this was the reason why he had so consistently neglected the navy. It was difficult for him to change his beliefs and methods in a few short months, and he failed in such efforts as he made. The war in which he found himself engaged was essentially maritime and colonial; he had, therefore, to produce both a navy and a plan, and his scrambling policy was the more flustered because of the yelps of the Opposition hounds hard upon his heels. What he produced was exceedingly vague and impressionistic, amounting to no more than this—that as South America and the Spanish colonies faced two oceans it would be as well to send expeditions to both the Atlantic and the Pacific. What the commanders were to do in those distant parts had better be left to their discretion. After all, Marlborough had never asked for instructions, and had done very well without them. So originated the exploits of Vernon at Portobello and Anson's famous voyage round the world, of which more anon.

In the meantime there was the home front to be considered. Here at least Walpole should have been in his element. For many years now he had been firmly in control; all administration centred in him; and he had unrivalled knowledge of the parliamentary machine. But with the change of policy, with the substitution of war for peace, his grasp relaxed, his resolution faltered. The picture of his fumbling has much of the pathetic in it, and would be tragic in the deepest sense if the alternative of resignation had not been open to him.

Instead of resigning he clung to office, though when Parliament met in November 1739 he showed himself strangely subdued. He hastened to agree with Wyndham's resolution that there should be no peace with Spain unless she renounced the right of search; he accepted, after a feeble show of opposition, Pulteney's Bill to surrender all prize money to the seamen instead of appropriating it as revenue; he dropped on the first sign of disapproval his own deeply considered and administratively wise measure for a general registry of seamen, and after laying an embargo on shipping, gave way to the complaints of the merchants. If he was feeble in the House, he was no more effective in the Cabinet. 'I oppose nothing,' he told Newcastle, 'I give in to everything; am said to do everything; am to answer for everything, and yet, God knows, I dare not do what I think right.'[1] And to the House he pleaded, 'as I am neither general nor admiral, as I have nothing to do either with our navy or army, I am sure I am not answerable for the prosecution of the war.'[2]

In other directions his past experience, and his present fears, led him wholly astray. He had long dreaded war not merely for its own sake but because of its possible consequences. Prominent among those possibilities had been the revival of the Pretender's claims. Yet during all the years of his power he had done nothing

---

[1] Coxe's *Walpole*, IV, 148.   [2] *Ibid.*, IV, 202.

to placate the Jacobites, and now that their opportunity seemed to be dawning, he neither knew how to restrain them, nor dared appeal to their patriotism. Yet their menace must be met and met at once. So in desperation he entered into a correspondence with the Pretender himself—treasonable in appearance, but obviously no more than a wild bid to prevent sedition at home. Whether his efforts had any effect it is hard to say. But this at least is clear —they did not suffice to prevent the '45.

Another of Walpole's fears had been that war with France or Spain would expand into a general European conflagration, and the thought paralysed him. It was not for him to ride that whirl-wind. Fortune saw to it that his fears should become fact. Barely a year after the outbreak of war with Spain, the Emperor, Charles VI, died, leaving his young daughter, Maria Theresa, heir to his rambling possessions. Her future had been his constant preoccupation for many years, and by his famous Pragmatic Sanction he had underlined the fact of her helplessness. The nations of Europe sat round the Emperor's deathbed with eager expectation; they were legacy-hunting, and when the will was not to their liking, determined to appeal to the law of might. England was caught in the toils. She had subscribed to the Pragmatic Sanction and been given her price; now she must abide by her bargain. It was, after all, Walpole himself who had guaranteed the Sanction by the Treaty of Vienna in 1731, and, ironically, it was largely his reluctance to become entangled on the Continent or to break with Spain which had induced him to sign. What he had hoped to gain, what he had indeed secured, was an immediate commercial benefit, and he had shut his eyes to the future. Now the future was upon him and added to his consternation. Yet this extension of the war at the end of 1740 did not spring out of England's conflict with Spain; and if rightly handled, might be made to favour England by distracting the Continent in general and the Bourbon powers in particular. They were too absorbed in the clash near at hand to notice the minor disturbances abroad, and England might have had a clear field in America. Yet the fascination of an expected horror blinded Walpole, and with the outbreak of the War of the Austrian Succession, England drifted away from the colonies towards the Continent. It was the War of the Austrian Succession and England's absorption in it, far more than the Spanish war, which gave the Pretender his chance. More-over, war on the Continent inevitably implicated Hanover, and

Walpole had at once to meet the urgency of the King and bear the odium of his policy. Too late he began to weigh up the possibility of severing Hanover from England. He might have arranged the matter without much trouble when George II and the Prince of Wales were at loggerheads, but in those days he had done nothing. Now he played with the idea of separation but in a nerveless fashion, flinging out the suggestion in private conversations, but finding himself unable or unwilling to carry the matter through.

All these difficulties would have mattered less if the war had been in any sense successful. But it was not. Walpole had little enough to show for his expeditions to the Atlantic and the Pacific. The former was entrusted to Vernon, who sailed in July 1739 and captured Portobello in the following November. So far all was *couleur de rose*, though Walpole gained small credit, since Vernon was an active member of the Opposition, and his success merely served as a text on which the Opposition could hold forth at length. However, reinforcements were sent to him, though without instructions, and with the arrival of the reinforcements things went from bad to worse. Vernon decided to attack Carthagena and failed dismally. He then received orders from home to attack Santiago in Cuba and failed once more. Thereafter he disappeared from sight and interest, except as a tavern sign.

The other expedition, under Anson, to the Pacific, suffered a precisely opposite fate. Vernon had been given what ships and soldiers there were. Anson had to make do with the leavings. Perhaps because he was not given proper forces, he was bothered and badgered by a plethora of conflicting orders. The result was that his gallant little squadron, largely manned by seamen dragged from the hospitals and reinforced by maimed Chelsea pensioners, did not sail till September 1740—fifteen months after Vernon—and had to round Cape Horn at the worst time of the year. From that moment England lost sight of it, till in June 1744 the *Centurion*, the sole survivor, anchored at Spithead, and Anson wrote deprecatingly to the Lord Chancellor, 'though the expedition has not had all the success the nation expected from it, which is a great misfortune to me, I am persuaded no misconduct can be justly laid to my charge'[1]—a sentiment that the world has admiringly endorsed. But Walpole by then was no longer in office, and had barely nine months to live.

[1] Yorke. *Hardwicke*, I, 346.

Anson pre-eminently, and Vernon to a lesser degree, suffered from the deplorable state to which the navy had sunk. No doubt both did their best, but they could not support Walpole's tottering credit. Now that he had to justify himself by deeds he stood miserably exposed, and it speaks volumes for his incomparable skill as a parliamentarian that he managed to maintain his position for nearly two and a half years, and at one point even seemed to have rehabilitated himself. The Opposition had been pressing him hard, and on the 13th of February 1741 staged what they hoped to be the final attack—a motion asking the King to remove Walpole from his presence and councils for ever—a motion which was lost by 290 votes to 106. Walpole had triumphed and by his triumph had secured another year of power, though hardly one of ease or contentment.

13

PULTENEY'S EARLDOM

Whatever those two and a half years may have been for Walpole, for Pitt they were years of striking development and still more striking experience. They came, too, at a point of time when he was exceptionally fitted to profit by them. He was in his early thirties, when the exuberance of youth first begins to be tinged with the colours of maturity. Moreover, he had served five years in Parliament, so that the initial strangeness had worn off and he was beginning to feel that inward poise which springs from an assured knowledge of skill and in its turn contributes to a sense of power. The malleable elements of his character were hardening into their final form, and it was particularly fortunate that the influences which bore upon him at that precise moment were all such as tended to prepare him for his future work.

The Opposition had never trusted Walpole and they did not overlook his failures. They had their own ideas both as to how the war should be run and what Walpole was likely to do. For military advice they could count upon the generals whom Walpole had cashiered. As early as December 1739 the veteran Lord Stair gave his views in a written memorandum. 'I shall take it for granted,' he wrote, 'that Great Britain has it in her power to make a prosperous war against Spain, spite of all the opposition that possibly can be made, even though France should meddle in the quarrel, by taking the Havannah, which can be done by raising troops in our colonies of America, headed by a very few regular troops sent from Britain. I mention the Havannah only, because *cela décide de la guerre*. The Havannah once taken, the body of troops can be employed in several other expeditions, which may be very useful and very practicable. I say nothing of the method of raising these troops in America; that is a consideration of another time and place. I shall only say, that by the means of our colonies in America Britain should get the better of any nation in a war in America.' Stair did not, however, believe that this was Walpole's

view or intention. He believed that Walpole's policy was 'to make
a treaty with Spain by the mediation of France,' and consequently
in his eyes 'the removing of Sir Robert' was 'a preliminary
absolutely necessary to the saving of the nation.' Here again the
old general had his schemes cut and dried. 'In the first place, there
must be a perfect union amongst the leaders of the country party
. . . all the operations must be directed by one common council.
Though there are many great and able men on the side of their
country, yet in my opinion the great strength of the party is the
people, who are entirely well-disposed to follow their leaders, to
save themselves and their country from impending slavery. If the
leaders will advise the communities to declare their sentiments on
a very few public points, and instruct their representatives in
Parliament accordingly, the strength of the country party will
very soon appear so very great, that it will very soon put Sir
Robert's gang out of countenance, and occasion a great many of
them to think of changing their side. . . .'[1] The quotation is long,
and would be over long but for the fact that in this memorandum,
which Pitt must have seen, lie the germs of his military and
political faiths. The influence which this expression of the old
veteran's beliefs must have had on Pitt can easily be imagined.
Stair was a great figure, and was still to be an active leader of
armies. In Pitt's eyes he was touched with the romance of
Marlborough's wars and crowned with the martyr's halo through
his dismissal at Walpole's hands. His words were steeped in
wisdom; his experience was vast; his advice Nestorian. The
memorandum was bread cast upon the waters.

The Opposition followed his advice as best they could, and
Pitt took his full share. More particularly he began to study the
problems of warfare, nominally and perhaps primarily in order to
bait Walpole; but the exercise must have been of the utmost value,
whatever the motive. 'Our time,' he declared, 'cannot be more
usefully employed during a war, than examining how it has been
conducted, and settling the degree of confidence that may be
reposed in those to whose care are entrusted our reputations, our
fortunes and our lives.' But the examination must be thorough
and factual; there must be no hushing up of faults, no whitewashing
of failure, no 'accounts obscure and fallacious, imperfect and
confused from which nothing can be learned.'[2] Concurrently there

---

[1] Papers of the Earls of Marchmont.
[2] Speech, 26th January 1741. *Parliamentary History*, Vol. XI

must be an open mind and a willingness to change opinions if the facts so demanded. Looking a little ahead, one may suppose that the most fruitful outcome of his researches was a growing conviction of the importance of thorough preparation and careful choice of objectives. Victories were not to be won at haphazard; carelessness would lose battles and throw away lives. It was some such thought which prompted him to demand why, when Walpole sent Admiral Hosier to Portobello in 1727, 'the Plate fleet was spared, our ships sacrificed to the worms, and our admiral and his sailors poisoned in an unhealthy climate.'[1]

Not many of Pitt's speeches during these two and a half years have been preserved, but those that have come down to us show, even in their imperfect form, a growing command of language, a new inventiveness in imagery, and above all an increasing readiness in retort. 'To tell us we must take this,' he said of the Government Bill for pressing sailors, 'because no other remedy can be thought of, is the same with a physician's telling his patient, "Sir, there is no known remedy for your distemper, therefore you shall take poison—I'll cram it down your throat." ' And in the course of the same debate he made his famous retort on old Horace Walpole, 'Sir, the atrocious crime of being a young man which the honourable gentleman has with much spirit and decency charged upon me, I shall neither attempt to palliate, nor deny, but content myself with wishing that I may be one of those whose follies may cease with their youth, and not of that number who are ignorant in spite of experience.'[2]

Although in Parliament Walpole managed to hold his own, in the country the Opposition were making steady progress. Their leaders were united for the moment by their dislike of Walpole and their hope of ousting him; they did their best to stir up the country, and found it increasingly easy. Walpole's conduct of the war was doing no one good. Admirals and generals were losing their reputations; soldiers and sailors were dying like flies; trade and commerce were flagging. 'The trade,' wrote a young Scot destined to future greatness, 'has suffered by captures to a degree that produces daily bankruptcies; and the merchants, enraged with the smart of their sufferings, impute most of the losses to neglect, in not stationing properly a few small ships, which was

[1] Speech, 13th February 1741. *Parliamentary History*, Vol. XI.
[2] Speech, 10th March 1741. *Chatham, The Modern Orator*, p. 11.

often desired to be done.'[1] The failures of Vernon at Carthagena
and in Cuba created discontent, the failure of Mathews and
Lestock in the Mediterranean led to squabbling and courts
martial. The Opposition fomented all discontents and the result
was that the general election of 1741 went against Walpole. He
faced a hostile House in December, failed to secure the election of
his nominee as Chairman of Committees and shortly afterwards
met defeat on the Westminster election petition. It was the
beginning of the end, and on the 11th of February 1742 he
resigned.

During the last few months of office he was barely engaged in
the war with Spain or the War of the Austrian Succession. He was
fighting disease, and more terrifying still, he was fighting to save
his own head. There were ugly cries from the more ardent of the
Opposition, and not least from Pitt; they seemed to be thirsting
for his blood. The bad old days of retribution were not yet over.
Impeachment, at least, was hanging over his head, and beyond
the trial before a packed jury loomed Tower Hill and the bloody
axe. Here was a fight which stirred Walpole's pulses, and one
which he knew how to wage. Here he was no longer dabbling in
the mysteries of army and navy and ordnance. Here he was
coping with parliamentary opponents, and his weapons were skill
in playing on human weaknesses and knowledge of the right
bribe. He clung to office desperately while he played out the
game. First he tried to bribe the Prince of Wales with an increase
of £50,000 in his allowance. But the Prince knew that he would
get as much or more from the Opposition. Then he turned to
Pulteney, the brilliant and unstable leader of the Opposition. He
dangled an earldom before him and hinted at a coalition. Pulteney,
wholly dazzled and half bought with the earldom, was more than
disposed to steal a march on his friends and join the great Minister.
Together what could they not do? And Walpole, smiling cynically,
knew that with his last fling he had won. When the bait had been
swallowed and the earldom was irrevocable, he slid out of office
secure in the knowledge that Pulteney's defection, incomplete
and disowned as it was, would cause heartburnings and divided
counsels, in the midst of which he would be forgotten, if he was
not forgiven. The crafty old fox was right—so great an error is
the acceptance of an earldom!

[1] William Murray to the Lord President in Scotland, 18th November 1741.

14

THE COMMITTEE OF ENQUIRY

Walpole had fallen but, like another Samson, he pulled down in his fall the Spanish castles of his opponents. Where was the new and incorruptible Ministry that was to succeed, and for which Opposition had been toiling all these years? As far off as ever. Pulteney had betrayed his followers and now deserted them. He took no pains to mould the new Cabinet. It was Walpole who created it from behind the scenes by means of his influence with the King. Walpole's main objects were to preserve the Whig flavour of the Ministry and secure an indemnity for himself. He had no intention of allowing uncontrolled power to fall into the hands of his enemies, and as he had fettered Pulteney with a peerage, so now he hobbled Carteret with a master. Carteret was Walpole's rightful successor, especially if Pulteney stood down. After all, it had been Walpole's failure to win the war and his feeble incursions into foreign affairs that had finally crushed him, and Carteret had been the chief exponent of a vigorous war policy and full-blooded intervention in Europe. Carteret undoubtedly hoped to become Prime Minister. But Walpole interposed; it was desirable for his own safety that the head of the new Government should be a nonentity; he chose Wilmington for the rôle and George II acquiesced. Carteret had to be content with the office of Secretary of State, where he could employ his time and talents on foreign affairs without too conclusive a voice in administration. Carteret accepted the position. With his undoubted abilities and without serious rivals, he may well have felt that sooner or later power would be his. But Walpole was not concerned with Carteret's ultimate destination; it was enough that the slight delay in his progress would give Walpole the breathing space that was so essential.

Amongst these changes—not so many, nor so striking—one fact stood out clearly. There were no appointments for the Patriots, for the small band who claimed to be unaffected by

bribes and unperturbed by menaces, and whose profession of
faith was reform at home and honour abroad. Some of them,
whose profession was perhaps stouter than their practice, complained to Pulteney in the presence of the Prince of Wales. But the
Prince had been won over already, reconciled to Walpole and the
King, and satisfied with the promotion of two young lordlings
from his household to be inferior members of the new administration. The deputation, including Pitt's two friends and mentors,
Cobham and Chesterfield, were sent empty away. Patriots with
cloudy ideas of purity in politics and prestige in foreign chancel-
leries were out of touch with the realities of life. They would
make a mess of administration and, worse still, they would
demand Walpole's head on a charger. At all costs they must be
excluded.

There was much to be said for this view. Walpole had claimed
sneeringly that 'it is but refusing to gratify an unreasonable or
insolent demand, and up starts a patriot.' Many of the small
band were men with a grievance; by no means all of them were
sincere; most of them were violent and uncontrolled. What is
more, they stood for something which they themselves had not
fully grasped. There was expectancy in the air, that strange,
restless ferment in the popular mind which presages revolution
and change. Twenty-one years earlier, when Walpole had come to
power, men's passions were still inflamed with dying loyalties and
outworn creeds, and the turgid swell was agitated by the huge
disaster of the South Sea Bubble; the world seemed to be falling
about men's ears and civilisation to be at stake. At all costs there
must be a period for settlement, for calmness, for rebuilding.
Any methods were justified that gave time for reflection. So
Walpole had proceeded with the weapons that he found to hand
—bribing, not widely but well, with the cynical wisdom of a
realist—a man with few ideals and none that were incapable of
fulfilment. He succeeded to admiration, but he left a trail of corruption behind which poisoned not only Parliament but the
Church and the People, and made reform necessary. The evil
which he had used had to be exorcised, and the vanguard of
reform was the small band of Patriots. They represented more
than a parliamentary Opposition. However inadequate their own
lives might be, however far short they fell of their professions,
however frequent their own backslidings, however profound
their own ignorance, they represented the highest and deepest

aspirations of the people—the instinctive dislike of corruption; the ingrained desire for freedom; the shy seriousness of national pride. Walpole had had perforce to stem these more generous instincts and wishes, substituting a flat and prosaic common sense that was philosophical in the pragmatic sense, and therefore doubly unsuited to the people he ruled, for the English are not philosophers nor pragmatists but a nation of poets tinged with a kindly idealism.

Walpole fell because his work was done. He had provided the necessary period of rest, which, if it had been broken by nightmares, had none the less performed its healing function. His fall should have been followed by a great outburst of reform; all the conditions were favourable. Yet nothing happened—or rather nothing seemed to happen. Walpole preserved the Whig Ministry, the old corruption, the bad methods as far as he could. What must change, must change—but let it be as little as possible. All seemed to continue as before; and yet his fall released two great streams of living spirit, the one political, the other religious. William Pitt and John Wesley, each in his own sphere, represented the awakening of England's soul in reaction against the dead hand of Walpole's system in Church and State. In the ensuing years Wesley was to breathe a lively faith through the countryside, raising and softening the individual toilers so that they might become worthy of the political heritage which Pitt was opening up for them. Henceforward the people were to grow equally in grace and power, and Parliament was to turn from a Venetian oligarchy full of intrigue and corruption to a popular assembly, dignified and impartial, at least in intention.

All this, however, at the moment was merely germinating. Not even Pitt, still less his colleagues, knew the full extent of their mission. And none of them, perhaps Pitt least of all, was free from the frailties of the flesh. Their exclusion from office filled them full of heats and undoubtedly inflamed their clamour for an enquiry into Walpole's conduct. Pitt was no more exempt from passion than the others—perhaps he was more violent—and it is sad to read his speeches at this time. Even in the bowdlerised form given to them by the Grub Street journalists, and for all the occasional flashes of profound truth and wise insight, they smell of resentment and revenge. Pitt knew that his case was bad, and deliberately used all his arts to make it appear good. He aped moderation and a willingness to admit mistakes, which his biographers have seized upon as forerunners of subsequent recantations. But alas! he made the subsequent recantations largely with his tongue in his cheek, and the present pretended moderation was out of keeping with the whole tone of the speeches. Now, if ever, he came within Burton's bitter description of an orator, 'a turncoat, an evil man, his tongue is set to sale, he is a mere voice . . . a corrupting cozener, one that doth more mischief by his fair speeches than he that bribes by money.'[1] A year earlier, in February 1741, while there was still hope of office, Pitt had spoken warmly on the motion for Walpole's removal, yet with a genuine moderation. Walpole, he had declared, had deserved to be 'deprived not only of his honours but of his life,' yet he demanded no such penalty; he was not incited by personal malice; he did not propose any arbitrary censure; he did not recommend an act of attainder or a bill of pains and penalties; all he asked was that 'the security of the nation may be restored and the discontent of the people pacified by his [Walpole's] removal from that trust which he has so long abused.' By March 1742 all had changed, and one must needs admit that the only apparent reason was Pitt's exclusion from office. He might pretend to be impartial, but that did not prevent him from basing his speech on the assumption of Walpole's guilt. There must be an enquiry, and 'the very design of an enquiry is to find out particular facts and particular proofs' —proofs in short of Walpole's misdeeds. Pitt might pretend to be waiting on the evidence, but that did not restrain him from enumerating Walpole's villainies and condemning him out of hand and without proof, nor from ending his speech with the ominous words, 'we must enquire, unless we are resolved to sacrifice our own liberties and the liberties of Europe to the preservation of one guilty man.' What he demanded now was that Walpole should be 'removed from the councils of our sovereign and condignly punished.' All of which sounded excellent in the onrush of Pitt's argument, until he suddenly recollected that Walpole was no longer a Minister. Nothing remained of his patriotic aims but the condign punishment, and with a wriggle of conscience Pitt turned to a half truth. 'If,' said he uneasily, 'we do not enquire, we shall probably remain under his guidance; because, though he be removed from the Treasury Board, he is not removed from the King's closet, nor will he be, probably, unless it be by our advice, or by our sending him to a

[1] Burton. *Anatomy of Melancholy*, I, 151.

lodging at the other end of the town [the Tower] where he cannot do so much harm to his country.'[1] It was a half truth, and was used with a great deal of insincerity.

The episode is not to Pitt's credit, though it was natural enough and no doubt of use in his education and for the ultimate benefit of constitutional practice. Walpole's assailants gained half their demand. They had clamoured for an enquiry into his conduct over the past twenty years. That was refused, but a second and modified demand for an enquiry into the last ten years was granted. A secret committee of twenty-one was appointed to sift the facts, and it is to the credit of the House that Pitt barely secured nomination to it. The first on the list obtained 518 votes, the last 258. Pitt was elected with 259 votes. The Committee never got very far, for all Pitt's efforts to galvanise it into action. Perhaps the majority were not anxious to press hardly on a defeated opponent, perhaps the majority had some inkling of his essential greatness and the place he was to occupy in history; perhaps the majority were moved by the kindly toleration of the ordinary Englishman.[2] But Pitt was not of that majority; he was fierce, uncompromising, indignant, hurt. He had not secured a post in the new Ministry; he was doubtful if the old abuses were dead, or even scotched; he was still nursing the grievance of his dismissal from the army; he was, let us hope, imbued with the reformer's zeal. But, alone, he could not open the mouths of reluctant and almost recalcitrant civil servants, or force them to give evidence against their old chief; alone, he could not call vengeance down on the fallen Minister's head. The enquiry lost itself in shallows and indifference, though it was not entirely without fruit. 'With the close of Walpole's administration,' it has been pointed out, 'and as a consequence, doubtless, of the appointment of the Secret Committee . . . there is a notable change in more than one respect traceable in the Treasury records. The total of the issues under the heads of secret service, special services, and of issues to the Solicitor of the Treasury for so-called law costs and charges becomes appreciably less.'[3] That result was

---

[1] Speech, 9th March 1742. *Parliamentary History*, Vol. XII.
[2] For the views of the ordinary Englishman and Walpole's neighbours, see Pyle's letter of 1st April 1742 : " Our great neighbour has little favour to hope for, and did not candid men believe he wants no favour, his case would be looked upon as hopeless. Yet . . . who is there that would wish him to undergo the fiery trial of an Inquisition. . . ." (*Memoirs of a Royal Chaplain*, p. 71.)
[3] *Calendar of Treasury Books and Papers, 1742-1745*, p. viii.

hidden from Pitt, and so the reforming zeal in his soul continued
to fizzle and sputter through one or two sessions, though it never
lit the bonfire which he had hoped. In the end he acquiesced and
came to reckon his old opponent more nearly in accordance with
his true measure. They pursued different aims in different ways at
different times, but both were great patriots and both were great
statesmen, the one mellow in his cynical quietness, the other
turbulent in his fiery strength.

15

THE BALANCE OF POWER

Though Pitt was undoubtedly chagrined at his exclusion from office, he cannot have been altogether surprised. Doubts had been lurking at the back of his mind throughout the last months of Walpole's Ministry, doubts that were not the less disturbing because they were shapeless and ill-defined. They had been sufficiently potent to make him press Chesterfield with increasing urgency, as 1741 progressed from summer to winter, to return from France and lead the Opposition. At first the wish was wrapped in friendly hopes that his health might soon be restored; then it became playfully serious—'It is reported here that you sup with ladies and keep ill hours. If you have health enough to live, not only with French men but with French women, I conceive the whole learned faculty will pronounce your health sufficiently confirmed. If this be your happy state, I do maintain (without talking patriotism) that your Lordship has more business which indispensably requires your presence here, than any man in England.'[1] Finally he grew anxious and argumentative, writing to 'sum up the great task which seems to require you, in the words of the litany, to comfort and help the weak-hearted, to strengthen them that stand, to raise up them that fall and finally to beat down Satan under our feet.' There should be no great difficulty, considering the 'numerous bands of upright spirits' which composed the House of Commons. And yet—and yet—'the Coffee Houses are filled with ingenious speculations. Some pretend the Minister of darkness may be able to amuse the credulous weakness of a few with the old charm of reversionary power, and by that means triumph over any numbers; this seems to me the worst that can possibly happen. Others suppose he may, by consent, make a quiet and safe retreat in the face of all these numbers, which will be bad enough but in my opinion much better than the former case, provided the evil spirit be effectually removed, and did not

[1] Pitt to Chesterfield, 10th September 1741. Chatham. *Correspondence*, I, 4.

change shapes, only to work destruction under a new name with a double weight of power and authority.' All was difficulty and doubt, and if good was to come of it, Chesterfield's 'hand will best mix the saving draught and heighten it with the necessary ingredients of honour and reputation.'[1] It was dawning on Pitt with increasing strength that other hands and voices were ineffective; he had already told Chesterfield that 'the Austrian thunder of my Lord Carteret has not yet waked the child in cradle';[2] that he was beginning to have doubts of his other quondam leaders may be inferred from the break which he was shortly to make with them.

And now events had shown that the speculations of the Coffee Houses and Pitt's fears had all hit the mark or come near it. Walpole had bamboozled Pulteney and Carteret with reversionary hopes; he had managed to slip off safely; and if he had not changed shapes himself, at least he had seen to it that the new Ministry donned most of his own cast-off clothes.

All that was left for Pitt was to sum up the new Ministry and define his own attitude towards it. As Carteret was clearly the moving spirit, it became necessary to know how far Carteret was involved with the old gang and its methods, and in what respect his foreign policy differed from Walpole's. Carteret was not one of Walpole's creatures. There had been a time nearly twenty years before when the two had been rivals, but Walpole had opposed and beaten him. Carteret had never recovered his balance, and now never would. For hard on twenty years he had been conscious of failure, and the secret admission of inferiority now made him accept the master whom Walpole placed above him. There was not a little of tragedy in Carteret's life, and not a little of irony in his posthumous reputation. He has come down the pages of history as a bright genius, whose promise was never fulfilled because of sudden and inexplicable flaws—a real figure of tragedy and yet brightened and lightened by a gay laughing spirit that refused to be broken by fate or browbeaten by misfortune— a brave battling spirit taking evil days lightly and unveiling in momentary glimpses the fertile fields of a lofty idealism and a colourful imagination—a wise and proudly aloof spirit sweeping the panorama of life with eagle eye and on his deathbed mingling the sonorous lines of Homer with the prophetic judgments of a

[1] Pitt to Chesterfield, 1741. Record Office. Chatham Papers.
[2] Pitt to Chesterfield, 6th August 1741. Chatham. *Correspondence*, I, 1.

statesman. Did not Pitt himself in a moment of forgiving candour
admit that Carteret had been his master in all the higher branches
of statecraft? A great soul, a flashing spirit! And yet, if underrated
in life, surely overrated in death. Carteret had once at the outset
of his career, when Ambassador in Sweden, shown himself pur-
poseful and tenacious and he had been rewarded by success; but
from that point onward his actions had been uniformly erratic,
infirm, and unsuccessful. His characteristics were in striking
contrast with those of his fellow-statesmen, and at variance with
the general characteristics of the age, but being attractive in themselves won a puzzled and not altogether sincere admiration from
his contemporaries. In an age that tended to be pedantic he
possessed the charm of manner which goes with genuine classical
learning; he had a sense of humour that was kindly in an age of
cynicism and satire; he was a gentleman by instinct in an age that
was gentlemanly by convention, and he stood for spiritual
optimism in an epoch of material gambling. His contemporaries
were half afraid and half contemptuous of the strange man who
could not only talk German to the King, but could rant and
rhodomontade when he was sober and break into poetry when he
was drunk. Carteret was a minor Elizabethan rather than a man
of the eighteenth century, and was not as able in action as he was
in vision. The political art *par excellence* of the Whigs and the
eighteenth century was the 'management' of the House of Commons, that system of bribery, sometimes in cash but more
generally in places and favours, which ensured the Whig majority.
Carteret, like Pitt, would have nothing to do with it, but only
because it was beneath his notice, not as in the case of Pitt
because it was utterly repugnant to his nature. Carteret had other
ideas; he was a big-game hunter and could not be bothered with
this shooting at clay pigeons. 'What is it to me,' he once cried,
'who is a judge or a bishop? It is my business to make kings and
emperors, and to maintain the balance of Europe.' And on another
occasion he burst out, 'I want to instil a nobler ambition into you,
to make you knock the heads of the Kings of Europe together,
and jumble something out of it which may be of service to this
country.' It was all very ideal, no doubt, but at the same time
windy and grandiose; for after all, knocking heads together is not
a noble ambition, and it is made no nobler by putting crowns
upon them. The saving grace in his foreign policy, the one point
to which Pitt must have looked with hope, was his determination

not to be overridden by France—'Will you submit to France or not? I will always traverse the views of France in place and out of place; for France will ruin this nation if it can.' And with this determination went a profound knowledge of European politics. The question, however, was whether this profound knowledge was really a blessing. For what was the sum of European politics? Big problems were not agitating, liberal ideas were not germinating. Europe in 1742 was much as it is today—a medley of would-be burglars, each intent on aggrandising himself, quickly and easily, at the expense of others. Perhaps Europe was better then than it is today, for the brigands made no secret of their intentions, and mouthed no nonsense of ideologies or the purity of racial blood. Kingdoms belonged to a hereditary caste, who were too self-confident to need the aid of political cruelty at home or political camouflage abroad. Europe was a vast scene of grab, and the game was one which showed no signs of finality and had no great attraction for this country. There had been a time when English kings had amused themselves with the vain hope of conquering France, and they had drained away the vitality of the country for generations in the attempt. But those days were long past. Consciously or unconsciously, England now felt that she had no place on the Continent. So little did she think of her chances, so slight were her desires, that she even thought more than once of surrendering Gibraltar. To a large extent the Continent reciprocated England's lack of interest. No one seriously wished to invade England, still less to conquer it. At most England's enemies contemplated a small expeditionary force to make good the landing of the Pretender, who thereafter must make his own way. England and the Continent were separated by more than the Channel. As a consequence England, perhaps only half consciously, developed an extra-continental policy. In Europe her main interest was centred, not on the shifting mass of the Holy Roman Empire, not in the rivalries of Bourbon and Hapsburg, not in the petty lordships of Germany or the coveted principalities of Italy, but in the Low Countries. Yet even here the interest was purely negative. She feared a possible invasion, and therefore she worked to keep the nearest ports out of the hands of the stronger powers. So long as the Low Countries were independent and weak, Great Britain was satisfied. Not that the fear was based on genuine grounds; it was the gaunt legacy of the Armada, which has overshadowed British policy from

Elizabeth onwards, and still holds sway. England, which has no interest in continental games of smash and grab, must yet play her part in the endless round because of the Low Countries and their ports!

In the eighteenth century this interest involved the political theory of the balance of power. England must prevent any single kingdom from dominating the Continent and so absorbing the Low Countries. It was a policy which must result in a constant change of loyalties, since no ally could be supported when he became too strong, and because no one could trust England for long it inevitably led to the taunt of 'perfide Albion.'

During the long reign of Louis XIV France so clearly dominated the scene that England could have no excuse for changing sides. But with the death of Louis the position was not so clear, and with the accession of the House of Hanover to the English throne the position became obscure. The interests of Hanover were essentially and inextricably European. She had no maritime interests, and no preoccupation with the Low Countries. All her thoughts, all her ambitions were centred in the Empire and the wrangling pettinesses and jealousies of the German states. In the welter of small principalities there was an excellent Tom Tiddler's ground where Electors might snatch handfuls of gold and silver. The first two Georges were far more absorbed in Hanover and the Empire than in England, and it was precisely the plotting and counterplotting of the Germanic states which Carteret had studied and understood. He was as wrapped up in them as George II; he was as convinced of their importance. Here were the kings whose heads he wanted to knock together; here was the jumble out of which a prize was to be shaken.

It is almost impossible, and certainly unnecessary, to describe the interaction of all these petty states, but it is important to grasp the broad European position. The wars of William III and Marlborough had been justified by the Whig theory of balance of power. France under Louis XIV was supposed to be aiming at European hegemony, and certainly desired to expand to her 'natural boundary' of the Rhine. As this involved the conquest of the Low Countries, England had forged the London-Hague-Vienna axis (to borrow a modern phrase) in order to reduce the overtopping power of France. The axis had proved successful, and in 1713 the Treaty of Utrecht had restored the balance by shutting France into her old territories, by separating the crowns

of France and Spain, by restoring the 'Barrier' in the Low
Countries, and by strengthening Austria in Italy. But the very
fact of success destroyed the *raison d'être* of the London-Hague-
Vienna axis and raised new objects of suspicion. Holland, of
course, was too small to be feared, but Austria was great and
growing. Care must be taken to see that she did not, in her turn,
covet the hegemony of Europe and make the Austrian Netherlands a source of disquiet. Hence the *entente* with France,
promoted and maintained by Walpole. Hence also his adherence
to the Pragmatic Sanction, in spite of the seeming contradiction,
in order to ensure that the Empire should not be disrupted on
the death of Charles VI—a catastrophe which would leave no
counterpoise to France. Other nations adhered to the Sanction
in their own time and in return for their own price, but when
Charles VI died on the 20th of October 1740 none of them felt
bound by their treaties, and all, with the exception of England,
were anxious to snap up any unconsidered trifles that might be
lying around. England's lack of interest was not necessarily due to
any higher code of morality. There were at least three good
reasons, besides ethics, why she should remain loyal to her
pledge. First, there was no part of the Empire which she coveted;
secondly, she was preoccupied with the Spanish war; and lastly,
a scramble for the Austrian possessions would overturn the
balance of power. The other nations had a more lively interest.
Prussia in particular was counting her chances. Her late King,
Frederick William I, had died in the previous March, bequeathing
to his son a full treasury and a splendidly equipped army. The new
Frederick of Prussia was young and as yet unknown. He had been
whipped, neglected, bullied, imprisoned and almost murdered by
his insane and ferocious father, and had early learnt to keep his
thoughts to himself. But beneath an impassive exterior lay a
cynical courage combined with a 'realist' view of life, sharpened by
the miseries and subterfuges of his upbringing. Frederick noted
the facts and on the 15th of December 1740 invaded Silesia.

To Walpole it seemed clear that if England took too active a
part in supporting Maria Theresa, Prussia would be forced into an
alliance with France, and perhaps also Bavaria, and the probable
result would be the dismemberment of Austria and the election of
a French candidate to the Imperial Crown. Accordingly, while he
acknowledged England's obligation to support Maria Theresa,
while he secured from Parliament a vote for an armed force and a

subsidy of £300,000, and while he set on foot negotiations for a Grand Alliance to crush Frederick, he also proclaimed his readiness to mediate between Prussia and Austria, persuaded Frederick to offer his vote for Maria Theresa's husband, Francis of Lorraine, as Emperor in return for the cession of Silesia, and urged Maria Theresa to accept this offer. She refused indignantly, with the result that Frederick entered into an alliance with France. Walpole's hesitating diplomacy had done nothing but antagonise Austria, while producing that alliance between France, Prussia and Bavaria which he so much feared. It was at this point that he resigned.

What line would Carteret take? The old theory of the balance of power no doubt demanded a strong policy in favour of Austria, but that in its turn would mean a continental war with France and Prussia on top of the existing war with Spain. Was England to plunge from one war into another? Was Walpole's policy of peace to be shattered in every direction? That was the question, and Carteret had no hesitations. His optimism, his upbringing, his Whiggism, all drew him on to one side, and he threw the whole weight of his influence into the Austrian alliance.

16

THE WAR OF THE AUSTRIAN SUCCESSION

The War of the Austrian Succession, in which Carteret was so determined to meddle, was simple in its broad outlines, however confusing in its details. The death of Charles VI had created a real problem. He had been the last male of the youngest branch of the House of Hapsburg. The choice of his successor therefore lay between his daughter, who was his natural heir, and a male descendant through the female line of one of the elder branches. It so happened that there were such male descendants of all the elder branches. True, the right of each one of them to succeed had been barred or renounced at some period in the past, but only in favour of a direct male heir. Now that cognizance had to be taken of the female side, it was not altogether unreasonable to claim that the whole position should be reviewed, and the inheritance if necessary divided. There were ample precedents. William of Orange and Louis XIV, to mention no others, were outstanding examples of potentates who had felt no compunction in carving up —at all events in intention—dominions which did not belong to them, regardless of the owner's wishes.

From the practical point of view there were other matters to be taken into account. There was, for instance, the problem of the Imperial throne. For centuries it had been filled by the House of Hapsburg and had given lustre to their dominions from which it derived its main strength. What was to happen now? Maria Theresa as a woman could not be elected herself, and her husband, Francis of Lorraine, was only one among several candidates. He might well fail to secure election, and in that event what territories could rightly be allotted to the new Emperor?

Then there was the problem of the Austrian inheritance itself, which was a medley of peoples held together more by habit than affection. It was commonly supposed that the accession of Maria Theresa would be followed by the defection of the Italian provinces and possibly also of many of the Germanic states. Chaos was only too likely to supervene, and the control of a strong male hand was therefore all the more desirable. There was much to be said in fact for making some reasonable arrangement instead of letting things slide in an atmosphere of sentiment.

Frederick of Prussia had been the first to move, but he was by no means the only interested party. Louis XV of France was equally engrossed and a much more important factor. Being descended from the eldest branch of the House of Austria, no doubt he had as good a claim as most, but he hesitated to put forward pretensions which would have united Europe against him. He thought it better to act the part of the honest broker, by which he hoped to secure a substantial advantage without incurring any odium. His plan, briefly, was to arrange for the partition of Austria between the various claimants, including Maria Theresa, the chief beneficiary being Charles Albert, Elector of Bavaria, who in addition to wide territorial gains was to be given the Imperial crown. Nominally, France was to get nothing beyond the incidental—and unmentioned—benefit which would accrue to her through the diminution of her rival's power, but Louis also had it in mind to snap up the Austrian Netherlands surreptitiously.

When Frederick had broken the uneasy spell following Charles VI's death, Louis set his plans in motion. His strategy was simple, He despatched an army of 40,000 men into West-phalia, which was admirably situated both to overawe the Dutch and to threaten Hanover. At the same time he ordered another army, of 50,000 men, to cross the Rhine and, in conjunction with the Bavarian and Saxon forces, to invade Bohemia.

At first all went well. The Dutch held back, and Hanover, terrified at the thought of invasion, promptly signed a treaty of neutrality. Most of the states of Europe entered into a coalition to dismember Austria. Frederick became master of Silesia, and Charles Albert, with the aid of the French, captured Prague, proclaimed himself King of Bohemia, and in January 1742 secured election as Emperor.

Of all the signatories to the Pragmatic Sanction, England alone supported Maria Theresa, and even England, under Walpole's guidance, did practically nothing but offer her a subsidy and try by diplomatic means to bring about a compromise with Frederick. By the end of 1741 her fortunes seemed at the lowest ebb; her army, never well found, was beaten and dispirited; her treasury was empty; her friends were few and faint-hearted; her enemies

many and eager; her territories largely overrun. Ruin seemed about
to fall on her, and in despair she made her dramatic appeal to
Hungary. It was a daring move, for the Hungarians were a proud
and independent people who had long chafed under the Austrian
domination. But it succeeded; the Queen's beauty and high spirit
stirred their chivalry and they rose as one man to right her
wrongs. Yet, for all their loyalty, there was little ground for
thinking they could stem the flood; at best their intervention was
likely to do no more than delay a destined end.

It was at this point, when all seemed dark, that Walpole fell and
Carteret assumed the reins. His decision to support Maria Theresa
had in the circumstances a touch of the heroic. He deserves the
credit which belongs to bold decisions, though in fact at that very
moment a harvest of other men's sowing was ripening for his
sickle.

His rise to power at once created an atmosphere of bustle, and,
more important still, a period of real activity. British troops,
16,000 strong, were despatched to the Continent; British money,
half a million sterling, was lavished on Maria Theresa; British
diplomacy was mobilised to form a great German confederacy
with the object of expelling the French from the Empire and
rousing the Dutch to the peril from the Bourbons. Even the
British Navy had its part to play, though it was a very minor part.
Captain Callis earned a gold collar and badge by burning Spanish
galleons in the French harbour of St. Tropez, and Captain Martin
won a niche in the temple of romantic history by placing his
watch ostentatiously on the cabin table as he gave Don Carlos of
the Two Sicilies one hour in which to sign an agreement to
withdraw his troops from Northern Italy.

There was a further problem which Carteret had to face, the
problem of Hanover. George II was determined to keep his
beloved Electorate safe and inviolable, and the difficulties which
arose out of this determination were twofold. On the one hand it
was necessary not only to distinguish between George II as King
of England and George II as Elector of Hanover, but also to
persuade other nations in general, and France and Prussia in particular, to accept this distinction. On the other hand it was
imperative to allay the jealousies and anger which the distinction
created in England. In English eyes it was anomalous, to say the
least, that England, with no direct stake on the Continent and
with her own private war on her hands, should spend money and

men and effort in lavish profusion, while Hanover in the midst of affairs and vitally concerned should bask in the sunshine of an artificial neutrality. Whether it was with some idea of reducing this anomaly, whether it was because of England's lack of military preparation, or whether it was merely to put money into George's electoral pocket, Carteret hired 16,000 Hanoverians and 6,000 Hessians to serve with the British forces in the Low Countries—and thereby increased the English irritation almost beyond bearing.

None the less he seemed to be gaining a large measure of success. The enemy advance slowed down, and by June 1742 he had persuaded Frederick and compelled Maria Theresa to come to terms, under which Frederick, in return for Silesia, threw over his French allies and withdrew from the war. Carteret preened himself on his success, and seems really to have believed that by a short war he could obtain terms for Maria Theresa which would leave her powerful enough to check France and at the same time by satisfying her opponents put an end to the various wars in Germany, Spain and Italy.[1] In effect he was usurping to himself Louis XV's self-appointed rôle of arbiter in the dismemberment of Austria.

But Carteret's success so far as he was concerned personally had more of appearance in it than reality. The fact is that the component parts of the enemy forces were becoming suspicious of one another and beginning to quarrel, while the French, on whom victory hinged, were suffering from an inefficient commissariat, and were wasting away through sickness and desertions. Hence the slowing down of their advance. Meanwhile, and from their point of view worst of all, Frederick was playing a subtle game which deceived friends and foes alike but was more hurtful to friends. He was the one realist on the Continent, and he showed his genius by keeping his ambitions within strict limits. He knew exactly what he wanted. He was determined to conquer and keep Silesia, but he had no intention of trying to bite off more than he could chew or of fighting to win prizes for others. If Carteret could and would arrange for the cession of Silesia, so much the better. Of course Frederick would then drop out of the war. What good would further fighting do him? It would merely serve to aggrandise France, and Frederick was a firm believer in a balance between his powerful neighbours. Too strong an Austria

[1] See Marchmont's Diary, 13th August 1744.

G

would jeopardise his latest acquisition; too strong a France would be a menace to his designs in the west. So he allowed Carteret to bargain with Maria Theresa on his behalf, graciously accepted Silesia at their joint hands, and cheerfully renounced further fighting which he had never intended to pursue.

So the first year of Carteret's administration drew to an end.

17

'A PROVINCE TO A DESPICABLE ELECTORATE'

Though Pitt had for some time misdoubted the wisdom and ability of Carteret, he did not at once oppose the new Minister. If his own exclusion from office left his heart sore, it did not swamp his reason—Carteret must be given his chance. It was not, however, long before the doubts deepened into distrust, and the distrust gave rise to opposition. Whatever Carteret might be doing abroad, at home he was not setting right the wrongs of which Walpole had been guilty. On the contrary, the change of Ministers seemed to be merely a substitution of King Stork for King Log. If Walpole had been too inert, Carteret was too active—in the wrong direction. This conviction forced itself steadily upon Pitt from more than one side. Although his eagerness to promote an enquiry into Walpole's methods had been sharpened and envenomed by his own private irritations, it had been founded in a burning desire to crush corruption and establish honest government. He had hoped much, and it was only by degrees that he realised that he had been tricked. Carteret's lukewarmness, the obstacles which kept supervening, the obstructive tactics of Walpole's old subordinates, were not inevitable, nor did they spring from feelings of humanity. The political conscience of the day would not have been unduly shocked if Walpole had been beheaded on Tower Green. What saved Walpole was the determination of the Whig oligarchy to remain in power, and their conviction that this could be achieved only by the 'management' of Parliament. Corruption as then practised was to continue, it was only the corrupters who were to change. It was essential therefore that there should be no disclosure of the methods lest the people, who were active enough in demanding reform, should have solid ground to go upon. Pitt fulminated and fretted, but there was no overcoming the weight of passive resistance. In a word Pitt had to recognise that 'the evil spirit' had not been effectually removed in domestic affairs. 'I hope indeed,' he had

said when Walpole fell, 'that I have at length lived to see the time
in which Parliament shall regain its ancient authority, when this
House shall be considered as the true representative of the people,
and when the laws shall be again observed rather from veneration
than from fear.'[1] But the hope was vain, and Pitt, for all his
obstinacy, had to admit it. Carteret might—as he boasted—be
busy banging crowned heads together but he was consenting to
the hidden greasing of dirty palms.

Nor did Pitt find the position any better when he turned to
foreign affairs. Carteret's energies were misplaced, and to make
matters worse he was afraid to trust to English armies. The hiring
of foreign mercenaries, which had been one of his first steps, was
not only a waste of money but an insult to the nation. To Pitt's
intensely patriotic spirit this contemptuous belittlement of
England's power was by far the most galling part of what he
believed to be a wholly wrong policy, and he waited with
impatience for the subject to be brought before the House. His
opportunity came on the 10th of December 1742 when a motion
for the payment of these troops was debated in Parliament.
'There was no necessity,' he declared,[2] 'for hiring auxiliary troops,
since it does not appear that either justice or policy required us to
engage in the quarrels of the Continent, that there was any need
of forming an army in the Low Countries, or that, in order to
form an army, auxiliaries were necessary.' So much for the
general premises. Having outlined his political and military
beliefs, he turned to the canker which lay beneath, and treated
Hanover to the full lash of his sarcasm. 'The troops of Hanover,
whom we are now expected to pay, marched into the Low
Countries, indeed, and still remain in the same place; they
marched to the place most distant from the enemy, least in danger
of an attack, and most strongly fortified if an attack had been
designed; nor have they any claim to be paid, but that they left
their own country for a place of greater security.' He would not
be surprised if, after such another glorious campaign, he were
told that 'the money of this nation cannot be more properly
employed than in hiring Hanoverians to eat and sleep.' All that
these redoubtable mercenaries were doing was to be 'a show to
our friends and a jest to our enemies.'

[1] Speech, 23rd March 1742, as reported in the *Gentleman's Magazine*, July 1743.
[2] Speech, 10th December 1742, as reported in the *Gentleman's Magazine*, February 1744.

From this contemptuous badinage about the inefficiency of Carteret's military plans and the ineffectiveness of his hired troops, Pitt turned to higher game. It was always his method to move directly towards the central point, and he realised that there was little to be gained, beyond atmosphere, in poking fun at the hirelings. England had long neglected her forces, naval and military, and it was likely enough that the Hanoverians, as troops, were better than a levy of raw English recruits. But in Pitt's philosophy the spirit was of infinitely greater importance than the material. High shakos might make a brave show, but it was high hearts that would make heroes. The Hanoverians were hirelings of the worst type, since they had no conceivable interest in the war; their Government had concluded a treaty of neutrality; their country would, or should, be left inviolate; their wives and children were safe; they were prompted by no stirrings of patriotism, no ideals, and no desires save the ordinary hope of making a living. Here was no material for glory or honour. And yet by their mere presence they stole the hearts out of Englishmen, by spreading abroad a false sense of security and the still falser doctrine that national safety and national honour can be provided by the laying out of money instead of by personal service. The fault lay, not in the mercenaries who were acting under orders, and indeed were following a dangerous occupation. The fault lay in the policy which produced these results—a policy mainly Hanoverian, both in its inception and in its working. The chief offender was the head of the Hanoverian state, the Elector. It was unfortunate that he happened also to be the King of England, but if that fact must cramp Pitt's style, he saw no reason why it should disguise the truth. He turned, therefore, resolutely to the dangerous task of baiting the King and belittling Hanover. It was all very well, he argued, to observe our treaties inviolably; it was very right to show an example of fidelity 'though we should stand alone in the practice of virtue'; but none the less we should not shut our eyes to the fact that 'the balance of power, the Pragmatic Sanction and the preservation of the Queen of Hungary' were of interest to other powers as well as Great Britain. We should be foolish to act 'as if they were to be the care of Great Britain alone; as if the power of France were formidable to no other people, as if no other part of the world would be injured by becoming a prey to an universal monarchy and being subjected to an arbitrary government of a French deputy.' England was not the only country to sign the Pragmatic Sanction. There was such a place as Hanover, and its Elector, like our King, had signed and 'was equally obliged, if treaties constitute obligation, to defend the House of Austria against the attacks of any foreign power, and to send his proportion of troops to support the Queen of Hungary.' Pitt with feigned humility professed not to know if those troops had been sent, but he added bitingly, 'since we have not heard them mentioned in this debate, and have found by experience that none of the merits of that electorate are passed over in silence, it may, I think, fairly be concluded that the distresses of the Queen of Hungary have yet received no alleviation from her alliance with Hanover, that her complaints have moved no compassion at that court, nor the justice of her cause obtained any regard.' From this indictment to an attack on the King himself was a short step, and Pitt took little pains to hide his meaning. 'This negligence of treaties,' he inferred, 'this disregard of justice, this defect of compassion,' must be due to the pernicious advice of the English Ministers who persuaded the King to hire to Great Britain the troops which as Elector he should have sent to the Queen of Hungary at his own expense, 'for it is not to be imagined that His Majesty has more or less regard to justice as King of Great Britain than as Elector of Hanover; or that he would not have sent his proportion of troops to the Austrian army, had not the temptations of greater profit been industriously laid before him.' Having crossed the Rubicon, Pitt grew bolder—almost reckless. 'Why,' he asked bitterly, 'should the Elector of Hanover exert his liberality at the expense of Great Britain? It is now too apparent that this great, this powerful, this formidable kingdom, is considered only as a province to a despicable Electorate.' The evidence of partiality was too open and obvious. It was not merely that unwanted troops were retained 'only for the purposes of Hanover.' There was much beside. 'I doubt not but most of those who sit in this House can recollect a great number of instances, from the purchase of part of the Swedish dominions to the contract which we are now called upon to ratify. . . . To dwell upon all the instances of partiality which have been shown, to remark the yearly visits that have been made to that delightful country, to reckon up all the sums that have been spent to aggrandise and enrich it, would be at once invidious and tiresome.'

Pitt's efforts were unavailing; the motion to pay the troops was passed by 260 votes to 193; and indeed he can hardly have expected any other conclusion. The payment of the troops was not the point at issue. More interesting was the proof of his final breach with Carteret. The two belonged to opposite schools, between which there could be no real compromise. Pitt was not wholly blind to the importance of the Continent; he was not fundamentally opposed to intervention in Europe, and within limits he accepted a policy of balance of power. But his emphasis lay in another direction. He believed the Tory policy of expansion overseas was right, and slowly he was building up on this basis his vision of a British Empire. All must be subordinated to that destiny, and Hanover first of all. He was already beginning to think that in the welter of Germanic rivalries it would be wiser to back Prussia than Austria,[1] and in the maelstrom of European strife to be freed from the dead weight of Hanover. Carteret belonged to the opposite school. He was wedded to the Whig theories, to the 'old system,' to Hanover. So far from desiring to be quit of the Continent, he revelled in its intricacies, certain that he was the one and only man able to unravel the skein and produce order. The two were drifting steadily apart, and while Carteret continued his preparations for the ensuing campaign, Pitt continued his attacks, growing daily in disfavour with the King and bad odour with the Government. But not with the public. 'Several of our young Members,' Montagu wrote to his wife,[2] 'have greatly distinguished themselves by their opposition. . . . But none has done it so eminently as Mr. Pitt who in the opinion of several, as well as me, is a greater man than ever I have sat with, and if he preserves his integrity will be transmitted to posterity in the most illustrious of characters.'

[1] See letter of H. Hastings to Earl of Huntingdon, 27th Sept. 1744. "Mr. P[itt] has been all along of opinion that P[russia] was to be gained upon any terms." H. M. C. Hastings MSS., Vol. 3.

[2] 21st Dec. 1742. Climenson, I, 137-8.

18

PELHAM RISING

The withdrawal of Frederick from the war in June 1742 at once
brightened Maria Theresa's fortunes, leading to the recovery of
her territories in the east. Carteret, meanwhile, had a golden
opportunity of striking at France in the west but failed to take it.
The Dutch were apathetic and without their active support he
would not allow a free hand to Lord Stair, now commanding the
forces in Flanders. So the army frittered away the autumn and
winter aimlessly at Ghent. It was a mistake. Inaction bred discord
among the allies and gave the French time to make new
dispositions.

When, at last, in the spring of 1743, Stair was allowed to move,
he prepared to march against the French under the Duc de
Noailles, but was much hampered by the Anglo-Hanoverian
bickering. His position was made no easier by the refusal of the
Hessians to fight and the failure of the Dutch to send their contingent. He suffered, in short, from the perennial troubles of an
English army meddling on the Continent. The nations of Europe
were well able to look after themselves; they had no taste for the
English conception of a balance of power, being intent on their
own aggrandisement, and knew full well that if English help
were needed, they would neither hesitate to demand it nor fail to
secure it. It was for them, not England, to choose the time. So
they lounged and took their ease while Stair did his best to reconcile the conflicting elements under his command. The arrival of
the King in person, accompanied by the Duke of Cumberland and
Carteret, had some modifying effect on the temper of the
Hanoverians, but it added nothing to the brains of the generals.
Ignoring Stair's advice, the army under its illustrious head
marched straight into a French trap at Dettingen and only
marched out again thanks to the rashness and disobedience of the
French general De Grammont. George II, unhorsed but not
unmanned, led his army to an undeserved victory and then

strutted on to another standstill. The war was petering out, and
would have died of inanition but for Carteret, who busied himself
creating new alliances. He tried, without success, to bribe Charles
Albert into renouncing the French connection—an unreasonable
hope, as the French were now the Emperor's only support—and
he managed to win over the King of Sardinia by a subsidy and the
promise of naval help. But the only effect of this rather mixed bag
was to blow up the embers of the dying war in a fresh direction.
Frederick's object in making peace—apart from the fact that he
had obtained Silesia—had been to depress France rather than to
raise Austria. He wanted neither of them to be paramount, and
now, alarmed at Austria's progress and Carteret's efforts to unite
a strong Empire in her support, he revived his alliance with
France, marched into Bohemia and renewed his war with Maria
Theresa. To add to Carteret's confusion, in October 1743 France
and Spain entered into the second of the Family Compacts.
Beyond a doubt Europe was rejecting England's intervention and
resenting the presence of her army.

Meanwhile the Opposition at home had not been without effect.
There was a growing reaction against the European entangle-
ment, a growing undercurrent of resentment against Hanover,
a growing dissatisfaction with the Ministers who could neither
'manage' the House of Commons to their own benefit nor knock
the crowned heads of Europe together for England's advantage.
In July 1743 Wilmington died, and the general discontent was
sufficient to thwart Carteret in the choice of a successor. Carteret,
revelling in the intricacies of the Continent, wanted a staunch
supporter at home, and pressed the King to appoint Pulteney,
now Earl of Bath, to be head of the Treasury. But the feeling at
home was too strong, and the King, after an anxious pause of six
weeks, promoted Henry Pelham, the Duke of Newcastle's brother.

Pelham was a colourless man with some pretensions to financial
acumen. Common sense was his strong point, but it was not bulwarked by much strength of character or forcefulness in action.
He could, and did, deplore many measures which were deplorable
enough, but when he found himself opposed in his endeavours to
check them, he washed his hands of the matter, falling back on an
acquiescence that was half resigned and half querulous. At this
juncture he was anxious to moderate Carteret's activities on the
Continent and bring the war within reasonable bounds. He was
also anxious to strengthen the administration at home and buy off

its opponents. Both tendencies pushed him towards the Opposition, with whom he seems to have carried on a vague, clandestine negotiation. It could hardly be called serious, because Pelham had little intention, if indeed he had the power, of widening the basis of government to real purpose; nor could it be called flirting, for the desire to treat was genuine so far as it went. Walpole, who, as Lord Orford, was busy behind the scenes, suggested recruits from the Cobham squadron, and referred specifically to Pitt who 'is thought able and formidable,' but with his old distrust of the Jacobites, bade Pelham beware of the Tories. Newcastle, whose opinion on parliamentary shuffles was as valuable as his opinion on policy was worthless, had no doubt that it was absolutely impracticable to win over the Cobham party without also accepting 'a mixture of Tories,' three or four at the least. This link between Pitt and the Tories deserves closer attention. Whilst Pitt on those comparatively rare occasions when he proclaimed his political faith referred to himself as a Whig, he emphasised that his Whiggism consisted of an adherence to what he called Revolution principles. These principles were by now the common background of all parties with the exception of the small and wholly discredited group of Jacobites. But while they formed a background, they exercised a rapidly diminishing influence over the Whig party proper. For the Whig magnates the Revolution principles meant very little beyond the charter of the existing Whig oligarchy. The flowers of liberty and toleration and ordered parliamentary government which should have sprung from those principles had withered in the bud, and in so far as they were cherished it was, willy-nilly, by the body of the oppressed Opposition—the Tories. Hence the feelers which Pitt found himself increasingly obliged to put out towards the Tories, with whom he found almost more in common than with his professed party.

To Pelham the idea of approaching the Tories did not appeal. He took Orford's advice to proscribe them, and thereby lost one more chance of strangling the '45 before it was conceived. The other part of the advice—to cultivate the Cobham squadron—he attempted to take, but only half-heartedly. He was hampered by his brother's warning, and perhaps still more by the uncompromising attitude which Pitt had adopted towards Carteret. Although Pelham knew that the Cabinet was divided and that he and his brother were at variance with Carteret, it was difficult for so timid and hesitating a man to push that variance into the open, let alone to extremes. An alliance with Pitt would have been too pronounced. Hence his overtures, whatever they were, proved to little purpose. Pitt recognised in Pelham someone who was less distasteful than Carteret, and in Pelham's policy something more nearly approaching a point of view which he could himself adopt. If he had to lean to either division of the Cabinet, there was something more than a vague preference to guide him, but for the moment he had no intention of leaning to either side.

With the opening of the new session in December 1743 Pitt made his views clear. In the Debate on the Address he made a passing reference to home affairs—'with respect to our domestic affairs, we have met with no change in our measures; we can now, I think, expect none. The same screening, the same plundering, the same prodigal spirit prevails; the same criminal complaisance is expected from Parliament; and to purchase that complaisance, we may depend on it, the same corrupt, extravagant and dangerous means will be made use of.'[1] All that was the usual dose of generalities. In much the same category but more interesting as a pointer was Pitt's complaint at the 'negative put upon every motion that may tend towards our acquiring any parliamentary knowledge of our late measures.' He was no doubt thinking primarily of the abortive enquiry into Walpole's administration, but the wrappings of personal bitterness were falling off, and the core of sound constitutional practice was beginning to appear. The Government had asked for approbation of its actions, and Pitt argued that the House could not, and should not, applaud measures of which it knew nothing except from the columns of public newspapers; to form a considered judgment it must be given full parliamentary information. Though Pitt used his argument merely as a stick with which to beat the Government, it undoubtedly contained the germs of his subsequent fight for the freedom of the Press and the reporting of debates. Pitt came more and more to regard the House as the trustee and guardian of the people, and as such no less the critic of the Government than its prop. If the Members needed information in order to pass judgment on the Ministry, equally the electorate needed information in order to pass judgment on its representatives. In a democracy there must be publicity.

That development, however, lay in the future. Pitt had not thought out his argument, though he expatiated on it—if the

---

[1] Speech, 1st December 1743. Almon, I, 144.

report of his speech is to be trusted—at wearisome length, and with a tendency to chop logic which was as surprising as it was unconvincing. It was a bit of byplay, and as such the prelude to his main line of attack. The sins of the Government lay mainly in their foreign policy and their handling of the war. Their strategy was too expensive and too extensive, and their tactics had been stupid and inhumane. Dettingen, on which they prided themselves, would have been a defeat if 'the courage of some of the French generals had not got the better of their discretion.' It could not possibly be called a victory; we had run away 'in such haste, that we left all our wounded to the mercy and care of the enemy,' and we had failed to pursue the French or improve our temporary advantage. So far from being a victory, the action could only be called a 'lucky escape' from a trap in which we had been caught. As for the Government's strategy, it was beyond the capacity of our forces, particularly as the Dutch would not move. Worst of all, this inept bustling was unnecessary as the French had evacuated the Empire. What must one think of Carteret who was responsible for it all? He was 'an execrable, a sole minister, who had renounced the British nation, and seemed to have drunk of the potion described in poetic fictions, which made men forget their country.' The old charge of being 'sole minister' came with a fresh meaning. Walpole had deserved the epithet because he absorbed all power into his own hands. No one could honestly or plausibly say this of Carteret. So far from absorbing power, he had just failed to secure the appointment of his own nominee as head of the Treasury. But in another, and perhaps more dangerous sense, Carteret was undoubtedly a 'sole minister.' He was sole in that his policy was concocted at Hanover in the closet of the Elector, and pursued without the knowledge or acquiescence of his colleagues, and indeed in flat contradiction to their wishes. Only recently (though Pitt did not know it) on finding that Pelham had managed to persuade the King that the separation of England and Hanover was desirable, Carteret 'had never rested night nor day, till he had got the King to alter his mind.'[1] And now he and the King were entering into alliances and promising subsidies on their own authority with the intention shortly of presenting Parliament with a series of *faits accomplis*. In foreign affairs, Pitt complained not unjustifiably, the administration had run from one extreme to the other; 'our former Minister [Walpole]

[1] Marchmont's Diary, 6th November 1744.

betrayed the interests of his country by his pusillanimity, our present sacrifices them by his Quixotism; our former minister was for negotiating with all the world, our present is for fighting against all the world; our former minister was for agreeing to every treaty though never so dishonourable; our present will give ear to no treaty, though never so reasonable.'

Pitt followed up his attack by sketching the policy which England should have pursued. He admitted that England had an interest in supporting Maria Theresa and seeing that her husband became the Emperor, in order to preserve the balance of power; 'but this was our only interest, and it was an interest we had in common with all the powers of Europe, except France.' There was no reason why England should bear the whole burden, and directly it became evident that Maria Theresa could not be established in all her father's possessions, we should have urged her to yield part in order to save the rest. Clearly the opponent to be appeased was the King of Prussia 'both because his claim was the smallest, and because he was one of the most natural, as well as one of the most powerful allies we could treat with.' His terms should have been accepted when first he invaded Silesia, and we should have seen that they were. So far, however, from taking this wise course and so securing a powerful ally and peace at one and the same time, we encouraged Maria Theresa to resist, we attempted to form a confederacy for checking and even dismembering Prussia, we promised money and we hired mercenaries, and then having stirred up France to action, we lost our nerve, dropped our schemes, forgot our promises to the Queen of Hungary, and 'after having led that Princess upon the ice, . . . we left her there to shift for herself.' We estranged Austria, we annoyed Prussia; we irritated France, and all that came of our efforts was the election of a Francophil Emperor and the despoiling of Austria. It was now hopeless to expect that Austria could be raised sufficiently to counterbalance the might of France. Fortunately a single potentate was not the only counterpoise; a well-connected confederacy would do equally well, and we should in the circumstances be working for peace in Germany and a strong confederation of German states. No such policy had been pursued. We had played into the hands of France by espousing the cause of Austria against Prussia and so promoting an internecine quarrel in Germany itself. That was bad enough, but what made it worse was that our actions were weak and aimless. We carried out a bad policy feebly. There could be but one end of such blundering—defeat and bankruptcy. And here Pitt indulged in a remarkable warning. 'In these circumstances, I must desire the real friends of our present happy establishment to consider, what might be the consequence of the Pretender's being landed amongst us at the head of a French army? Would not he be looked upon by most as a third saviour? Would not the majority of the people join with him, in order to secure the nation from those that had brought it into such confusion?' It was a strange argument coming from Pitt, who had pooh-poohed similar warnings from Walpole in the past. Pitt himself felt the incongruity, and expressed the hope that this danger might be 'one of those that may be called imaginary.' None the less, he had an uneasy feeling that the course which Carteret was pursuing gave point to the danger by entangling us in a continental war which would absorb our forces without producing any result. It was likely enough that France would seize the opportunity of our preoccupations to promote internal difficulties through the Pretender.

Pitt's warning was based on the French activities at Brest and Dunkirk, which he had noted, though without being much perturbed. The Government, on the other hand, had been far too much interested in Hanover to observe them at all, or at least to pay them proper attention. Yet they arose naturally out of the course of events on the Continent. In January 1743 the aged Cardinal Fleury had died after a long tenure of office which had coincided largely with Walpole's. The two had had much in common: both had striven earnestly but in vain to preserve peace: each had been forced into a war which he had handled without much skill or conviction, and each had been succeeded by a Minister eager to prosecute it vigorously. Fleury's successor, Tencin, happened also to be indebted to the Pretender through whose influence he had obtained a cardinal's hat. In other circumstances this indebtedness might have escaped his memory, but now everything conspired to bring it to the front. The French had fared badly throughout 1743; they had been compelled to withdraw from Germany; their allies had been unsuccessful in Italy; their enemies had crossed the Rhine and were threatening Alsace. Gone were the days when hopeful and carefree incursions could be made into Bohemia. France must now fight in Flanders, perhaps for her existence, and the English as the mainspring of the attack must be harassed and hampered by every possible means. The known discontent of the English at the favours shown to Hanover gave Tencin good grounds for hoping that they might actually welcome the return of the Pretender. His restoration would mean peace, and even if the attempt failed, his landing would certainly create a diversion and might lead to the recall of the forces in Flanders. Tencin easily persuaded Louis XV that France had everything to gain and nothing to lose, and, with his consent, in the early summer of 1743 disclosed his plan to the Old Pretender at Rome, suggesting that Prince Charles Edward should come at once to Paris, so as to be on the spot and ready to lead an expedition against England. James, intrigued but cautious, replied that when the preparations were complete, the Prince would come. Hence the stir and bustle on the coast.

By the close of 1743, when Pitt made his speech, a force of 15,000 men had been collected at Dunkirk under the Maréchal de Saxe, and a fleet of twenty-four sail at Brest under Admiral de Roquefeuil.[1] In spite of Dettingen, war had not yet been declared between England and France. Each of them pretended that they were acting merely as auxiliaries to the main combatants, though it was clear that, both in fact and of intent, the two nations were at war with one another, and that the formal declaration could not be long delayed. None the less the English Government allowed themselves to be deceived. They ignored the fleet at Brest. If they showed any concern at all, it was rather with another and a smaller French fleet at Toulon, which had betrayed a disposition to collaborate with Spain. To meet any possible threat from that quarter they had sent reinforcements to the tempestuous, but not very wise, Admiral Mathews, who in February 1744 fought an inglorious and indecisive action in the Mediterranean. Just before that action the Brest fleet sailed up the Channel with the intention of protecting the Jacobite transports from Dunkirk. By the 3rd of February it was off the Eddystone, and by the 24th it had reached Dungeness. The Government, now thoroughly alarmed, collected a fleet hastily together in the Downs, and placed Sir John Norris in command. Perhaps fortunately, this veteran, eighty-four years of age, was never put to the test. Once more the winds and waves came to England's rescue; Roquefeuil was driven by storms back to Brest, and such transports as survived were obliged to return to Dunkirk. The danger was over for the time being, but a startling light had been thrown on the policy which the Government were pursuing, and as though to emphasise and underline their lack of preparation they felt it necessary at this juncture to hurry Dutch troops over to Sheerness in order to protect England against invasion. Carteret might well have fallen at once, had not France now stepped into the open with a declaration of war. As always happens in times of crisis, people felt that national affairs should be put on a firm basis before party politics were resumed.

Had Pitt been so disposed, he might have said 'I told you so,'

[1] Hannay. *Short History of the Royal Navy*, II, 111.

for in a series of speeches throughout December and January he had developed an argument which, if accepted, would have put an end to the danger before it had arisen. The object of the war, he had declared, had been attained by the expulsion of the French from the Empire. Any attempt to penetrate into France itself would be exceedingly difficult and even more meaningless. English troops in Flanders could do no good to anyone. If it were still really necessary to help Maria Theresa, that help should take the form of subsidies—by which she could hire plenty of troops in Germany, 'that great market of men'—and naval support by 'our squadron in the Mediterranean.'[1] Perhaps his speeches had carried the less conviction because he had embellished them with diatribes against Hanover, for whose benefit, he asserted, all our actions were at bottom designed, and opprobrious attacks on Carteret, who, he said, was not only depriving Parliament of control over the conduct of the war but had failed to take any steps to gain the confidence of the public or ascertain their wishes. But however little the speeches may have influenced opinion, they displayed clearly his conviction that the time had come to make peace with France and slide out of the German war.

His advice had not been taken and he might have emphasised the fact. Instead he preferred to take his stand on national honour and national sufficiency. On the 15th of February 1744 the King sent a Message to the House informing them that the Young Pretender was about to invade England 'in concert with disaffected persons here.' The House promptly drew up a loyal Address, to which Waller, a member of the Opposition, wished to tack a demand for an enquiry into the state of the navy. Pitt supported the Address wholeheartedly, becoming for the nonce almost a fervid Hanoverian. He would take, he declared roundly, 'this and every other occasion of expressing the most disinterested duty to the present royal family'—a sentiment which however true in spirit was unusual in his speeches. It must have surprised the King, though he was perspicacious enough not to be convinced, knowing full well that Pitt was moved not by any love for the House of Hanover nor by any hatred of the Stuarts, but solely by his intense loyalty to the country of his birth whose shores must be preserved inviolate. The support which Pitt gave to Waller's proposed addition, though genuine, was half humorous and much less serious. He would have liked to press it, for the neglect of the

[1] Almon, I, 194.

H

navy was in his eyes one of the Government's major sins, but he recognised that this was not the time. On one point, however, he was emphatic. The reference in the Message to disaffected persons was for every reason to be regretted. If there were such persons, it was impolitic to refer to them; and if, as Pitt believed, there were none, then 'how monstrous a thing it was in any Minister to poison the fountain of truth, and fill the nation with mutual jealousies and distrusts.'[1] It was no doubt these hesitations and reserves which made the speech sound more cold than it was, and gave the impression in some quarters that, as Lady Hervey wrote, 'Mr. Pitt has done a right thing with as ill an air as he could contrive it; it is like giving a purse by throwing it at one's head.'[2]

So much for the loyal Address. Nine days later, on the 24th of February, there was another debate. It took place while the French were still in the Channel and the issue still lay in the balance. Oppressed by this knowledge, Parliament debated, in a spirit of apprehension almost approaching panic, a motion asking the King to augment his forces by sea and land in such manner as he might think proper and necessary. As the King obviously needed no such prompting, the motion had a touch of the ridiculous about it, and the debate little meaning beyond the opportunity which it provided for Members to express their individual opinions. Pitt seized the chance to review the military situation calmly and realistically; it was the first occasion on which he had given any indication of his grasp of military as opposed to political strategy. It was a time, he agreed, 'to be alarmed, to be upon our guard, and to take all proper precautions,' but emphatically not a time 'to be terrified as if the danger was of the extremest sort.' The fleet stood between us and the enemy and would probably be sufficient; but even if hostile troops were landed, we had 'no inconsiderable body of forces in the island and might recall for our own defence what numbers we pleased out of those abroad.' It was of course one thing to throw a small expedition ashore, and quite another to support it. 'No military man,' Pitt declared, 'could be very uneasy about the event.' Satisfied on the point of danger, Pitt searched round for the underlying motive. If France could hardly hope for military success, what was her real object? The answer was not in doubt. She had two objects in view; she hoped to discredit us in the eyes

[1] Speech, 15th February 1744. *Parliamentary History*, Vol. XIII.
[2] Letter of 27th February 1744. *Letters*, p. 41.

of our allies, so that they would no longer place any confidence in our support, and she wanted to frighten us so that we might in fact withdraw our troops from the Continent. The two objects were complementary. Pitt, in a word, saw through Tencin's scheme and published it abroad, believing that good might come out of evil if the threat to our shores united the nation. As indeed it must, for 'no one could be so desperate or mad as to think of joining the attempt.'[1]

He emphasised this serene confidence in English loyalty once more on the 3rd of April 1744 when the mutual declarations of war were debated. Pitt recognised that war was inevitable and that being so was anxious to give 'a cheerful and ready testimony of duty to His Majesty and of zeal to support him.' He wanted also to record his great pleasure at noting that the King in his Speech had expressed his reliance on the affection and loyalty of all his people; the more so as this seemed a tacit recantation of the previous reference to the 'disaffected persons here.' He could not, however, refrain from pointing out that such reliance did not chime in with the demand for Dutch troops. If more troops were needed, we could easily have recalled our army from Flanders, more easily, indeed, than we could summon the Dutch from Holland, and with greater assurance of their arrival on the scene. And when they arrived they would fight with greater vigour and enthusiasm.

But Pitt's duty to the King did not include confidence in the Minister of his choice. In the same speech Pitt 'threw out a political prophecy at Lord Carteret, and said perdition would infallibly attend the rash author of those measures which had produced this disastrous, impracticable war.' He gave warning that he would oppose similar measures in the future, and he reserved to himself full right to promote enquiries into the management of the forces and all branches of public expenditure.[2]

This reference to public expenditure is of more than passing interest. One of the commoner charges against Pitt is that in his heyday he failed to appreciate the effect of war upon the finances of the country and refused to cut his coat according to his cloth. Subsequent historians have supported the charge, which seems to be confirmed by his own ostentatious denial of responsibility for the Exchequer, and perhaps even more by his own virtual bankruptcy

---

[1] Speech, 24th February 1744. *Parliamentary History*, Vol. XIII.
[2] Speech, 3rd April 1744. *Parliamentary History*, Vol. XIII.

at death. Yet in fact Pitt had a shrewder and more profound
idea of finance than many of his contemporaries. He looked upon
it, however, as a means to an end, not as an end in itself, and consequently the Treasury appealed to him only in so far as its operations affected matters in which he took a deep interest—more
particularly the armed forces and the colonies. Its other mani-
festations and duties left him comparatively cold, which is no
doubt the foundation of the charge against him. The effects of
finance on colonial policy and Pitt's reaction to them belong more
properly to a later period of his life, though it should perhaps be
mentioned in passing that in February of this very year he had
opposed a tax on 'muscovado sugar' because of the excessive
burden which it would place upon the planters.[1]

In March and April Pitt had an opportunity of discussing the
finance of the war in debates on the 'Army Extraordinaries.' The
specific points on which he pounced were in a sense immaterial,
what counted was the underlying principles. He emphasised two
in particular—the lack of parliamentary control and the lack of a
sense of proportion, both of which led to extravagance and might
well lead to malversation. He objected to the hasty offer of subsidies to all and sundry, especially Hanover. He objected even
more to the unauthorised disbursement of money by the Government as the result of exaggerated fears. Take for instance the
money paid on Lord Stair's warrant to meet the needs of the
Austrian troops in Flanders, for which the Government wanted
covering authority. The expenditure was very possibly justifiable;
certainly no objection could be based on the facts, because the
facts were not known, the information given being altogether
insufficient. It was, however, abundantly clear that Parliament
could have been consulted in advance. If there had been real need
or urgency, he would 'go as far as any man in defence of any
extraordinary measures . . . the utmost stretch of the prerogative
is then constitutional.' But where there was no overwhelming
need, a tight check must be kept on expenditure. Here the money
had been paid out precipitately and the whitewashing unduly
delayed. To attempt, as the Government apologists did, to com-
pare action which might be justified by the fear of invasion with
action prompted simply by the wants of Austrian troops in
Flanders was merely ridiculous. In any event, there had been a
five months' interval between the issue by the Paymaster and the

[1] Add. MSS. 9198, 95-6.

Order by the Treasury. It had not been unknown in the past for money in the Paymaster's hands to be misapplied. What had happened in the past might easily happen again if the Commons were deprived of the right of granting and appropriating money. That right should not be made 'a mere cobweb limitation.'[1] So for the first but by no means the last time Pitt protested against extravagance whether actual or potential. Waste of money was far more likely to have an adverse effect on our war effort than lack of means.

Pitt was voicing the general feeling of England. Carteret and the war were falling lower in popular estimation, and in its own indefinable fashion popular feeling was influencing the House. The breach in the Cabinet widened as 1744 advanced. The contest between Carteret and the Pelhams on its lower plane resembled the old contest between the Cavaliers and the Roundheads. Carteret was brilliant and careless; Carteret was contemptuous. 'Lord Carteret,' Egmont noted in his *Diary*, 'speaks of Harry Pelham in very contemptible terms; he said he was only a chief clerk to Sir Robert Walpole, and why he should expect to be more under me, I can't imagine; he did his drudgery and he shall do mine.' It seemed not unlikely when the King, as Egmont also noted, 'said the other day to the Duke of Newcastle that my Lord Carteret was a Minister to his own heart, for he was a man of sense and understood Foreign Affairs,' which the nervous and easily startled Duke took, probably with justice, as a reproach on himself. But if the Pelhams were dashed, they were also persistent. With a mole-like burrowing into parliamentary 'management' and an ever watchful eye on the constituencies, the brothers built themselves into a position that was impregnable to anything but popular sentiment. They kept a tight hold on their majority in the House and left Pitt to undermine their rival.

Pitt's efforts were seconded and enforced by the fact that the war was not successful and showed no signs of improving. Rarely, if ever, had England's naval and military forces been worse found or worse led. The Ministry thought the generals and admirals on the fighting list either incompetent or politically unsound, and so were forced to recall old veterans from Marlborough's wars to lead the troops and manage the fleets. These stricken dug-outs did their best; but after all they were not the great generals of a past age but only the then subalterns who had just grown older; with

[1] Speeches, 19th March and 10th April 1744. *Parliamentary History*, Vol. XIII.

the lapse of time their limbs had become stiff and their brains unnimble. They had nothing with which to work but the dim reflection of a faded glory. None the less they deserve gratitude from a later generation for the negative blessing of preventing harm even if they failed to produce good.

Pitt had also the active support of the popular voice and the negative aid of the Pelham faction. Hitherto his main opponents had been the King and the Prince of Wales. Carteret had been a connecting link between this ill-assorted couple. They had both believed in him, and on his appointment as Secretary of State the Prince of Wales had tried to muzzle the Opposition. Only Pitt and Lyttelton had flouted his instructions, and there had been a time when the world at large expected the Prince to dismiss these two recalcitrant servants. But now the Prince's favour towards Carteret was beginning to evaporate. In September Pitt told the Earl of Marchmont that 'the Prince's attachment to Lord Carteret was much weakened; that he bore to be talked to about it; that the Prince had talked to him of him only as a man of great ideas in foreign affairs, and had not been offended when he said he would soon be as much exploded as Horace Walpole [Sir Robert's brother], and that the events that showed his inability were none of 'em fortuitous, but the natural effects of the measures he pursued.'[1]

With the Prince's support going, Carteret's prospects were much dimmed, so much so that the Pelhams and their inseparable adviser, Hardwicke, began seriously pondering the best method of forcing him out altogether. They had been hinting to the King of their disapproval for a long time past: 'My brother,' Newcastle wrote to Hardwicke on the 8th of August, 'had a longer audience, and . . . had several flings at Lord Carteret's conduct and manner without naming him.'[2] Now they decided to take more open and definite action, and throughout the late summer were interminably concocting a memorial. It needed much care, but as Fortune would have it, Hardwicke was laborious and plodding. 'I am sensible,' he wrote to Newcastle on the 20th of September, 'the paper is too long, contains both too much and too little, and must have many things pared off, others polished, and the whole made fitter for the condition of Majesty and of ourselves.'[3] On the 1st of

[1] Papers of the Earls of Marchmont.
[2] Harris. *Life of Hardwicke*, II, 74.
[3] Hardwicke to Newcastle, 20 Sept. 1744, Harris, II, 77.

November 1744 it was ready. Newcastle presented it to the King, who returned it a few hours later without comment. But having taken the plunge, the brothers were not prepared to turn back. The King was importuned on every opportunity, and finally gave way. On the 23rd of November 1744, four days before Parliament met, the King took back the seals from Carteret, reluctantly and of necessity.

For the second time Pitt had been instrumental in securing the
downfall of a Government, and no one could deny the importance
of the part he had played. Indeed he had worked hard, and with
an energy that was all the more damaging because it was dis-
criminating as well as strong. So long as danger was at a distance
and might be parried he had fulminated against the policy which
was keeping us unnecessarily at war, but with the nearer approach
of danger he had rallied to the side of the Government, giving
them firm if tempered support while putting off to a more convenient season, but certainly not discarding, the demand for a
new and a better policy. His whole conduct had been independent
and fearless, and perhaps a bit puzzling to his friends. He had, for
instance, joined with them in pooh-poohing the Ministry's doubts
of the loyalty of the common people, but he had refrained from
opposing, as they did, the temporary suspension of the Habeas
Corpus Act, though he would not actively support it. When,
however, the Government went farther and wanted to visit the
sins of Jacobite fathers upon the children, he resisted warmly and
indignantly.[1]

By the end of this strenuous session he was exhausted, and a
violent attack of gout drove him to Bath, where he drank the
waters hopefully, but none the less remained in a poor state of
health for the rest of the year. He was therefore absent from Town
while the Pelhams were working upon the King and laboriously
gaining their ends, but when Carteret fell everyone recognised the
part he had played and the world at large expected him to receive
his reward. 'Mr. Pelham,' wrote Walpole, that sounding board of
polite gossip, to his crony Mann, 'must bring in Lord Chesterfield,
Pitt, the chief patriots and perhaps some Tories.'[2]

In spite, however, of expectations, Pitt did not receive office.
Pelham formed an administration popularly dubbed broad-

---

[1] Coxe's *Pelham*, I, 148.   [2] Walpole to Mann, 26th November 1744.

bottomed because it was supposed to include all the warring factions, even the Tories and Jacobites, or at least those members of the factions whose power, influence or talents might make them dangerous. But he omitted Pitt, whose power and talents, if not his influence, made him the most dangerous, as he was becoming the most dreaded, of opponents.

There were two reasons for this omission, the one political, the other springing from Pitt's character. Walpole writing to Mann at the end of December combined the two in one of his less perspicacious comments. 'You perceive,' he said, 'the great Mr. William Pitt is not in the list, though he comes thoroughly into the measures. To preserve his character and authority in the Parliament, he was unwilling to accept anything yet; the Ministry very rightly insisted that he should; he asked for secretary at war, knowing it would be refused—and it was.'[1] That was no doubt one view of the situation, but it hardly carries conviction. Pelham, of course, would have welcomed Pitt with open arms, but bearing in mind the many aspirants to office whom he had to satisfy if his Ministry was to be truly 'broad-bottomed,' he would have welcomed still more a refusal which was accompanied by a promise to 'come thoroughly into the measures.' What more could he want? At one and the same time he had Pitt's support and Pitt's vacancy! As for Pitt himself, it is difficult to see why acceptance of office should have been more damaging to his character and authority than acceptance of measures. The former would at least have explained the latter, which otherwise might well look like a belated bid for recognition. Nor, *prima facie*, was there any good reason to suppose that the office of Secretary at War would be refused. It was a minor office for which there was little competition and not much consideration, and one with which incidentally Pitt's name had long been coupled in the public mind.[2]

The reason must be sought elsewhere, and is to be found in the King, who, without finesse or beating about the bush, refused to have any dealings with the outrageous demagogue who had times without number insulted him personally and defamed his beloved Hanover. The royal displeasure was not only peppery but adamantine, and had some excuse if not much justification. The King was being pressed hard. It was bad enough to find Tories and Jacobites proposed for a number of minor offices and Court

---

[1] Walpole to Mann, 24th Dec. 1744.   [2] Williams, I, 130.

appointments. It was worse still to be asked to restore Cobham to his regiment and accept Lyttelton at the Treasury and George Grenville at the Admiralty. To all that, chafing and fuming, he had agreed. But there was worse to come. When Pelham mentioned Chesterfield and Pitt, George II shied like a startled horse. At first he would have nothing to say to either. By degrees and with much trouble Pelham and Newcastle placated his wrath until finally he consented to make Chesterfield Lord Lieutenant of Ireland. After all, Chesterfield was a distinguished nobleman and Ireland was not unlike exile. But the fact that he had given way over Chesterfield made it the more essential for him to hold out against Pitt. The line had to be drawn somewhere if the Royal Prerogative was to have any meaning. And Pitt was no peer but a commoner, a violent, opprobrious ranter, reckless of truth and regardless of feelings. George would have none of him. At last the Pelhams desisted; after all they must be reasonable; the King must be given some sop; there must be some compromise, and if Pitt was formidable, he was now isolated; his friends had been won over, his relations with the Prince were a little strained, and his own party were a trifle jealous of him. So they sacrificed him in fact while they tried to soothe him with promises.

Strange to relate Pitt was ready to be soothed, and when the House met stood forth as a champion of the new Ministry. More than that, he seemed to eat his words, and now that Carteret had fallen, seemed to support most of Carteret's measures. The wits made merry at his expense, and Pitt accepted their thrusts with humility. For the first and almost for the last time, he offered the other cheek, and when attacked in the House 'carried himself,' as Yorke noted, 'with all the art and temper imaginable; he soothed and complimented.'

Why was Pitt so acquiescent? Why did he accept the rebuff so humbly, without apparently striking a single blow on his own behalf? It was certainly not, as Walpole thought, to preserve his character and authority, for, in spite of the curious inferiority complex which dogged him all the days of his life, he had a lofty and unshakable belief in himself and his own powers. Obstruction stirred him to the soul and drove him, now to new heights of eloquence, now to violence and exaggeration, but never to a tame acquiescence. Nor was it indifference to money, titles and position. It is true that he revolted from any form of bribery or corruption, whether direct or indirect, whether allowed by custom or sanctioned by precedent, and rather enjoyed flaunting his purity in the face of the public, but all the same he was by nature a spendthrift, avidly hungry for honours and unduly impressed by outward trappings. Money and office, therefore, were not indifferent to him, and when honestly offered became objects of desire. There must have been some other reason, and it is to be found in a concatenation of unexpected events which set him upon a fresh road.

He had gone down to Bath in May 1744 ravaged with illness but sustained by a sense of mastery over friend and foe alike, conscious of his powers and hopeful of success in the near future. While there his personal position had been strengthened by a sidewind of fortune. On the 18th of October the old Duchess of Marlborough died, and in her will left Pitt £10,000 'upon account of his merit in the noble defence he has made of the laws of England and to prevent the ruin of his country.' It was a splendid gesture and was made the more dazzling by certain contingent legacies. She had named him as heir presumptive to large properties in Buckinghamshire, Staffordshire and Northamptonshire, in the event of her own family dying out, and she had procured for him similar prospects in Sunderland. None of these properties ever came to him, but at the time the prospects seemed good and Pitt may well have built high hopes in his mind, which was as prone to be sanguine as it was apt to be vague in his own financial affairs. Any hopes he may have formed were bulwarked, and in part materialised, by an annuity of £300 per annum from the Duke of Bedford which was settled by a document signed actually in the following March, though no doubt discussed about this time, and which appears to have been connected in some way with his prospective claims under the will.[1]

But whatever hopes he may have built, his first feelings seem to have been mixed. He did not appear to be unduly elated by the sudden affluence which had come to him, and in acknowledging the bequest to Lord Marchmont, the executor, was brief and ambiguous. Mere politeness made him speak of the Duchess's 'great goodness to me,' but it must have been either an uncommon reserve or a pungent sarcasm or perhaps a mixture of the two which made him add 'the sort of regard I feel for her memory, I leave to your Lordship's heart to suggest to you; besides the many reasons there are for bearing that regard to it, I hope you have

[1] Williams, I, 126.

likewise some of the same which she has been pleased to honour
me with.' Pitt was fully aware of the value of his services and was
anxious enough to be paid, but the acceptance of the price was a
sad affair; it savoured somehow of corruption and Pitt did not
like the appearance of being bought, even posthumously. Earlier
in his life he might possibly have refused the legacy; but he was
now thirty-six, his fortune had not been made, and the cares of this
life could not be ignored. Pitt's relations with the Prince were
not entirely happy, and if he lost his post as Groom of the
Bedchamber his income—apart from the legacy—would drop to
its original minute proportions. The legacy gave him ballast and
an element of freedom which he had never enjoyed before. Now
he could maintain his principles, without the gnawing fear that
they would involve starvation; and better still, he could reject
compromise.

This sense of freedom was undoubtedly present within a few
days of the receipt of the legacy, and undoubtedly coloured his
vague negotiations with the Pelhams. His attitude stiffened.
Bolingbroke was anxious to come to terms with them; he thought,
as most people did, that Carteret might fall and that then there
might be a favourable opportunity of returning to power. He was
busy salting the ground. On the 6th of November he visited Pitt
at Bath and told him that 'he saw but one way of getting ourselves
out of our miserable state, and that was by taking the pathetic
style and endeavouring to soften the old party, without the
opposition departing from their own principles, but acting with
moderation, if a concert could not be obtained, so as to be able to
take advantage of the breach in the Ministry.' 'Taking the
pathetic style' was not likely to appeal to such a fire-eater as Pitt
at any time. It was doubly distasteful to him now that he had been
savouring in anticipation the freedom conferred by his legacy.
Pitt was brusque if not downright rude to his old chief. He said
bluntly that 'the ministers who seemed desirous to form a concert
with the opposition, were weak men, and incapable of it, and in all
their steps insincere; and that he thought any union with them
quite impossible; that they were contemptible; and he was angry
with such and such of 'em, and particularly with Pelham; that he
had seen Lord Cobham, and had had much treaty with the
Grenvilles, who were obliged to follow Lord Cobham; and that
he saw the Opposition designed to move questions little, if at all,
inferior to high treason; that the best method possible must be

used to stop 'em, and to moderate, but that they must preserve
the coalition.'[1]

Here was an outburst. The legacy revealed Pitt's inner feelings,
as though he had been a palimpsest. He despised the Ministry; he
was clearly breaking with Cobham; he obviously would not submit to any 'obligation' to follow a leader; and he must have his
own way.

One would like to have been a spectator at this meeting when
the fiery, gout-ridden young man flew out so unexpectedly at the
veteran and soured statesman of an older generation. One would
like to have noted the play of their countenances and read the
emotions that coursed over them. Whatever may have been true
of Pitt, Bolingbroke was certainly hurt to the quick, and after
repeating his original proposition in a half-startled, half-querulous
fashion, took it upon himself to admonish his young friend. He
told Pitt that he was 'a young man and should not mingle passion
with business, nor act out of anger to one or to another man,' and
when he came away complained to his friends that 'Mr. Pitt was
extremely supercilious; and that when he was a young man, Sir
Edward Seymour, and Musgrave, and such, heard him with more
deference than Mr. Pitt had done'; 'that Mr. Pitt was a young man
of fine parts; but that he was narrow, did not know much of the
world, and was a little too dogmatical.' Evidently the old man
was hurt.

His rebuke, however, was not without its effect. At the moment
Pitt had quietened down and said no more than that 'they could
only wait for some such conjuncture as would form a new epocha,
such as the death of the King; but in the meantime go on without
any object beside,' but there can be little doubt that he took note
of the advice and pondered over it. While he was so doing, Carteret
fell. The 'new epocha' was upon him, and he was sufficiently
chastened to listen to Pelham's advances. He was ready to accept
office on reasonable terms, and in accordance with his natural
instincts asked for the office of Secretary at War. Pelham promised,
but was unable to perform. Meanwhile Pitt's friends had been
placated and Pitt, still smarting under Bolingbroke's rebuke,
stood alone. What part was he to play?

[1] Marchmont's Diary, 6th November 1744.

SEEMING INCONSISTENCIES

If Pitt looked round the political arena, one fact must have stared him in the face, and one question must have pressed for an answer. For just on ten years he had been in Opposition, and no one, least of all Pitt himself, could deny that he had risen to the top. No one was his superior and few could pretend to be his equal in debate. No one had contributed more to the overthrow of two separate Ministries. No one was more formidable in talent and reputation. Yet twice when opportunity offered his claims to office had been ignored. Was there to be no end? What could he do to secure proper recognition? The only answer which seemed to hold out a spark of hope, the only answer which had not been well weighed and found wanting, was Bolingbroke's advice—he must not mingle passion with business; he must be humble; he must be less dogmatical; perhaps he should take the pathetic style.

There was a pause while he pondered it in his mind. He was still at Bath, where it was possible to lie low and wait, and he took full advantage of the fact, though probably there was little hesitation. The King's attitude coming on top of Bolingbroke's rebuke must have had a profound effect. It showed Pitt as nothing else could how negative had been the results of his past policy. He could turn Ministers out, but never create them; he could destroy, but never win the chance to build. Henceforward he must move along a new path, and he gave the first hint by acquiescing in the King's veto. If he would not accept Pitt willingly, he should not be coerced but wooed. Pitt would stand down for the time being. Having made that gesture, he retired into his shell in order to readjust his views.

When he had finally made up his mind, he proclaimed it to the world, characteristically, in dramatic fashion. Pelham had not begun too successfully. He was neither a colourful nor a strong man, and his brother, the Duke of Newcastle, was a weak and querulous man, clever only in underground lobbying and the 'management' of the constituencies. Neither of the brothers was likely to adopt striking policies or capture the imagination of the crowd. They owed their present success far more to Carteret's mistakes than to their own merits, far more to clever electioneering than to constructive statesmanship, and when the House met in the winter of 1744 the Opposition, composed of disappointed place-hunters, seemed likely enough to grow powerful and troublesome. If Pitt joined them, as they no doubt hoped and expected, the Pelhams could be driven from office more speedily than either Walpole or Carteret. They leapt to the chase with a will. 'On the first tinkling of the brass,' Walpole wrote to Mann,[1] 'all the new bees swarm back to the Tory side of the House.' The Broad-bottomed Administration seemed to be no more firmly based than any other. On the contrary, Walpole and Carteret had been obvious masters of men; so long as they were in a ministry they were admittedly supreme. Now, there were no giants; and each petty chieftain thought—with justice—that he had as much right to lead as any other. A broad bottom of nonentities is not half so broad as the solid foundation of a single genius.

The first hint of disintegration coincided with Pitt's final determination, and gave him the chance he needed. The task of bolstering up a falling Ministry was something new; it would come with a shock of surprise, and Pitt intended to heighten the shock. He appeared suddenly in the House on the 23rd of January 1745 wrapped in flannel and looking (what he was) an invalid risen from a sick-bed. He emphasised the effect of his appearance by declaring that if this was to be the last day of his life, he would spend it in the House of Commons, since he judged the condition of his country to be worse than that of his own health. This was not the first time that he had traded upon the sympathies of his audience —he had done it when cashiered from the army—but it was the first time he had deliberately flaunted his physical infirmities. It was a trick which he repeated at intervals, and one peculiarly liable to the law of diminishing returns. But on this occasion it was fresh and paid a handsome dividend. The world might—and did when it had time to think—twit him with inconsistency, with place-hunting, with disloyalty to the shade of Duchess Sarah; but in the first flush it admitted the stark effectiveness of his intervention. He saved the Ministry and placed them upon the road to security and strength.

[1] Walpole to Mann, 1st Feb. 1745.

Pitt was twitted at the time with inconsistency and has been roundly accused of it since. 'A severer judgment may be passed,' wrote Lord Rosebery, 'when it is seen that the policy remained substantially unaltered and that Pitt found himself able to discriminate between Carteret's policy with Carteret in office, and the same policy with Carteret out of office.' The charge is worth examining because this was the first though not the last occasion of Pitt's seeming inconsistency.

No one who has studied Pitt's life would be disposed to deny that he held certain principles in the deepest veneration. On the other hand no one can deny that he had little difficulty in changing his opinions and eating his words. Consistency for its own sake meant nothing to him. It was no virtue; it was just obstinacy.

Accepting this, was Pitt at this moment of his life sacrificing a principle, or merely changing an opinion? Was he genuinely convinced, or was he simply pushing his own fortunes? His first speech under Pelham's leadership was on the army estimates, and in it he supported a vote of 28,000 men for Flanders. In other words he apparently approved the war and the sending of British troops to the Continent. The year before, when Carteret had been in power, he had opposed both measures. Was this a complete *volte face*? It seemed to be, and perhaps Pitt gave shot to his opponents by stressing 'how much the question was changed from what it was last year.' That may be regarded as a tacit admission of guilt, and indeed has been. But it may also conceivably represent Pitt's real belief. It is worth while assuming for a moment that Pitt meant what he said. Where would that lead?

In Pitt's view there had been an entire change of emphasis. The same motions might be performed, but with a different aim, and so to speak from a different angle. There had in fact been a change of heart. Pelham was not so much carrying on a continental war as liquidating Carteret's policy. It was not possible to ignore the existing situation; it was not possible to withdraw the troops from the Continent overnight and act as though the whole world was plunged in profound peace. The war must obviously be continued until it could be concluded. If therefore Pitt was to support Pelham, he must support the war. Was he to support Pelham? The answer can hardly be in doubt. There was no reasonable alternative. Walpole was too old; he could never return and was soon to die; Carteret had just been hounded from

Furis—whore my reco[...]

Dss of Marlborough left Mr Pitt by will £10,000 "for defending the Laws of his country."

Ungrateful, Pitt,—	And did Obtain.	Three Thousand a Year,
You have me Bitt!	The long sought gain.	You have got a Year,
Ten Thousand Pound,	Then forc'd your Way,	Since Fear nor Shame,
My Will you found.	To C—t for Pay.	Can you reclaim;
		I Brand your Name.

Publish'd for L.R.aymond. April ye 15th. 1746.

Vide Forehe

THE GHOST OF THE DUCHESS OF MARLBOROUGH APPEARS TO PITT

from a contemporary cartoon

office; the squabbling chieftains of the Whiggish clans were all on a level, a slightly lower level than Pelham and Newcastle, and their policies would not be different. The only alternative would have been Pitt's own friends, and they had been absorbed and given office. Pitt could have seen no party to replace Pelham now that Bolingbroke had consented to the coalition and Chesterfield had been placated.

Here was a reason for support, if not a very strong reason. It was enhanced by the offers that Pelham made. Not only had he included Pitt's friends in his Cabinet, not only had he promised Pitt office as soon as the King could be persuaded, but he had at least paid lip service to Pitt's theories, and gone some way to show that his inclination followed his words. Pelham had no taste for continental adventures; he was anxious enough to end the war, and he proposed to take the quickest means of doing so. One of his first actions was to dispatch Chesterfield as an Envoy Extraordinary to Holland, charged with the duty of persuading the Dutch to take their fair share of the war. If England and Holland acted with energy and in close alliance they could easily manœuvre themselves into a position where reasonable terms of peace could be obtained. Here was an example of energetic action on right lines prompted by sound policy, and Pitt saw no reason for traversing it. As he himself explained, 'The object seemed then [under Carteret] to be the multiplying war upon war, expence upon expence, and the abetting the House of Austria in romantic schemes of acquisition, such as the recovery of the *Avulsa Imperii*, without regard to the immediate interest of Great Britain. The object now was, by connecting ourselves closely with Holland, to arrive at a situation which might enable us to hold out fair and reasonable terms of peace, both to our friends and enemies, and not to prosecute the war a moment longer than we could obtain an equitable and sufficient security for our own rights and those of our allies.'[1] The question was in fact much changed from what it had been the year before, and the emphasis was wholly altered. Pitt's argument, whether genuine or not, was sound, and that being so, he cannot on this occasion be justly accused of betraying his principles or even in any true sense of the word of altering his opinions. At most he was realising that the irresponsible words of Opposition are not always easily squared with the facts of administration. They may lead to seeming

[1] Speech, 23rd January 1745. *Parliamentary History*, Vol. XIII.

inconsistencies. This period of Pitt's life should be regarded as the initial stage in his transition from a firebrand of Opposition propounding general policies to a constructive statesman adapting those policies to the facts.

The first speech passed off well enough, and in fact saved Pelham's Ministry. The second was more difficult. In February Pelham brought forward a double-barrelled proposal which was not without its element of chicanery. On the one hand he proposed to get rid of the Hanoverians in English pay, while on the other he proposed to increase the Queen of Hungary's subsidy, so that she might take them over. This indirect hiring of the unpopular Hanoverians gave Carteret (now Lord Granville) and his friends ample scope for mockery. It looked bad, and when Pitt rose to defend the measure, he did not make too good a case. He was clever rather than convincing. The Queen of Hungary, he argued, must not be compelled to take them, but no more must she be prevented. 'God forbid,' he went on, with a pious tongue in his cheek,' that those unfortunate troops should by our vote be proscribed at every court in Europe.' It was unfair to turn them into pariahs merely because we had no use for them. All of which, of course, was much beside the point, and if he had left the matter there, he might justly be charged with levity as well as with inconsistency. But he did not leave the matter there. He hinted at his real motive. 'It was sufficient,' he said, 'that the ill consequences which were apprehended from the voting them year after year as part of our own army, and upon the foot of a rival establishment, had been removed by His Majesty's wisdom and goodness.' Here, once more, a trifle of imaginative insight discloses the workings of his mind. Objects are more important than methods; motives than actions. Pelham was liquidating the past, and on the whole he was doing it cleverly. There must be a transitional period and he was using it not only to end the war but also to emphasise the gulf between England and Hanover. Transitional periods are never very logical, but life is not ruled by logic alone, and in England compromise has always appealed; it saves face, it lets people—and kings—down lightly; it makes for peace and happiness and the smoothing of ruffled feelings.

So, one may believe, Pitt argued to himself, and in so arguing taught himself a new art, the suavity of conciliation. If he over-acted at times, it is forgivable; more interesting is the ease with which he adopted the new rôle. It was to form an important

element in his career. As a Minister he showed a yielding side to
the people he governed, and more particularly an understanding
sympathy with the underdog. This pleasant and eminently practical trait was the obverse of the intolerance, flaming and inflexible,
which he showed invariably towards England's enemies, and was
inclined to show towards his personal opponents.

One further point is worth making. If Pitt was inconsistent, it
can only have been for personal ends, that is, to obtain office.
The fact remains that he did not obtain office until February 1746,
and then for other and special reasons. More than that, so far
from gaining office, Pitt resigned his employment in the Prince's
household. The legacy enabled him to do it, and his determination
to support Pelham against Carteret made the step desirable. The
Prince had always favoured Carteret, and Pitt's views had led to
a growing estrangement. It speaks well for the Prince, and throws
an interesting light on Pitt's private character, that the Prince
had not dismissed his Groom of the Bedchamber. There was no
reason why Pitt should not have retained this office unless and
until turned out, but in April 1745, after mature deliberation, he
left of his own accord. It was a minor burning of his boats, and
as such is evidence of his feelings. For good or ill, he felt it right
and necessary to support Pelham.

The value of that support can be measured by the shoals and rapids that Pelham had to negotiate. His first year of power was a testing time, and by all ordinary standards he came out badly. Success eluded him; fate was against him; fortune played him false. It almost seemed as though Pitt alone stood between him and his downfall.

The year started with one brief flash of hope. The Emperor died on the 20th of January 1745, and Maria Theresa at once pushed the claims of her husband. For various reasons neither France nor Frederick thought it worth their while to oppose, and he was duly elected to the empty dignity, though not until September. Apart from this solitary flash, all seemed unrelieved gloom, which grew ever more gloomy. Abroad there was a total lack of success, turning steadily to disaster. In Flanders the allies were pressed continuously back. Fontenoy, that strange mixture of victorious defeat, took place in May, when the Duke of Cumberland, being no match for the French Maréchal de Saxe, lost with the aid of his allies what the English infantry had won. Equally without meaning, Tournai fell to the French in June, Ghent and Oudenarde in July, and Ostend in August. No one in England cared, for the war had lost what little popularity it had possessed. If there was no success in Flanders there was almost less in the other theatres of war. In Italy the King of Sardinia was defeated at the Battle of Bassignana, and the Franco-Spanish forces entered Milan in triumph, while in Silesia Frederick defeated the Austrians at the Battle of Hohenfriedberg. Only in two directions was there any comfort to be found. At sea the English fleet gained the upper hand in a few minor encounters, and across the ocean the English colonists captured Louisbourg. It was little enough, but by contrast it emphasised both the expediency and the rightness of a maritime as opposed to a continental policy. Diplomatically also there was one unexpected gain. In August

Frederick of Prussia, who recognised that he had blundered in renewing the war, was induced through fear of France's growing strength to sign the secret Convention of Hanover, which led in December to a fresh peace between himself and Maria Theresa.

Meanwhile as the year progressed, with its failures and its follies, a greater cloud was spreading over the horizon. It burst in July when the Young Pretender landed in Scotland to set up his father's standard. The fortunes of that elusive Prince, half Ariel, half Caliban, belong to another tale. Suffice it here to record that by mere charm he raised a band of ragged Highlanders, and by bold bearing imposed himself upon the Whiggish tradesmen of Edinburgh. On the 21st of September his Highlanders, still wild for all their sojourn in a great city, and still gallant and brave for all the glamour of Holyrood nights, swept Cope and his rustic recruits into headlong flight at Preston Pans. In a few brief minutes they had raised their Prince from a poor joke to an invading King, and revived the faded glories of Anglo-Scottish warfare. Charles Edward crossed the border and, after the manner of the old forays, seized Carlisle with its castle of terrible dungeons. Thence he marched through Lancashire, by way of Preston, Wigan and Manchester, to Derby, which he reached on the 4th of December 1745. It was the ultimate point of invasion. Charles wished to penetrate farther, but the Highlanders only understood border raids; they were lost in this vast country with its puzzled and polite tradesmen, its industrious and small-minded mechanics, its imperturbable and grumbling farmers. They wanted to return with their fame and their spoils, and return they did. The dream was ended; the cold morning had broken, and at Culloden on the 16th of April 1746 the Duke of Cumberland exacted usury for all his ill-success in Flanders, buying with it the title of Butcher. But Charles, broken, defeated and without an army, won a different title to fame by captivating one faithful heart the more, the heart of Flora Macdonald, who wove a veil of glowing romance for him, which softens, if it cannot hide, the drunken features of his latter end.

Meanwhile, what of Pitt? And what of the Government? To the Government the landing in Moidart seemed uncommonly like the beginning of the end. The King was in Hanover, and did not return till the 31st of August; the army was being rapidly pushed by the French out of Flanders; the navy was in the doldrums of the Mathews-Lestock affair, bristling with courts

martial and disgusts; the countryside seemed paralysed. All this
gave the Government their cue, which can be summed up in the
words of one of their latest recruits. Henry Fox, who had become
a Lord of the Treasury in December 1743, expressed the ministerial—and incidentally the military—view in a letter to Hanbury
Williams: 'England, Wade says and I believe, is for the first
comer; and if you can tell whether the six thousand Dutch and the
ten battalions of English, or five thousand French or Spaniards
will be here first, you know our fate.'[1] Later (in September) he
wrote: 'Had 5,000 landed a week ago in any part of this island, I
verily believe the entire conquest would not have cost them a
battle.'[2] Newcastle, notorious for his dejection, had given up hope
before the Pretender landed; he apparently thought that the
Maréchal de Saxe was destined to conquer England with the rest
of the world. 'I don't know what,' he wrote, 'can stop that victorious army; I am sure ours in Flanders cannot.'[3] With such
invincible enemies advancing like a juggernaut, the possibility of
local trouble in Scotland hardly seemed to count, and indeed it
was the carrying out of Newcastle's defence policy that kept
George II in Hanover for the first month of the '45. The Pelhams
had felt that the only hope of curbing France was to detach
Frederick from the war, and they had consequently urged the
King to negotiate with Prussia. It went much against the grain
with him, for as Elector he saw in the maintenance of strife
between Frederick and Maria Theresa a possible means of
improving the position of Hanover. None the less, as King of
England, he had to give way, though he did so with a bad grace.
Negotiations began in June, and on the 27th of August the
Convention of Hanover was signed. With the Convention settled,
the King could return to meet the trouble from Scotland. Unlike
his Ministers he was not impressed by it. 'Pho!' he is reported to
have said, 'don't talk to me of that stuff'—and the remark smacks
of his testy, but rather lovable, intrepidity.

The immediate effect on the Government of the Pretender's
landing was a state of nerves, which became something like panic
after Preston Pans. They clamoured for mercenaries from the
Dutch and ordered Cumberland to send back ten battalions of
English troops. The history of the mercenaries makes curious
reading. The Dutch garrison of Tournai had recently surrendered

---

[1] Coxe's *Memoirs of Lord Walpole*, II, 113.   [2] Williams, I, 137.
[3] Charteris. *William Augustus, Duke of Cumberland*, p. 197.

to the French, and their general with every appearance of content had agreed that the troops should be disqualified from military service till the 1st of January 1747. As they were thus temporarily out of the continental war, they seemed to George II and the Dutch authorities eminently suitable for export to England to make up the contingent required by treaty obligations. They were duly shipped over, and had hardly landed before they were recalled in deference to representations from France that their presence in England on behalf of the Hanoverian dynasty was contrary to the terms of the capitulation. War in those days was gentlemanly to a degree! As however the Dutch had thus proved broken reeds, urgent requests for troops were sent to Hesse. Charles Edward, in short, had plenty of justification for the taunt in his proclamation at Edinburgh in October—'Let him [George II] send off his foreign hirelings, or put all upon the issue of a battle, and I will trust only to the King my Father's subjects.' He had more justification than he realised, for there was a section of political thought (including Granville and Fox) which objected to the use of English soldiers against the Highland clans.[1]

The panic grew calmer when on the 23rd of September Cumberland's ten English battalions landed at Gravesend, but it speedily returned and rose almost to frenzy when on the 6th of December (Black Friday) news came that Charles had slipped past Cumberland's army and had arrived at Derby on his way to London. The fear was so universal that even in remote country places such as Dersingham in Norfolk terrified ladies could be found packing up their valuables and burying their plate in the garden.[2] Of course the panic was not justified. There was only one possible source of fear, and that was a genuine French invasion. But the French had no intention of moving; to put or keep the Stuarts on the throne of England was never as such an object of French policy, but merely an adjunct.

[1] Riker. *Henry Fox*, I, pp. 60 and 62.
   Memoirs of a Royal Chaplain, pp. 56 and 113.

23

THE '45 AND ITS EFFECTS

The danger from the '45 is seen in retrospect to have been laugh-ably small, but its threat at the time loomed gigantic. It was a stern test of loyalty and the country rallied with remarkable unanimity to the King. Offers of assistance both in money and men poured in from all sides. Amongst other offers the great Whig landowners volunteered to raise troops, and Chesterfield from his exile in Ireland despatched a couple of regiments from Dublin and called out the militia.

The part which Pitt played in the midst of this bustle shows not merely his own views but the reputation which he had made for himself. In times of difficulty men turn instinctively to the leader whom they hold in greatest respect, and his advice carries the greatest weight. It is therefore highly significant that in the second half of 1745 Pitt was approached by practically all parties and exercised an influence second only to that which he was to exercise during his own great administration.

Parliament met on the 17th of October, and with the delightful if unconscious irony of the eighteenth century, Sir Francis Dashwood, founder of the notorious Hell-Fire Club and sensualist of the loosest life, was spurred by the common danger to move an amendment to the Address praying for purer elections, shorter Parliaments, and an end to bribery. It was the old case of the Devil was sick, the Devil a monk would be. Pitt disposed of the amendment summarily. He was, he said, a friend to everything that could be reasonably offered for securing the independence of Parliament, but popular as this amendment might be, if his advice had been asked he would have made use of 'all the little rhetoric I am master of, to persuade the hon. gentleman not to offer such an amendment at such a dangerous conjuncture'; it was 'like a man sitting down to think of ways and means for preventing his being cheated by his servants, at the very time that thieves were breaking into his house.' When everything was

at stake no contentious measures should be introduced, and
nothing done which might 'raise discontents among the people,
or lessen their confidence in those who are placed in authority
over them.' The people knew well enough that there must be
national unity in the face of national danger, and were showing
their wisdom by refraining from demands for reform and by
turning their attention to the defence of their sovereign and
themselves 'against those who have traitorously conspired to rob
him of his crown, and them of their liberties, properties and
religion.' There would be other opportunities when the rebellion
had been crushed; perhaps—who could tell?—before that session
was over, and then he would gladly give his support.[1] His words
carried conviction and the amendment was withdrawn.

Six days later he moved for the recall of all the troops in
Flanders 'to protect us from immediate danger.'[2] The Earl of
Shaftesbury says that this was moved 'in very respectful terms,'
but it was not without artfulness. Although Charles Edward was
still marching south, Pitt knew perfectly well that there was no
real danger, immediate or otherwise. The Highlanders numbered
less than 5,000 and were advancing into a country which was
negatively unfriendly, if it was not positively hostile. They were
opposed in the north by an army of 9,000 men, under Wade, and
by another army of 10,000 or more which Cumberland was leading
from the south. Their days were numbered. None the less, the
country was alarmed and Pitt's motion was popular. He put it
forward deliberately, because in his eyes the rebellion offered an
excellent excuse for dropping the continental entanglements. By
this time Carteret's war had been largely liquidated. The Convention with Frederick must result in an end to the Austro-Prussian
war; and thereafter in the making of that peace among the German
states which Pitt felt to be the essential basis of England's foreign
policy. Allied to a united Germany, England could view the efforts
of France on the Continent with equanimity, and without further
hesitation pursue her true destiny on the sea. Now was the time
to clinch matters, and by withdrawing from Flanders to take the
first step towards a wiser future.

His move frightened the Pelhams; they were not prepared to
follow so fast; they were obsessed by the old bogy of the French
occupation of the Austrian Netherlands; and they wanted peace

---

[1] Speech, 17th October 1745. *Parliamentary History*, Vol. XIII.
[2] Malmesbury. *Letters*, I, pp. 7-8.

between Prussia and Austria to be a fact and not merely an
expectation, however reasonable. So they manœuvred against
Pitt and managed to side-step his artful motion by putting the
previous question. But they carried the day by only twelve votes.

The large measure of support which he had received on this
point, combined with the general want of success at home and
abroad, made Pitt impatient, while at the same time it drove the
Pelhams towards him. At a later and a greater crisis Pitt said that
he alone could save England, and no one denied it. At this point
Pitt did not make any such claim, but the Government were
beginning to think it. They were weary of ill-success; they were
growing tired of the King's ill-humour. He was beginning to call
them names. 'We are now come to bad language,' Newcastle
complained to Richmond. '*Incapacity* to my brother. Spectator of
other people's policy and measures, and yesterday *Pitiful Fellows*.'
Flesh and blood, or at least Newcastle's flesh and blood, could
not be expected to bear it, and the Pelhams were eagerly anxious
to share their responsibilities with Pitt. Their difficulty was, of
course, that they had not only to come to terms with Pitt, but
thereafter reconcile the King to the terms he had exacted. Pitt was
not growing more amenable. He felt that the rebellion justified
and underlined every point of his policy—the need to get out of
the Continent, the need to stir up the latent vigour of the people,
the need to conciliate and win the affection of the poorer partner
of the Union. Neither King nor Parliament understood the secret
of his glowing patriotism, which not merely wanted the best for
his own country but believed the best of his own countrymen
and resented as an insult the hiring of foreign mercenaries to
protect our shores and revolted at the sacrifice of British lives to
forward the ambitions of Hanover.

If he was growing impatient, his reputation was daily increasing.
The Pelhams were not the only people to believe that Pitt alone
could save the situation. Perhaps the most significant, certainly
the most startling, fact of Pitt's life during those turbulent months
of 1745 was the attitude towards him adopted by the Scottish
peers and Members of Parliament in London. Ever since Walpole's
Excise scheme in 1733 there had been a coterie of Scots in
opposition. At that time they were nominally objecting to a
financial measure which they believed to be undesirable, but what
really influenced them was their discontent with Walpole's treatment of their country. He might have used the long years of peace

to bind Scotland with hoops of steel; instead, he had held her at arm's length in a species of subjection galling to a proud and talented race. The Scotch Members felt his rule to be painful and humiliating; they looked askance at his methods, which they considered unworthy of respect; they resented his policy as tending to degrade their fellow-countrymen, and they secretly deplored a course which was likely to alienate rather than win the Highlands, so making the prospects of Stuart intervention the more possible, if not probable. They had consequently given up office and the hopes of preferment for opposition, and they had gladly welcomed the advent of the Boy Patriots. Since that time there had been opportunities in plenty for them to observe Pitt and note his general policy and his particular applications of it. They realised that his outlook—at least so far as Scotland was concerned—was far wider and far wiser than Walpole's; they responded to his embryonic feeling after the British Empire, and appreciated, as only those conscious of unmerited disdain could, his bold and statesmanlike sympathy with British subjects struggling to wrest a living out of a hard soil in the outlying parts of the Commonwealth. They turned to him as the needle turns to the pole star.

And now with the coming of Charles Edward their fears had materialised. They yearned over their deluded country; they shuddered at the possible results of the rebellion, and they determined to do their best to obliterate the past and redeem the time. If it were left to them, there would be less prospect of bitter animosity and ferocious punishment. It would be better for their country and for themselves to declare their loyalty and take over the work of pacification. But how to do it in the inevitable atmosphere of suspicion? It was to Pitt that the perplexed Scottish leaders turned. If he would support them, they would ask for a Parliamentary Committee before whom they could first prove their own loyalty to the Crown, and then expound their views for raising volunteer regiments as the English peers were doing, and their reasons for thinking that the measures being taken against the rebels were insufficient. But without Pitt's aid and support they felt helpless.

Pitt, on being approached by the Duke of Queensberry, said there were 'niceties and difficulties,' and suggested a small meeting at which he, Lord Barrington and Lyttelton could discuss the matter with a small number of Scottish peers. There were anxious consultations on this proposal, such as one might expect among fearful and agitated men. Pitt's advice they wanted—desperately —but who were Barrington and Lyttelton to be dragged in so unnecessarily? In the upshot Lord Marchmont pointedly declared to his fellow peers that Barrington and Lyttelton 'were influenced by Mr. Pitt, so that it was only multiplying himself, and that none of them could have objected niceties and difficulties to him; these must have come from himself, and therefore were to be discussed with him alone.' Marchmont, for his part, 'would walk bare-footed from one end of the town to the other to gain Mr. Pitt to it, but would not spoil business by meetings.' With Pitt he would gladly consult at any place and at any time, 'but no number however small.'[1]

Pitt's first hesitations were characteristic of him. He had no doubts himself of the general loyalty of Scotland, but he very much feared the enflamed state of feeling in England. Unless the Scottish peers could put forward convincing evidence, they might easily do more harm than good; and if their evidence were convincing, they might expose the well-affected families in Scotland to the resentment of the rebels. They satisfied him however and he promised to help. But on the appointed day Oswald, one of the Scottish Members, in seconding the motion, made a violent attack on the Government, thus falling foul of Pitt, who consequently withheld his support. Without Pitt's support the motion fell through, and the Scots feeling that they had not received proper recognition were disposed to retaliate and attack the system of the volunteer regiments raised by the English peers. On the 4th of November Hume Campbell, Lord Marchmont's brother, moved that the officers in these newly raised regiments should be given only temporary commissions.

Whatever merit there was, and certainly there was some, in striving to distinguish between the holders of regular and the holders of war-time commissions, it was vitiated by the spirit in which the motion was moved. Pitt opposed violently, but not altogether convincingly. It was easy for him to deplore anything which might tend to damp the ardour of enthusiasm or affront the men of standing whose influence was important for procuring volunteers, but it smacked of special pleading when he argued that veteran regulars who found themselves outstripped in rank by newly commissioned novices could feel no genuine grievance

[1] Marchmont's Diary, 22nd Oct. 1745.

because 'this arbitrary distribution of preferments' was not uncommon in the army and was accepted with submission even in times of peace and safety. It would have been different if he could have argued that they were passed over on merits. However, whether his argument was good or bad, he carried the House with him, and the motion was rejected. It is an indication of the respect felt for Pitt that Lord Marchmont told Lyttelton a day or two later 'that as Mr. Pitt and we began the world together, and I had hoped, we should go through it in friendship, since we thought in the same manner on public matters, I should be sorry, if the heat on Monday last between him and my brother was to leave any rancour in his mind.' Lyttelton assured him that 'it left none, and was all over,' which is interesting when one bears in mind Pitt's haughty and sensitive temper.

Having given vent, unsuccessfully, to their momentary feelings of spite, the Scottish peers returned to their first proposals, and urged Pelham to allow them to raise regiments. Pelham replied that if larger forces were wanted, he should advise the King to bring over the Hessians. One can appreciate the fumblings of the nervous Pelham; he was not the man to win the Scots by a genuine belief in them. But one can also appreciate the feelings of his audience. Stair burst out indignantly 'that everybody would think, and he did think, this was plainly giving the exclusion to the whole Scots nation, and done only for this, although their zeal for the King could not be called in question.'[1] Pelham, anxious and shunning responsibility, at last promised 'that the alternative should be proposed to the King, either to accept of these regiments, or to send four or five battalions from Wade's army to give the superiority in Scotland to the King's friends, or to send for the Hessians.'

The King's decision could not for a moment be in doubt. He plunged for the Hessians, and by so doing brought Pitt into the open. Hitherto Pitt's conduct had been exemplary. He had declared unhesitatingly his loyalty to the Crown; he had supported every measure designed to overcome the rebellion; he had curbed the over-zealous and heartened the cowardly. But there were limits, and the idea of substituting Hessians for loyal Scotsmen was too much for him. His growing impatience exploded and he began to treat the Government roughly. His speeches have not been preserved, even in the fanciful form of the eighteenth

[1] Marchmont's Diary, 26 Nov. 1745.

century. There is nothing but tantalising hints in letters that could have told us so much. On the 4th of November, for instance, Horace Walpole gave Mann a trifle of news. Pitt, he said, is at last to be Secretary at War. The news was something which Walpole could not know for certain, and as it happens he was mistaken; but he added something which he could and did know from personal observation. He mentioned parenthetically that Pitt had alternately bullied and flattered Mr. Pelham. The bullying continued, for on the 22nd of November Walpole wrote 'yesterday they had another baiting from Pitt,' and added that 'they'—Pelham and his brother—wanted to get Pitt appointed into office, 'but as a preliminary, he insists on a declaration of our having nothing to do with the Continent.' Indeed he went farther than that, for while washing his hands of the Continent, he moved for an increase of our naval forces, which he declared was the only method of putting an end to the rebellion. Walpole, who was no friend of Pitt, waxed merry over this conceit. 'Ships built a year hence to suppress an army of Highlanders, now marching through England!' But Walpole, as usual, was the gossip of today; Pitt was the far-sighted statesman. A strong fleet was the best method of ensuring the end of the starveling rebellion, for it ensured the country against a French invasion, which alone held out a prospect of restoring the Stuarts to the throne. If Walpole's comments were shallow, his description of the scene in Parliament was none the less amusing. He tells how his uncle, the elder Horace, attacking Pitt, 'congratulated his country on the wisdom of the modern young men; and said he had a son of two-and-twenty, who, he did not doubt, would come over wiser than any of them. Pitt was provoked, and retorted on his negotiations and *grey-headed* experience. At those words, my uncle, as if he had been at Bartholomew Fair, snatched off his wig, and showed his grey hairs, which made the *august senate* laugh, and put Pitt out, who after laughing himself, diverted his venom upon Mr. Pelham. Upon the question, Pitt's party amounted to but thirty-six. In short, he has nothing left but his words, and his haughtiness, and his Lytteltons, and his Grenvilles.' There were not many who foresaw Pitt's future, but it is pleasant to be able to pause for a moment on this picture of his temporary confusion, and pleasanter still to record that he could laugh at his own discomfiture and laugh it off. There was a lighter side to his portentous majesty.

Meanwhile the attacks on the Government and the increasing

public uneasiness drove the Pelhams, half eagerly, half fearfully, to negotiate with Pitt. They must do something to relieve the strain on themselves, if not to save the country. The devoted band of Highlanders were marching rapidly south; panic was rising; Government was paralysed; the King was passing from testiness to abuse. The Broad-bottomed Administration, which contained all the talent, seemed woefully light compared with the strength and solidity of the one rejected genius. The Government found Pitt essential, so essential that they opened direct negotiations, and pressed them forward. Pelham saw Pitt alone, and Pitt laid down his main conditions. They were three in number and at first sight seem rather mixed. He demanded the removal of all Carteret's adherents from the Court. Secondly he wanted 'a total alteration of the foreign system': on the Continent we were to act only as auxiliaries, sending not more than 10,000 men to the help of the Dutch, 'and to act as principals at sea in the war against France and Spain. For a peace with France, at present, was not to be thought of.' Thirdly there must be a Place Bill to exclude from Parliament all junior officers of the two services.

These three conditions were not so haphazard, nor so vindictive, as they appear. They were in fact three facets of the same object—the liquidation of the continental war. If this was to be achieved, three different authorities must be brought into line— the King, the Government, and Parliament. The King was interested in the continental war because he was wrapped up in Hanover, and his interest was fostered by Carteret, who in spite of his fall from power still kept his influence in the Closet, both personally and through his friends and adherents—particularly the two Finches, William, the Vice-Chamberlain, and Edward, Groom of the Bedchamber. George II was 'difficile,' and the best hope of softening his animosity against Pitt and Pitt's policy would be to insulate him from the insidious advice of Court officials. Hence the first of Pitt's conditions. The Government, of course, must be dealt with directly and must accept the new foreign policy which Pitt laid down—hence the second condition. Parliament was more of a problem. The system of party government had not yet been evolved; the Cabinet did not necessarily command a majority, nor would they necessarily resign if the House refused to support them. After all foreign affairs were— and are—essentially a matter for the Executive, since Parliament cannot legislate for foreign nations. But if the House refused support, the Government could not carry on for long. The Members must therefore be 'managed,' and Place Bills were not consequently popular with the dispensers of patronage. In war-time, however, it was undesirable that the House should be crowded with officers—especially junior officers. Their place was at the front, and if they appeared in the House it was too often as spokesmen, not of their constituencies, not even of the army, but of the higher command, whose interest in the continental war was obvious. It would be going too far to forbid any officer to stand for Parliament, but it was not unreasonable to attempt the exclusion of the more irresponsible element at a time of crisis. Though Pitt's view could hardly be justified today, it had much to be said for it in the light of eighteenth-century conditions, and perhaps the best comment is that no one with whom Pitt negotiated showed the least hesitation in accepting that particular demand. Of greater interest is the reflection that if such a Place Bill had been in force some dozen years earlier, either Pitt would have remained in the army and outside Parliament, or, if he had entered the House, Walpole would have had no opportunity of cashiering the 'terrible Cornet of Horse.' Looking back those few years Pitt must have realised that, however honest he had been in his views, the influence of his colonel, Lord Cobham, had not been negligible. He had begun to shake off that influence, but others, with less strength of character and perhaps with less luck in the testamentary lottery, might not fare so well.

At all events Pitt laid down his conditions, and after various conversations a final meeting took place on the 16th of November. Pelham and Newcastle were supported by the Chancellor (Lord Hardwicke) and the Lord President (Lord Harrington). Three other members of the Ministry, Lord Gower, the Duke of Bedford and Lord Cobham, were present, but were regarded as Pitt's friends, or at all events as speaking to some extent for the Opposition. Pitt put forward his three demands and gained a promise of the Place Bill with ease. On the second point—the removal of Carteret's friends—the Cabinet, being desperately afraid of irritating the King, gave way with reluctance. On the third point —the change in the foreign policy—any appearance of unanimity quickly vanished. All were agreed that Austria might be left out of consideration. Since the Convention with Prussia in June, England had been urging Maria Theresa to come to terms with Frederick, and the Government felt that peace was in sight, or at least ought to be. But after all, the war in Germany had never concerned England directly. Our forces were in Flanders and our interests, as represented by the orthodox and traditional party, lay in keeping France out of the Netherlands. We must, Newcastle insisted, support Holland in a defensive war, and for that purpose the 10,000 troops suggested by Pitt as a maximum were quite inadequate and would not content the Dutch. Even if circumstances at home made a larger force impracticable we ought to show a disposition to help to the utmost of our ability.

To Pitt, a purely defensive war seemed nonsense. It could never lead to peace, and since the Dutch were always evading their responsibilities, any general disposition to assist them would land us in infinite obligations. We must limit the help to the Dutch very precisely, and meanwhile bring to bear the immense pressure of sea power.

At this point Pitt lost the support of Bedford. That pacifist, whose influence was destined to have the most malign effect on English history, was ready to support Pitt in ending the continental war, and not less ready to support Newcastle in frittering away the maritime war. Bedford was an exponent of peace at any price and at the first possible moment. In the strange workings of fate he had been appointed First Lord of the Admiralty, and as such now informed Pitt that it was impossible to increase or improve the navy—apparently oblivious of the fact that at that precise point of time it had sunk nearly to its lowest pitch of inefficiency. Newcastle welcomed Bedford's unexpected support; he was for ever grateful for signs of 'proper' conduct on the part of his colleagues, and for ever fretful at the least appearance of contradiction. With his tenacious and very exact memory, he should have recalled Bedford's words precisely a month later when the Admiralty ordered him, as Vice-Admiral of Sussex, to lay an embargo on ships in Sussex harbours laden with food, because, alas! 'several of His Majesty's ships have been detained in port for want of provisions, when the service required their being at sea.' That, however, is a digression.

Pitt did not accept the arrogant pessimism of the First Lord of the Admiralty. He knew by instinct if by no other means that the navy could be vastly improved. He did not believe for a moment in the bogy of Newcastle's imagination—that, if the Dutch in high dudgeon at our lack of effective support made a separate peace, and left us at war with France and Spain, those two

K

powers, 'by being absolutely disengaged from all expense on the Continent, would soon be able to be superior to us at sea.' His mind was full of the other side of the picture. To Newcastle's dismay he 'talked much of the general impression we could make upon France when our efforts were singly at sea,' and refused to be convinced to the contrary by the Government's idle fears and forebodings. As Newcastle wrote to Chesterfield (20th November 1745) 'we were not able to prevail'; and again 'to bring Mr. Pitt in against his own will is impossible'—a comment to be remembered whenever Pitt is accused of giving up principles to obtain office.[1]

Having failed to win Pitt, the Government fell back on the hope of making peace with France. Secret feelers were thrown out, but progress was slow. There proved to be a 'great difficulty,' as Newcastle called it, which was simply 'that Mr. Pitt and his friends are more averse at present to the treating of a peace than to anything else.' Yet Government could have expected nothing else. Pitt had made his views abundantly clear at the abortive negotiations. Like Carteret he was strongly opposed to France as the domineering nation on the Continent and the cause of the European unrest. He was sure that conclusions had to be tried with her sooner or later, and every quality he possessed drove him to believe that the sooner the better. It was not the war that worried him, but the methods adopted. 'A peace with France at present was not to be thought of.'

So, one way or another, the feelers led to nothing. Nor did the Government find much comfort in other directions. Pitt remained 'cold and reserved,'[2] while the Dutch not only demanded more help than ever but failed to understand why English troops should be withdrawn from the Continent to suppress the Jacobite rebellion. That rebellion continued its triumphant course, and on the 6th of December 1745 London experienced its famous Black Friday. News arrived that Charles Edward had given the slip to the unwieldy Cumberland and had arrived at Derby, with nothing between him and London but the trained bands still to be gathered on Finchley Common. Terror reigned supreme and the Bank of England stemmed the rush upon it only by doling out payments in sixpenny bits. Newcastle was so scared that he had no time to think even of Pitt.

---

[1] Add. MSS. 32,705.
[2] Newcastle to Chesterfield, 30th Nov. 1745. Add. MSS. 32,705.

But from that point the tide of disaster turned. The rebellion ebbed back towards its source; the panic died down; and on the Continent Frederick and Maria Theresa spent Christmas Day signing the Treaty of Dresden. Even the King was showing signs of grace and beginning to overcome his prejudices. Early in January 1746 he told Newcastle in an expansive moment 'that he would do everybody justice: that Lord Chesterfield had done extremely well in Ireland; that his notions were very right as to England, and should be followed.'[1]

There can be little doubt that Pitt viewed these developments with mixed feelings. It was all very well for the rebellion to be crushed, and for the continental war to die of inanition. He probably expected as much. But with the passing of the panic, his own chances of office were passing also. And Pitt was very human in his weaknesses. The haughty pride and dignity with which he surrounded himself were mostly a matter of self-defence. Underneath the grand exterior lay a soul hungering for wealth and honour, hungering for human love and happy friendship. Pitt was desperately lonely and, fighting a lone hand, he did not always find it easy to hold the torch of patriotism aloft. Very human cravings cut athwart his austerely splendid façade. He wanted office; he wanted recognition; he wanted an opportunity of displaying his gifts and powers; he wanted to aggrandise his country; he wanted so much that was a mixture of self and selflessness. And the tide of seeming disaster which had been carrying him so rapidly towards all his goals was receding and in its ebb leaving him more isolated than ever. Something had to be done.

Pitt acted without hesitation, but also with the angularity common to men who mingle the shyness of frustration with the conscious knowledge of capacity. After having kept himself haughtily aloof from all Ministers for some time, he suddenly swallowed his pride rather as though it were a fishbone, and made dark and distant overtures to Bedford. He expressed an inclination to know the Government's foreign schemes; he showed a disposition to acquiesce; he wished that someone in authority would have a talk with Lord Cobham, who was the leader of the little band of Patriots. In short, he did his best to woo the Government, and they were still sufficiently alarmed to welcome his addresses. Newcastle hurried to Cobham, who was more suave

[1] Newcastle to Chesterfield, 6th January 1745/6. Add. MSS. 32,706.

than Pitt, more able to appear natural and at ease. He even took the war into the enemy's camp and told Newcastle, with a delicious touch of condescension, that the Government's foreign policy was much more reasonable than he imagined they could have made it; and that if the Continent had to be supported, he thought it could not be done in a better or cheaper manner. That being so, he was graciously willing to throw in his lot with them. As a reward for this disinterested service, he demanded that Pitt should be appointed Secretary at War, and Barrington a Lord of the Admiralty, while his nephew, James Grenville, should be given a job worth £1,000 a year. Other points 'he flung out,' but fortunately 'not as points absolutely to be insisted upon.'[1]

Newcastle was overjoyed. He and Pelham, mortified by the King's asperities, had long been contemplating a fall with him. Their scheme was to threaten resignation, and if necessary to resign, so as to bring the King to heel and force him to accept their views. But first they wanted to establish themselves beyond the possibility of defeat. Actually, they had little to fear since there was no practical alternative to them. The Broad-bottomed Administration included all the Whig factions and all the Whig magnates except Granville. At other times the King might possibly have resorted to the Tories, but not in the midst of rebellion. His only hope, therefore, lay in Cobham's connection. That hope was slight enough, bearing in mind the King's known repugnance to both Cobham and Pitt; but the hope, such as it was, had now vanished. There was no one to whom the King could turn but Granville and Bath, both of whom were discredited and unpopular.

Perhaps the King had some inkling of the cage in which he was enclosed. Perhaps, too, his experience of Chesterfield had softened him. At all events, he was far milder than Newcastle had expected. He agreed to everything except giving Pitt the particular office of Secretary at War. That was too much. Any other office Pitt might have and welcome, but not the office which controlled the army. It was intolerable to think of discussing strategy and tactics, commissariat and uniforms—the great love of his life—with his soul's abhorrence. Oil and vinegar would mingle more easily and sweetly.

The Pelhams, having gained the first round, pressed hard upon the King, who put up a spirited rearguard action. From a blank

[1] Newcastle to Chesterfield, 18 Feb. 1746. Add. MSS. 32,706.

refusal, he passed to a threat that he would use Pitt ill, if he were made Secretary at War—a threat that seemed vague enough, but perhaps for that very reason frightened Newcastle the more. In any event it was not an offer that the brothers felt justified in reporting to Pitt. So the pressure was continued, and at last the King was driven one step farther back, a step which must have cost him a great pang. He would give Pitt the office, but with the gift, he would relinquish his own interest in army affairs; Pitt must carry on as best he could, since George II would not admit him to his presence. The army in short must be reduced to pure routine.

The Pelhams were still unsatisfied, and the King though 'very uneasy' and full of complaints at the pressure brought to bear on him, was wavering when Bath intervened. It was scandalous, he declared, that the King should be so bullied. He should send the Pelhams packing and summon Granville and Bath to his aid; they would mould an administration more to his heart's desire.

George was no fool. It is customary to belittle him in order to commend his wife, that famous virago Caroline of Anspach, but remarkable as she was, it still remains a fact that the most glorious years of George II's reign occurred after the Queen was dead and buried. George had a sound common sense, even if he was irritable and testy and often let his feelings get the better of him. It is quite on the cards that he knew how hopeless it was to dismiss the Pelhams. But George was no coward, and, besides, he was 'extremely irritated,' so that when Bath gave him that word of encouragement, he determined to try his luck. His attitude stiffened and the Pelhams began to contemplate resignation. Pitt thereupon intervened. He wanted desperately to obtain office, he was ravenous for it, to use Walpole's expression, but he disliked the gamble of resignation at such a moment and he shrank from coercing the King. He therefore renounced all his pretensions to the particular office of Secretary at War; but it was too late. The Pelhams and their followers resigned in a concerted order, leaving the King without Ministers and almost without speech. None the less he accepted the resignations with spirit, and without further ado appointed Bath First Lord of the Treasury and Granville Secretary of State. If only they could bestir themselves, he would have men about him of far higher talents than the humdrum Pelham and the fussy Newcastle, and what was more, men infinitely more to his liking, men who understood him and sympathised with his ambitions.

Granville, whose capacity was being undermined by drink and the luxury of wealth (he had succeeded to his title in October 1744) accepted office laughingly and as laughingly laid it down four days later when it became abundantly clear that he had no followers. Bath had already sneaked down the back stairs. So the King's conspiracy failed, and the Pelhams' conspiracy succeeded. They were recalled, grudgingly and of necessity. George, with the happy conviction that his *obiter dicta* would circulate round the town, sooner or later reaching the appropriate ear, fumed to Newcastle that Harrington was a rascal, and roared at Harrington that Newcastle was a fool; and generally bedaubed all his returning Ministers with shrewd, if libellous, epithets. Meanwhile he urged Bath to write a full account of their scandalous behaviour. 'Rub it in their noses,' he said, 'and if it be possible make them ashamed.' But, for all his wrath, he knew himself to be beaten. Pitt could have had the Secretaryship at War if he had pressed for it, but on the 22nd of February 1746, with exemplary moderation, he accepted the meaningless office of Vice-Treasurer of Ireland, till a more suitable post or a better opportunity should arise. Pitt was rarely wise in negotiation, and perhaps never when his own interests were concerned.

24

THE PRICE OF OFFICE

Having made his choice, Pitt lost no time in proclaiming his views to the world. Early in March he made what Lord Hastings described as 'a florid oration in favour of the Court, which has made him the ridicule of everyone. . . . It is reckoned one of the most barefaced impositions on the public that has been known lately.'[1] The speech is lost, but the buzz of comment implied by Hastings' letter must have shown Pitt what he had to expect. Possibly it was this very fact which drove him on; for his next speech, which must have been more than usually difficult, was unnecessary and seems to have been deliberate. It was made on the 8th of April. The subject was the hiring of Hanoverian troops, a subject notoriously distasteful to Pitt, and one on which he might reasonably have kept silence: yet he spoke, and spoke in favour of the motion. If he did not do so deliberately he can have done so only under direct orders from Newcastle or Pelham—an unlikely event.

Whatever Pitt's motive, the problem was one which the Government had to face, and the answer must depend at least in part on the progress of the war. On the Continent hostilities were dragging out their weary length. Most of the nations—England, Austria, Holland, Sardinia, France and Spain—were nominally at war, but there was no clear-cut division and in fact fighting was practically confined to northern Italy and Flanders. It would have been difficult to say what the fighting was about. None the less until peace was actually made, some forces had to be provided, and in April the question came up for debate in the House. The new campaign would shortly begin, and though it was probably too much to expect Pelham and Newcastle to evolve any strategy, at least they must arrange something, however makeshift. What they decided was that a 'great effort'—that magnificent cloak of emptiness—should be made in Flanders. There was to be an army

[1] Hastings to Earl of Huntingdon, 13th March 1746. H. M. C. Hastings MSS.,Vol. III.

of 90,000 men or more, provided mainly by the Dutch and Austrians, but including 18,000 Hanoverians. These Hanoverians were England's contribution. There were no English troops to spare until the Jacobite rebellion had been finally quashed; and since their place was to be filled by Hanoverians, it was right that England should pay for their hire.

As members of the Government the Cobham connection had to acquiesce. Most of them did so silently, but Pitt, with his ingrained wholeheartedness in any project which he adopted, was not prepared to vote without at least an explanation. He therefore spoke in support. The speech has not come down to us, but there are two short and well-known descriptions. 'Pitt,' wrote Walpole, 'was the only one of this *ominous* band that opened his mouth, and it was to add impudence to profligacy; but no criminal at the Place de Grêve was ever so racked as he was by Dr. Lee, a friend of Lord Granville, who gave him the question both ordinary and extraordinary.'[1] To Pelham this mixture of impudence and profligacy showed 'the dignity of Sir William Wyndham, the wit of Mr. Pulteney, and the knowledge and judgment of Sir Robert Walpole.' Newcastle, speaking from secondhand knowledge, did not attempt to describe the manner; but he praised the purport, declaring that Pitt said 'all that was right for the King, kind and respectful to the *old corps*, and resolute and contemptuous for the Tory Opposition.'[2]

It is a pity that Pitt's own arguments are not forthcoming, as they would have shown if his speech was a mere recantation or something wholly different. Certain points, however, may be tentatively suggested. Pitt was never frightened of inconsistency. He realised that the consistency which may prove an admirable buckler for a timid and short-sighted politician tends to degenerate into a mere lack of imagination when used by the statesman. Facts change and with them the statesman's attitude should also change. The right policy today may easily be the wrong policy tomorrow. Besides, politicians as well as ordinary men grow wiser with experience. Pitt accepted the fact of his inconsistency as something in the course of nature, and so far from attempting to gloss it over, proclaimed that he spoke with an 'unembarrassed countenance'— a rash phrase, which gave an opening to the caricaturists. It is ironical to think that the dead and damned lampooners have kept

---

[1] Walpole to Mann, 15th April 1746.
[2] Duke of Newcastle to Duke of Cumberland, 17th April 1746.

alive the only genuine phrase of the speech, and one moreover which throws light on a dark place.

For the phrase suggests, if it does not prove, that Pitt did feel some embarrassment. This in turn suggests that his advocacy was not based entirely on conviction. He was paying the price of office. Yet the sin, if it be such, was not without its merit. Pitt was showing, and showing boldly, something that was new in English politics. Hitherto the idea of Cabinet responsibility had been practically non-existent, or if it did exist, had arisen through the authority of the King rather than the adhesion of the Ministers. The curse of eighteenth-century politics was the innumerable Whig factions, each loyal only to its own leader, each intriguing in the Cabinet to thrust out its political colleagues and bring in its personal friends. It was a system which could work only under some outstanding genius such as Walpole. Under lesser men it led to chaos and therefore was a phase that was bound to pass. Pitt was one of the first, if not the first, to realise the need for Cabinet responsibility and as a corollary Cabinet agreement. His 'unembarrassed countenance' is the forerunner of the possibly apocryphal remark of a later Prime Minister that it did not matter much what the Cabinet said, so long as they all said the same thing.

Apart from this conviction, which undoubtedly grew, Pitt could have found some justification for his change, if he had wished. The war was not over and must therefore be supported. He had always agreed—however reluctantly—to a force of 10,000 men; he had always agreed to England's playing the part of an auxiliary on the Continent. At the moment, with the rebellion still smouldering in the Highlands, it might reasonably be argued that England could not spare even 10,000 men. At all events no English troops were going to the Continent. Further, Pitt had been told but a few months earlier by Bedford that the navy could not do real damage to France. There is no reason to suppose that he believed Bedford, but acceptance of his statement might be politically expedient. Unless, therefore, the Hanoverians were hired, it seemed as though England must do nothing.

Whether or not Pitt used any such argument, certainly in this speech he changed his views officially, and whatever reasons may be guessed or suggested, it can hardly be doubted that one reason at least was the obligation to pay for office. Another reason must surely have been the desire to placate the King. From that point of view, it may be said that he was attempting to buy preferment.

If he was trying to curry favour, beyond doubt he succeeded. The King was so much surprised at the speech, and so much pleased, that he suggested Pitt for the honour of proposing the parliamentary grant to the Duke of Cumberland after Culloden (16th April) and it was only the Duke's own objection that quashed the proposal. Further, when a fortnight later Winnington's death made vacant the lucrative office of Paymaster to the Forces, the King had no qualms about allowing Pitt to succeed. He kissed hands for the office on the 6th of May, becoming at the same time a privy councillor. The King is reported to have shed tears of vexation as Pitt knelt before him, but the report does not bear the stamp of truth. At the moment the King felt towards him much as he felt towards Chesterfield. He would do him justice and admit that he was not so bad as he had been painted. If quick returns are a sign of success, Pitt's first speech as a Minister was an overwhelming triumph.

But he had to pay the price, and it came in a temporary loss of popularity. The Government's acceptance of him into their ranks was said to have given 'vast offence to some of their best friends,'[1] and now his apparent apostasy from his previously proclaimed views brought on his head a furious outcry from the Opposition. In a word he had no friends and many enemies. There was a spate of lampoons, in verse and prose, written not only by the unknown purveyors of scurrilous broadsheets but also by men of literary talent such as Hanbury Williams. The fact that his recantation came so soon after his legacy from the Duchess of Marlborough, and the fact that he had lighted on so infelicitous a phrase as 'unembarrassed countenance' gave endless scope to the wits and caricaturists, and the Opposition journals abounded for weeks in satires, sometimes humorous, sometimes virulent, and in either case generally coarse, as was the custom of the age.

[1] Malmesbury. *Letters*, I, 33.

25

PAYMASTER PITT

Pitt remained Paymaster for nine and a half years (6th May 1746 to 20th November 1755). The office itself was something in the nature of a rich sinecure. As Paymaster he was responsible for distributing regimental pay and pensions, and handing over subsidies to the agents of foreign princes; the work was routine and was conducted automatically by the staff. Incidentally, James Grenville was made Pitt's deputy, at a salary of £1,000, thus obtaining the perquisites demanded for him by his uncle, Lord Cobham. Pitt could do as much or as little as he chose; and whichever course he adopted could feather his nest successfully. The salary, £3,000 a year, was out of all proportion to the work and yet was augmented by various allowances which raised the total remuneration to something over £4,000. Munificent as that sum might seem, it paled into insignificance beside other emoluments of office, which were allowed by custom and were not illegal. The Paymaster held large balances and it was accepted practice for him to use these balances for his own personal profit until they were required. Furthermore, it was usual for the Paymaster to take a commission on the payment of subsidies. Even at one-quarter of one per cent. this commission ran into considerable money when reckoned on subsidies of a million and over. In short, the office was a recognised plum, and in able financial hands could and did lay the foundation of large private fortunes. No better example can be found than Henry Fox, first Lord Holland. He was Pitt's rival, and in 1746 snatched the office of Secretary at War from under Pitt's nose. But in the hurly-burly of fate he succumbed before Pitt's genius, and in 1757 was glad enough to accept the office of Paymaster. There he remained to amass the vast wealth which financed the endless dissipation of his sons.

Fox and others of his kidney no doubt showed financial genius in handling their opportunities. In that direction they outshone Pitt. He was not particularly clever at money matters, though equally he was not so obtuse as he was pleased at times to pretend and as his biographers have since asserted. But if there was one direction more than another in which his lack of financial skill, or perhaps mere carelessness, was specially evident it was in con- nection with his personal affairs. In public finances he showed greater interest and some degree of perspicacity. Certainly it was impossible for his restless soul to labour at the Paymaster's office and leave no trace. Even routine had to bear the mark of his genius. Unlike the majority of his contemporaries, Pitt was a strenuous worker; success did not come easily, nor did he expect it to. Each step had to be prepared; each plan had to be pruned; each letter had to be revised and polished and perfected. Later on he was to wear out his colleagues with the multiplicity of detail, but in these early days there was not the same scope. None the less he found much to do in reorganising the office and initiating reforms. Pitt took his duties seriously and surprised the various agents and officials by insisting that they should report direct to him. He scrutinised the claims, cut down unwarranted demands, and generally tightened the control over expenditure, eliminating waste and extravagance. Side by side with this desirable measure of economy, which was no doubt most galling to the army agents, went a determination to make prompt payments, especially to the officers and men. Accounts in the leisurely days of the eighteenth century were tiresome things that everyone put off till the day after tomorrow. When therefore Pitt insisted on speed and economy he was throwing a stone into a stagnant pool, and the ripples spread in ever-widening circles. Fox and Rigby might revert to the old ways, but the effects of Pitt's régime were not dead, and the demand for reform grew—a reform which would not depend solely on the goodwill and character of the individual Paymaster—until it came to fruition after Pitt's death.

Side by side with the tightening up of administration went two reforms eminently characteristic of Pitt. The one was a measure of human charity which alleviated the worries of the Chelsea out- pensioners. Those unfortunate veterans were paid their pensions annually in arrear, and in order to tide over the waiting period of twelve months betook themselves to moneylenders. Perhaps it would be truer to say that the moneylenders took advantage of this lacuna to introduce themselves to the pensioners and buy up the pensions at a cheap rate. At all events the upshot of the system was that the veterans, in their ignorance if not their innocence,

THE PAY OFFICE IN THE EIGHTEENTH CENTURY

became inextricably tangled in the usurer's net and for ever after contributed largely to his upkeep. Pitt, according to his own statement, and probably in truth, had it much at heart 'to redeem these helpless, unthinking creatures from their harpies,' but for some time allowed himself to be foiled by the obstacles which are liable to spring up in the path of reform; he could not 'devise any practicable and effectual scheme.' Ultimately, however, for a somewhat surprising reason (see p. 259) he applied himself seriously to the problem, and found no real difficulty in discovering a satisfactory remedy. In November 1754 he introduced a Bill, which was passed, providing for half-yearly payments in advance, forbidding mortgages on pensions and stopping the exaction of commissions by the pensions officers. This care for the underling marked Pitt out from the majority of his contemporaries. The others were not inhuman or cruel; they were very normal Englishmen, disposed to be kind and not ungenerous. But they were completely lacking in imagination, and as members of a very exclusive and self-sufficient caste drew in with their mothers' milk an insouciant belief that the masses outside their immediate dependants whom they knew and liked were little more than pawns in the game of life. Pitt was not untouched by the spirit of exclusiveness; he kept himself very much to himself; he was haughty and distant to his immediate subordinates, being very fearful of losing face if he were not starched and stiff. But where his own personal dignity was not concerned he displayed a deep understanding of the people, a profound sympathy with their sufferings, and an appreciation of their ideals and aspirations. Pitt envied and aped the aristocracy but he sympathised wholeheartedly with the common people, from whom he derived his strength.

The other reform was personal to himself, and sprang partly out of his natural uprightness and partly out of his showman's instinct. From the moment of entering office he put by the perquisites; he refused to touch the balances; he refused to divert any portion of the subsidies granted by Parliament to allies and foreign powers by taking the usual commission. The King of Sardinia was the first to benefit by this surprising new régime, and he was so startled and perhaps so frightened of what it might portend that he first urged Pitt to deduct the usual commission, and failing in that tried equally unsuccessfully to bribe Pitt with a handsome present.

Pitt was, of course, acting as civil servants and Ministers are now expected to act. But at the time his attitude created a sensation. It cut across all precedent and practice; it seemed so unnecessary as to be almost priggish; and worst of all, in Pitt's hands it took on a flaunting theatrical air which appealed to the melodramatically minded gallery but rasped the more sophisticated stalls with a mixed feeling of pricked consciences and the malaise that springs from a social solecism. In matters political Pitt did not believe in hidden virtue or private charity. Politics were essentially public and demanded publicity. The time was to come when Pitt would stretch out his hand in the House and, waggling his fingers, solemnly declare that no gold stuck to them. It was clever publicity and as such it paid, but it was vulgar and pharisaical.

26

HISTORY'S 'HORRID EXAMPLES'

When his departmental functions have been described, little remains to be said of Pitt's activities as Paymaster, at all events during his earlier years in office. The mere attainment of office, aided no doubt by the concomitant loss of popularity, seemed to damp down his fires and blight his energies. One might almost think that he was a little overawed at finding himself one of the country's rulers. Perhaps for that very reason his attitude was 'correct.' His first step was to break with the Prince of Wales and then with Cobham, who countered by calling him 'a wrong-headed fellow.' Henceforward he was to be a King's man and have no dealings with Opposition; henceforward he was to be a loyal colleague and a firm supporter of the Government. More strange still, with this access of mildness, Pitt seems to have given up ambition. Apparently he saw little or no prospect of rising to any of the great offices of state, let alone the premiership, and he contented himself with the conscientious performance of his duty in a subordinate capacity. He effaced himself; he did the Government's dirty work; he acted time and again as a peacemaker, oiling the wheels and resolving the grit; and he seems to have asked for neither recognition nor reward. On the contrary, he seems to have subscribed to the view held by others that he had obtained 'a great and sudden rise,'[1] or as the Duke and Duchess of Bedford confided to one another, with a faint flavour of upturned aristocratic noses, that 'the orator is so vastly well provided for.'[2] He told Sir Thomas Robinson on the 17th of May 1746 with an unusual tone of humility, 'I heartily wish I had as much reason to be contented with the state of the Public, as I have to be so with my own.'[3] Pitt realised that he had forced an entry into a world into which he had not been born, and he felt the paralysing mixture of humility and irritation that always descended on him

---

[1] See Legge to Duke of Bedford, 3 May 1746. Bedford. *Correspondence*, I, 89.
[2] Bedford. *Correspondence*, I, 93.   [3] H. M. C. Trevor MSS.

in high society. Besides it was difficult, even on a calm review, to see what prospects he had of further advancement. Pelham was Pitt's senior by some twelve years; but he had only just reached the fifties and there was no reason to suppose that his florid and robust strength would succumb much, if anything, before Pitt's sickly and delicate frame. Pitt's opportunity of stepping into his leader's shoes seemed small enough, and even if it arose would still be subject to the King's prejudice. Pitt might justly doubt whether the King would choose him voluntarily as his chief Minister. It was true that George II was old and might die, but if he did, Pitt had broken with Frederick, the Prince of Wales, and could not reasonably expect to be taken back again into favour by Frederick the King. His prospects, in short, were bad, look at them how one would; and this fact, combined with his content-ment at his sudden access of wealth, kept him quiet and watered down his ambition. It was the course of history and not his own fiery spirit which was to give him his great opportunity, and it is therefore the more essential to look closely at this course which was to prove so important.

Pitt's first year of office was not remarkable in itself, but the historian looking back cannot fail to observe that both at home and abroad it presented Pitt, at what must have been an impres-sionable stage, with 'horrid' examples—examples which he noted and put to good use when his own time came.

At home the year saw the end of the '45; it gave Cumberland his solitary victory, Culloden, and his soubriquet of Butcher. The victory was hollow enough, since there was little of permanent interest in the crushing of the Jacobites. They had never been formidable, and might have been killed with kindness years before. As a power they were negligible from the first, and as an oppor-tunity they had so far been overlooked. But the horror and the folly of the treatment meted out to them did not escape Pitt's eagle eye. He noted and disapproved—though in silence. Sub-sequently he was to show a newer and a better way of treating them, and his success, compared with Cumberland's failure, was to mould his views on America and give birth to a new conception of imperial duties.

Abroad, the year was to offer Pitt much food for contemplation. It opened with something approaching a plan. Whilst the Jacobite rebellion had been absorbing England's energies, a body of American colonists under a colonial officer, Colonel Pepperell, had taken a sudden hand in the war, and captured Louisbourg (17th June 1745). No one in the home country was quite sure whether this proved the prowess of the colonists or the feebleness of the French Canadians, but on the whole English opinion, which was generally supercilious towards the colonists, inclined to the latter view. If prowess came into the picture at all, it was called to mind that the colonists had been stiffened by a body of English marines from the squadron under Admiral Warren. The capture, however, was very popular, becoming, as Chesterfield said, 'the darling object of the whole nation';[1] and this success, exposing as was imagined the degeneracy of the Canadians, raised warlike thoughts in Bedford, who nine months later, in March 1746, threw out an undigested proposal that an expedition should be sent forthwith from England to reduce Canada. Indeed, so pressing had the matter become at the very moment of its conception, that nothing should be allowed to postpone the embarkation 'though but for twenty-four hours.' In Bedford's opinion 5,000 troops were enough; they should, if no time were lost, arrive at Quebec not later than July, and would then have 'more than sufficient time to complete the reduction of Canada before the commencement of the winter.'[2] Among other minor suggestions Bedford expressed the belief that 'the Indian nations in alliance with us may be of great use in scouring the woods and reducing the open country of Canada, and we know no more likely method of gaining them than the directing the several governors on the continent to invite them into it, by the promise of plunder, and some small presents, such as powder, ball, firearms, etc., in order to enable and encourage them to act vigorously in conjunction with his Majesty's troops.' The scheme fell through, as was natural, considering the want of precision, the lack of preparation, and the deplorable state of the navy. None the less, while impossible of performance under such men as Bedford and Newcastle, the idea was right; it turned England's attention away from the Continent towards the countries overseas. Bedford himself did not appreciate the benefits of his own proposal. He put it forward, as he explained later in the year, in order 'to strike such a blow to the French maritime force they may never be able to recover; whereas, in all probability, if something of this sort is not done, their maritime power must increase in proportion to

[1] Lodge. *Studies in Eighteenth Century Diplomacy*, p. 134.
[2] Bedford. *Correspondence*, I, 67-8.

L

the decrease of ours, and how much ours depends on the security
of our northern colonies, I think I need not mention.'[1] It was of
course easier to attack and destroy the French Navy at sea than in
Canada, but Bedford in his sudden fit of urgency could hardly be
expected to realise this. But, if his proposal was put forward for
wrong reasons, it was put forward at a crucial moment. The
scheme was proposed a few days before Pitt became Paymaster,
and was being actively canvassed when he entered office; it must
have been one of the first measures which he was called upon to
consider in an official capacity. He came to it with the freshness of
a new broom and found it invested with the glamour of greatness.
He embraced it with ardour. It touched his imagination; it helped
to germinate the seeds of empire lying in his brain. If Bedford
was destined in the end to undo much of Pitt's work, at least he
gave that work a fillip at the beginning. Pitt recognised at once
the value of the idea. He hoped ardently that we should have
'facility and resolution to pursue firmly those great and practicable views in America, which, as far as they have gone or are to
go, we owe to your Grace alone. You are alone, however,' he
added, 'but in one place, for the nation is certainly with you; with
such a second, your Grace can surmount all obstacles.'[2] But
Bedford failed to take his chances; he was too easily diverted.
His scheme was put off, and apparently he largely forgot it. Later
in the year there was a faint echo. The threat of a French squadron
sailing for Acadia stirred George Grenville at the Admiralty to
hope that in 1747 the colonists would be assisted with both troops
and money from England. Bedford agreed, languidly, but thought
that the colonists should pay for their own troops. And so the
matter dropped.

The proposed expedition against Canada was not the only
feature of interest in Pitt's first year of office. The ships and troops
which Newcastle did not care to despatch so far from England—
and perhaps rightly, considering the inefficiency of the home fleet
—had to be used somewhere, and were in fact ordered to make a
descent on the coast of France. It is tempting to think that the
suggestion came from Pitt; at all events it is the forerunner of his
own policy some twelve years later, and was undertaken for
precisely the same reason. The war on the Continent was going
badly. The Maréchal de Saxe had, in a most ungentlemanly

[1] Bedford to Stone, 10th Nov. 1746. Bedford. *Correspondence*, I. 183.
[2] Pitt to Bedford, 19th July 1746. Bedford. *Correspondence*, I. 132.

manner, ignored the usual cold weather recess, and renewed his operations in mid-winter, whilst England was still in the throes of the Jacobite rebellion. By this unexpected course he had managed to overrun the Austrian Netherlands, capturing Brussels as early as the 20th of February, and thereafter mopping up Antwerp, Mons and Charleroi. The allies seemed powerless, and were destined in the autumn to suffer a serious reverse at Roucoux. To relieve the pressure, the expedition to Quebec was diverted against France. Admiral Lestock, flushed with the undeserved results of his court martial, was put in command of the ships, and General St. Clair of the troops. The expedition sailed on the 14th of September, without any definite orders, but with plenty of discretion to attack the coast of France wherever they thought fit. What they did was to land troops near l'Orient on the south side of the Brest Peninsula, cleverly enough so far as the dis-embarkation went, but with no foresight or clear plans. Finding themselves unable to make an impression on l'Orient, they re-embarked, made a futile landing a little farther south in Quiberon Bay, and returned home without glory but also without loss. The failure of the expedition was at least as much the fault of the Government as of the soldiers and sailors. According to Hume, who took part in the expedition as St. Clair's secretary, the general 'lay under positive orders to sail with the first fair wind, to approach the unknown coast, march through the unknown country, and attack the unknown cities of the most potent nation of the universe.' If this description is a trifle picturesque, it is none the less true that the plans were very ill-digested and worse prepared. The Powers that Be appeared to think that pilots and guides were unnecessary and the absence of maps and plans could be made good by reconnoitring. The mere lack of success was something not unsubstantial; it showed that descents on the coast of France could be made with impunity; and it suggested that they might be made with success, if properly prepared and ably led. At all events Pitt seems to have been disgusted rather than dis-appointed with the results. 'In the gloomy scene,' he commented to Grenville, 'which I fear is opening in public affairs for this disgraced country, there is nothing to rest upon but the pleasure of esteeming and sharing the esteem of those who deserve to have lived in better days.'[1]

Perhaps owing to the yeast of Pitt's personality, or perhaps to

---

[1] Pitt to Grenville, 29th Oct. 1746. *Grenville Papers*, I, 52.

the vague fumblings of Bedford, the Government was sufficiently stirred to end the year with good intentions. The King's Speech at the opening of Parliament in November 1746 breathed a spirit of resolution. Six million pounds were voted for the army and navy; subsidies were offered with a lavish hand, and the Duke of Cumberland was sent over to Holland to reanimate the wavering Dutch and settle a plan of campaign. By January all was cut and dried—on paper. England was to provide 13,000 native troops and 24,000 Hanoverians and Hessians, while Austrian and Dutch contingents were to raise the army to 138,000. Cumberland himself was to assume the supreme command, and it was his firm intention to strike an early blow—something maybe as crushing as Culloden—something which would not only enable England to dictate terms of peace but also enhance his own reputation. He left to take up his command in February 1747, no doubt in the best of spirits.

27

THE TREATY OF AIX-LA-CHAPELLE

Pitt, at the time, was staying at Bath in a vain attempt to ward off gout. In spite of a tendency, as the years passed, to a mild hypochondria, understandable if not altogether excusable, Pitt was amazingly patient under his affliction and more than a little optimistic. 'I am at present,' he wrote to his cousin John in January 1747, 'far from well, and unless I find infinitely more amendment the next week than I have hitherto done since I came hither, I fear I am not able to get through one day's attendance in the House. However, as I gain ground, I have reason to hope that, by a little more time here, I may get rid of my disorder quite, before it fixes, as it did once, upon a part so hard to dislodge it from.'

He was still in poor health when the Government decided to dissolve Parliament and appeal to the country. The reason appears to have been the false dawn of success given by Anson's victory off Finisterre in May (1747). It had been known that the French were despatching to sea a fleet covering transports and merchantmen, half to sail to America and the other half to India. Anson fell in with the enemy and being far superior in strength was able to gain an overwhelming victory, taking six of the nine French men-of-war and capturing four of the merchantmen. It was a shrewd blow. 'I most heartily wish your Grace joy,' Pitt wrote to Newcastle, 'of this total defeat of the naval designs of France for this year, which, I conceive, cannot fail to have considerable effects on their affairs in general.'[1] For almost the first time in the war the Government had something to put in the shop window, and they felt rightly that they should make the most of their fleeting advantage by presenting themselves to the public in the hope of securing additional strength. The idea was said to have been suggested by Thomas Sherlock, then Bishop of Salisbury, and the story gains weight by the fact that his son was at once given

---

[1] Pitt to Newcastle, 17th May 1747. Add. MSS. 32,711.

the Deanery of York and he himself was translated to London the next year.[1] But, with or without Sherlock's prompting, Newcastle, who was both unrivalled in the art of managing the House and a hard bargainer in the dispensing of ecclesiastical preferment, recognised his chance and seized it. Parliament was dissolved forthwith and fresh elections took place in June. Newcastle was only just in time, for the mirage of victory was dissipated on the 2nd of July when Cumberland sustained another defeat on the Continent, at Laffelt; none the less he was in time, and he had more than one reason for his move. Besides the hope of gaining greater numbers, Government needed the wholehearted support of the country for the definitive peace negotiations which all hoped would spring out of the pourparlers which had long been proceeding on the Continent. The Government would clearly be in a much stronger position if they had seven years of office in front of them instead of the prospect of an election in a few months' time.

The election found Pitt without a seat. Now that he had broken with the Prince of Wales, his brother was not prepared to renew the gift of Old Sarum, which was dedicated to the Prince's party and Opposition. Newcastle, however, came to Pitt's aid and offered him one of the two Seaford seats. Sussex was very much under the wing of the Duke of Newcastle. He was Lord Lieutenant of the county, owned large properties there, and assiduously nursed the various constituencies through his agents. But if he nursed them, he also expected them to pay prompt obedience to his wishes. On the 20th of June he wrote to the Corporation in mild and gracious terms; the goodness which the Corporation had showed him on all occasions encouraged him to recommend Mr. Pitt to their favour; Mr. Pitt's well-known qualifications would doubtless make him as agreeable to the Corporation as their choice of him would be serviceable to the public; he intended to bring Mr. Pitt down and introduce him to the electorate; and their favour to the Duke's two nominees—Mr. Hay was the other—would ever be gratefully acknowledged.[2]

It was all very dignified, very polite and charming, very eighteenth century. It was no less eighteenth century, though much less dignified and neither polite nor charming, for the Duke to fall into transports of indignation when the Opposition refused

[1] *Memoirs of a Royal Chaplain*, p. 127.   [2] Add. MSS. 32,711.

to recognise his preserves and put up Lord Gage's son and the Earl of Middlesex as rival candidates. What is more immediately interesting is the evident doubt of victory which assailed both Newcastle and Pitt. 'Whatever the event,' Pitt declared, 'I shall with great pride meet any persecution in which I have the honour to be joined with your Grace and Mr. Pelham'; and in spite of his ill-health he obeyed Newcastle's instructions to hurry down to Seaford. 'I have,' he wrote, 'sent on horses to East Grinstead, and a Post chaise in case of rain, which I am too infirm to stand.' Newcastle accompanied him and, once at Seaford, not only urged Pitt's candidature, but, quite illegally, took a seat on the hustings and scrutinised the votes. The obsequious electors knew too well the probable results of falling foul of the great man, and on the 29th of June duly elected Pitt—apparently to his great relief. But the opposing candidates were rightly annoyed at this flagrant breach of the law and lodged a petition. In those days when election petitions were settled by the House, minority claims could not hope to succeed, but this petition was not without its influence on the future. Pitt made light of the charges, and so brought down on his head a well-deserved rebuke in a maiden speech from a young parliamentarian, Thomas Potter, the son of the Archbishop, who was said to have spoken 'well and bitterly.'[1] Pitt accepted the rebuke in silence; possibly it chimed in with his true feelings; possibly it opened up new vistas. At all events he adopted Potter's views and on a subsequent occasion used them with devastating effect. This rebuke was the beginning of a deep and lasting friendship.

Apart, however, from these details, the election suggests that Pitt's popularity was still in eclipse. Indeed his lot was bound to be uneasy. His strength came from the people, as all the world appreciated. But just in so far as the Whig magnates adopted him, in order to placate the people, so his popularity waned, and his usefulness to the Ministry grew smaller. There was real dilemma here, and it was the cause of much that appeared to be inexplicable not only in Pitt's own actions but in those of the other actors in the drama.

Meanwhile the international situation during the interval between the election in June and the meeting of Parliament in November (1747) was far from encouraging and was the more confused because all the nations concerned in the war were

[1] Lady Hervey's *Letters*, p. 111.

angling for position so that they could secure better terms of peace.

As already mentioned, Cumberland on the 2nd of July added Laffelt to his long list of defeats, and his conqueror, the Maréchal de Saxe, moved to the siege of Bergen-op-Zoom, which fell in September. Realising that no further action of moment could take place that winter, the French then proceeded to create a panic in England by massing troops on the coast. The Cabinet believed invasion to be imminent and when they dared to turn their eyes from the Channel glanced nervously in the direction of the Highlands. The Jacobites—poor hunted devils—seemed to Newcastle's feverish imagination to be 'uppish and stirring everywhere.' To add to the feeling of depression, reports from America were discouraging, when they were not bewildering. When Bedford in the previous March had flung out his suggestion of an attack on Canada, Newcastle had been galvanised into a few jerky actions. Communications with America were slow, and the results of Newcastle's actions were only now beginning to be reported. The reports puzzled and distressed him. He had, amongst other arrangements, appointed one, Benjamin Wheatley, to be Naval Officer of North Carolina, and the Governor wrote in perplexity 'I am at a loss to admit him, for there is no such office here.'[1] The Governors, too, acting on vague instructions and with their customary want of tact, managed only too frequently to exasperate the colonists under their charge and to stir up trouble. They wrote peevishly of obstruction and want of support. 'I have been met,' said Governor Clinton, 'with a most vile and insolent treatment from both Houses of Representatives of this Province [New York] for no other reason than my endeavouring to support His Majesty's prerogative and forwarding the service commended to me.'[2] From India, too, the news, though out of date and misleading, was a cause of depression. The brilliant but unfortunate Governor of the French Islands, La Bourdonnais, had cowed the pusillanimous Peyton, whom chance had placed in command of the English squadron in Indian waters, and had captured Madras in September 1746. The arrival of reinforcements under Griffin gave temporary relief, but the East India Company none the less sent urgent petitions for more effective Government succour, and Government felt obliged to fit out and

[1] Governor Johnston to Courand, 3 April 1747. Add. MSS. 32,711.
[2] Clinton to Stone, September 1747. Add. MSS. 32,713.

despatch a powerful squadron under Boscawen. It was not however ready till the end of November 1747, and no one could say
what had happened in India during the long months of preparation or what the admiral would find when he reached Indian
waters. Maybe the rich resources of Indian trading had been lost
for good. There was plenty of room for depression and perhaps
amongst the weaker brethren for despair. Only in one direction
was there a ray of hope. In European waters, if not in Indian, the
English Navy was still able to hold its own, in spite of Bedford's
timid handling. Anson was always at his elbow, and his efforts
and perhaps still more his example were bearing fruit. Since his
victory in May there had been two respectable skirmishes, in one
of which (June 1747) Commodore Fox had met and scattered the
convoy from San Domingo, and in the other of which (October
1747) Hawke had smashed six of eight French vessels convoying
the outward-bound trading ships to the French West Indies.
Besides these three actions, which were comparatively large, the
navy and privateers were snapping up individual merchant
vessels in considerable numbers. French commerce was disap-
pearing from the seas, and France was beginning to feel the effect.
The pressure of sea power was making Louis anxious for peace.

Peace might have come more quickly if the Cabinet had been
more united, or if the negotiations had been in other hands. The
two Secretaries of State were Newcastle and Chesterfield. The
latter had succeeded Lord Harrington as Secretary for the
Northern Department in November 1746. While Lord Lieutenant
of Ireland he had shown himself a strong and able administrator,
making so good an impression that even the King was inclined to
hope great things of him in this new appointment. The war and
the peace negotiations both came within his province, and by way
of assistance for the handling of these matters was the fact that
he was versed in Dutch politics. He had therefore plenty of
experience and plenty of opportunity, but he failed to profit by
either. No doubt there were many explanations. He had been
seriously ill the previous summer, and this may have impaired his
abilities. His heart, too, was not in his new work. He left Ireland
with reluctance, looking back regretfully to a country where—to
use his own words—'I thought I could, and began to hope I
should, do some good.' By contrast he found his new post 'a
laborious employment,' and seems to have been oppressed with a
sense of inadequacy both physical and mental; 'it requires,' he told

his son, 'more strength of body and mind than I have, to go through with it.' But the outstanding difficulty came from a different quarter. In Ireland he had been for practical purposes his own master; now he was continually thwarted by Newcastle, who had long fancied himself as Foreign Secretary and could not refrain from meddling. He had driven Harrington from office by secret intrigues, and now he applied the same underhand methods to Chesterfield. That astute politician realised what was happening but was either too weary, or too indifferent, or too weak to resist. He contented himself with playing a minor rôle. 'I wish,' he wrote to Dayrolles in July 1747, 'I could see a plan for either a vigorous war or a tolerable peace, or rather, a plan eventually for each. . . . All this *entre nous* absolutely; for I meddle very little; I execute orders quietly; and give no advice.'[1] None the less he grumbled at Newcastle's activities; and when Pitt began to criticise he felt angry and resentful, and complained irritably that Pitt was 'most extravagantly proud.'

The position was exasperating enough and called for help from anyone who could give it. The Cabinet were fundamentally divided, Pelham and Chesterfield longing for peace, while Newcastle and Hardwicke, the Lord Chancellor, wanted to prolong the war in the hope of obtaining better terms. This division of opinion spread downwards to the diplomats and officials, each of whom followed blindly the wishes of the particular Minister—Chesterfield or Newcastle—to whom he was responsible. Even the soldiers were in two minds, since Cumberland, having failed as a general, nourished fitful hopes of regaining his reputation by success as a negotiator. What was true of the English authorities was true also of the allies as a whole. The Dutch, Maria Theresa, the King of Sardinia, and for that matter George II in his several capacities as King of England and Elector of Hanover, all had different aims and aspirations. They were all intriguing to a greater or less degree. They were all highly suspicious of being double-crossed, and by no means averse from double-crossing. The results could not fail to be shifting and chaotic.

Pitt had definite views. He would have been glad enough to force victories which should give England a commanding position at the conference table, but he saw no prospect of winning that enviable advantage. The navy seemed under a cloud; the

[1] *Letters*, II, 826.

most it could do was to frustrate French schemes and so give the Government a little kudos. Commodore Fox's 'falling in with the St. Domingue Fleet,' Pitt told George Grenville,[1] 'is a little cordial, and comes most critically for the elections.' But, like the rest of the Cabinet, Pitt had no conception of the pressure which sea power could exert. That the Whig magnates should have been ignorant is not surprising, since their interest in commerce was slight: for them incomes and pensions came from Government appointments and sinecures. But that Pitt should have remained so long in ignorance is the more remarkable since he had from the first a close connection with the City. At the recent elections the City had returned as one of its Members Alderman Beckford, the representative of the West Indian interest, who from the first attached himself to Pitt, and not only supported him with unswerving loyalty, but always made him free of his own great knowledge of commercial affairs. Pitt was possibly misled by the emphasis which the eighteenth century placed on the fisheries. The effect which a share in the Newfoundland fisheries must have on the naval power of France was a self-evident proposition in an age when the navy was recruited by the press gang from merchant ships—not for long service but simply as required. Without the fisheries the French marine would simply disappear—or so the eighteenth century argued. Pitt was undoubtedly much influenced by this view. It was to colour and indeed to occupy an undue prominence in his negotiations with France at a later date. In short, like most of the things which he borrowed from the Whig magnates, it was to do him more harm than good. It was precisely in so far as he broke from the Whig tradition that he saved England and created the Empire.

For the moment, however, he was a member of a Whig Government, and looking at facts from that angle, he found little consolation, and no real assistance, in the navy. Turning from the sea to the land, he found less consolation and no more assistance. 'It is agreed,' he told Newcastle, 'by everybody that we should bring considerable or superior armies into the field; but the plan for so doing, I fear, creates much difference of opinion, as to its timely effects; I confess, for one, I see no probability of it.'[2] Pitt's objection was based on simple observation. The allied armies in Flanders never came up to expectation. Under their

---

[1] Letter of 30th June 1747. Grenville. *Correspondence*, I, 67.
[2] Letter of the 5th December 1747. Add. MSS. 32,713.

various conventions, which were annual affairs, the greater part
of the forces were to be supplied by Austria and Holland. England's contribution was mostly in money or mercenaries. But
Austria was far away, was not much interested in the Netherlands,
not even in that part which she owned, and believed her efforts
should be concentrated mainly on the Italian battlefields, where
she very much hoped to recover the Kingdom of Naples. Hence
her contingents to the army in Flanders were never up to promise
and never up to time. The Dutch contingents were little better.
It is a favourite theme with Whig historians that the Dutch were
unreliable and lazy. Perhaps they were, but after all Holland was a
very small country, on the verge of bankruptcy after the struggle
with Louis XIV, and now fighting unwillingly and without much
faith in the necessity for war. It was perhaps in any event unreasonable to suppose that Holland could raise a larger army than
England; and quite lacking in all sense of realism to continue year
after year trusting to promises which were given only to secure
English subsidies. Pitt, at least, would have none of them. The
army in Flanders existed only on paper. 'I see no probability
of it.'

These factors formed the basis of Pitt's policy. The country was
rapidly being exhausted in a war which she could not win and
which did her no good. Peace, therefore, which in 1745 was 'not
to be thought of,' had now become essential, and it could not be
secured merely by maintaining existing alliances. Instead, therefore, of meddling in Flanders, which resulted in pinpricks for
France and humiliation for ourselves, we must seek some other
method of ending the war, and that method could only be some
movement from Prussia. 'I will sum up my whole political creed,'
he told Newcastle, 'in two propositions; this country and Europe
are undone without a secure lasting peace; the alliance, as it now
stands, had not the force ever to obtain it, without the inter-
position of Prussia.' How, then, could Prussia be induced to
move? Only by being offered security in Silesia. Frederick had
grabbed Silesia, and Maria Theresa could not bend her stubborn
mind to submission; she must, in the interests of peace, be made
to submit. 'The umbrage of that Prince [Frederick],' wrote Pitt,
'justly taken at the language of the Court of Vienna ever since the
cession of Silesia, once effectually removed, it is his interest, and
therefore his inclination, to see Europe pacify'd, and France
contained within some bounds. I am not sanguine enough to

imagine he would, on any account, engage in the war, but I must believe, if the proper steps were taken, and taken in earnest, he might be brought to declare for such a peace as we ought to think ourselves happy to obtain.'[1]

Such were Pitt's views. They were not entirely his own nor yet altogether new. As far back as 1740 old Horace Walpole had been advocating an alliance with Prussia, and in December 1743 Pitt himself had declared that 'the claimant whom we ought first to have thought of taking off, was, certainly, the King of Prussia; both because his claim was the smallest, and because he was one of the most natural, as well as one of the most powerful allies we could treat with.'[2] Recently old Horace Walpole had returned to the attack with growing insistence. In October 1746 he had written a passionate letter to Philip Yorke, Lord Hardwicke's eldest son, and had sent a copy to Pelham, in which after setting out the deplorable state of Europe, he had continued, 'But you will say, where is the remedy to this calamitous situation? To which I reply, Prussia, Prussia, Prussia! Real friendship and strict alliance with that crown might have prevented these misfortunes; that only can now retrieve them.'[3] The next month he was writing in the same strain to the Duke of Cumberland, and no doubt, like any other superannuated enthusiast, to anyone who would listen to him. His efforts, however, had been wholly in vain; indeed matters had gone from bad to worse, and since November 1746 England had been unrepresented at Frederick's court. Pelham told him on the 15th of October 1747, a little sadly but with every appearance of finality, that 'there is nothing so evident as that you are in the most parts in the right, and yet nothing more certain than that your advice will not, or cannot be followed,'[4] and a month later the younger Horace Walpole was assuring Mann with equal conviction that 'there is not a glimmering prospect of our sending a Minister to Berlin.'[5] Opposition came not only, or mainly, from Ministers such as Pelham, who on the whole was inclined to agree. Much more devastating was the repugnance felt by the King for anything to do with his Prussian nephew, and hardly less obstructive was the dislike which Newcastle felt for anything which would weaken the ties with Austria or threaten the 'old system.'

---

[1] Letter to Newcastle, 5th December 1747. Add. MSS. 32,713.
[2] Speech, 1st December 1743. Reported in the *London Magazine*.
[3] Coxe's *Memoirs of Lord Walpole*, II, 166.
[4] Coxe's *Pelham*, I, 376.   [5] Walpole to Mann, 24th Nov. 1747.

It was at this point that Pitt threw in his weight. He took up the idea again, basing himself upon the logic of facts, and pressed his views upon Newcastle respectfully but firmly, and even with a suggestion that he was the only obstacle to peace.[1]

Newcastle, in whose hands England's foreign policy lay, was the reverse of a realist. He lived perennially in a land of phantasy —sometimes a land of dreams, more often a land of nightmares, but very rarely a land of vision. His policy was an affair of make-belief, which he toiled unceasingly to bring to life, without much regard to facts and with no regard for his colleagues. At this point of time he, like Pitt, believed that the existing alliances were not sufficient. Unlike Pitt, he did not look for help towards Prussia. His idea was much more daring; he proposed to separate Spain from France. The Spanish King, Philip V, had died in July 1746. Pitt had hoped that the occasion might be improved by pursuing a resolute policy in America,[2] but Newcastle thought otherwise. Far from attacking the Spanish colonies, he proposed to buy Spain out, and seems at one time to have toyed with the proposal of restoring Gibraltar. Fortunately no such sacrifice was required. From negotiations which, for reasons known to himself alone, he started simultaneously at Breda through Lord Sandwich and at Lisbon through Benjamin Keene, he found that Spain was prepared to acquiesce in the loss of Gibraltar provided she could obtain more valuable acquisitions elsewhere—in the shape of some suitable provision for the new King's half-brother, Don Philip. Although the provision would have to be made in Italy and at the expense of either Austria or Sardinia, Newcastle eagerly absorbed the hint and began an exciting game of carving up Italy. 'My scheme,' he wrote complacently to Cumberland,[3] and the emphasis should be laid on 'my,' 'is shortly this: Parma and Placentia to Don Philip, to revert to the present possessors when Don Philip succeeds to Naples and Sicily. The Queen of Hungary or the Great Duke of Tuscany to have the Stato della Presidii as an indemnification for Parma and part of the Plaisantine; and the King of Sardinia to be indemnified for his part by Savona and the Ponente. By this means,' he added—quite untruthfully—'every Power contributes something to this establishment; and the Allies have the benefit of having effectually, I hope,

[1] See letter of the Duke of Newcastle to Cumberland, 4th March 1748. Add. MSS. 32,714.
[2] Pitt to Bedford, 19th July 1746. Bedford. *Correspondence*, I, 132.
[3] 13th October 1747. Add MSS. 32,713.

separated Spain from France. This,' he concluded with a premature touch of jubilation, 'would give us great éclat here; and
enable us to carry on the war, if France in the winter did not consent to reasonable Terms of Peace.' The proposal, however, did
not appeal so strongly to either Maria Theresa or the King of
Sardinia.

In developing this policy Newcastle stood practically alone, but
he was the more dangerous because he was acting outside his own
province and by means of secret agents and clandestine correspondence. As already explained, he was steadily ousting Chesterfield, in whose department the business lay and whose one reason
for accepting the post of Secretary of State had been to bring
about peace. Newcastle succeeded first in disgusting him and then
reducing him to impotence, until in February 1748 he resigned
—curiously enough, to Newcastle's surprise and consternation.

Pelham, who as Prime Minister should have been in full control, was timid and fretful. He disapproved of his brother's policy
and still more of his actions, but could not assert himself effectively and never succeeded in doing more than squabble and sulk.
At this crucial moment he and his brother were hardly on speaking
terms. 'Lord Chesterfield told me,' Marchmont recorded in his
Diary (27th Oct. 1747) 'that Mr. Pelham and the Duke now conversed only through Mr. Stone, being apt to fall into a passion
when they conversed together.' Pelham himself corroborated the
lack of union when he wrote, 'it is a greater pleasure to him
[Newcastle] to put me in the wrong for an hour or a day, than to
be in the right himself for months and years.' The estrangement
of course left Newcastle free to follow his own devices.

Nor did he suffer any check from Bedford, who succeeded
Chesterfield as Secretary of State. Bedford was the obverse of
Newcastle; instead of living in a phantasy with no regard for fact,
he was tossed to and fro by every breath of wind. Though an
ingrained pacifist, his suggested terms rose with each semblance
of victory and fell with any hint of reverse. 'Your Lordship
judges very right,' he wrote to Sandwich in November 1747,[1]
'that though I am strongly inclined for peace, yet I am not for
one *quovis modo*; and I flatter myself our late great successes at sea,
and the vigorous measures[2] now pursued both by England and

[1] Bedford. *Correspondence*, I, 299.
[2] It was typical of Bedford, and indeed of the Whig magnates generally, to
imagine that a few resolutions in the House of Commons were 'vigorous measures.'

Holland, will conduce much to make the French listen to reasonable terms of accommodation.' Two months later (January 1748) he was not so sure; 'your lordship will . . . begin to think me one willing to consent to a peace *quovis modo*'; that, however, was not the case; he pinned his faith to Newcastle's phantasy and was confident that England might make a separate and good peace with Spain by giving up Gibraltar. In February and March, however, the desperate plight of Holland was revealed, and so by April (1748) he had lost all hope and become panic-stricken; 'the result of this long detail (to which I could add reams of paper) will be, my laying before you the absolute necessity, I must own I see, of coming to an immediate conclusion of the war upon the best terms we can get; and without this, I must own to you I do not see any hopes of salvation for us.'

With such weak and wavering Ministers, such poor generals, and such fumbling at the War Office and the Admiralty, there seemed little enough hope for the country. Only one man in office had definite views and stuck to them—Pitt. His proposals began to be universally adopted. His letter to Newcastle of the 5th of December (1747) in which he revived the idea of an approach to Frederick was followed after an interval by letters from others. Hardwicke wrote at the end of the month: 'Is it not therefore absolutely necessary to hasten the sending of your minister to Berlin *immediately*, and that the States-General should send one at the same time? That they should jointly be instructed to tranquilise the King of Prussia. . . .'[1] A week later Richmond was writing in nearly the same strain: 'I do not think you have pushed enough in the Closet for the means to gain Prussia.'[2] Another week and even Bedford was supporting the Prussian project and actually claiming that it had long been his opinion— though one carefully concealed from the world![3] The pressure increased and Newcastle gave way to it grudgingly, but having done so he characteristically tried to curry favour with Pitt on the strength of his action. Pitt had been drinking the waters at Bath and returned to find a letter from Newcastle dated the 19th of January 1748: 'During your absence,' said the archhypocrite, 'I have not failed to use my best endeavours towards promoting a perfect union and good correspondence with Prussia. I have, in some measure, succeeded beyond my expectations,

---

[1] Add. MSS. 32,713.   [2] Add. MSS. 32,714.
[3] Bedford to Newcastle, 10th Jan. 1747/8. Add. MSS. 32,714.

though I cannot say I have had much assistance in it.'[1] Pitt wrote a grateful letter of thanks, before returning to Bath and the everlasting fight against gout. His policy, however, succeeded.[2] Prussia became interested in the promotion of peace, and seems even to have attempted to infuse some iron into Newcastle's flabby mind. 'The Prussian Secretary,' Newcastle confided to Cumberland in February 1748, 'has sounded me about our Conditions of Peace. His Master thinks we shall not be willing to restore Cap Breton [Louisbourg], having been able to gain such advantages at sea over the French; so that I believe that concession will not appear such a trifle as it has been treated here this winter.'[3] The last words were characteristic and summed up the views not only of Newcastle but of the magnates. America was a trifle and India on the whole a nuisance. Much more important was the hiring of 30,000 Russians to raise the siege of Bergen. If the town fell—as it did—long before they could arrive, none the less they were tramping somewhere about Europe and English money was being spent wisely and well!

The desire for peace, however, was strong in every country. England had forgotten how the war had begun and why she was fighting. The French, 'beaten at sea, driven from Italy, deserted by Prussia, and weakened by the accession of Ferdinand VI of Spain, were ready to discuss terms.'[4] The Dutch were worn out and bankrupt; Spain was indifferent, and Austria tired. Peace supervened rather than was made. No side felt able to claim the advantage, and so after years of aimless endeavour the *status quo ante* was restored between England and France, and between England and Spain. The Assiento was confirmed, but the right of search which had begun the war was forgotten or ignored. Nobody gained anything out of the pother except Frederick, whose conquest of Silesia was made absolute, and curiously enough Don Philip of Spain, who had contributed nothing either to the fighting or to the peace, but who, none the less, received not only Parma and Placentia, but Guastalla as well. This acquisition was the sole result of Newcastle's meddling, and the outstanding fact about it is that whilst it failed to reconcile Spain to England it succeeded in embittering Austria and Sardinia. So much for Newcastle's policy.

---

[1] Chatham. *Correspondence*, I, 27.
[2] That it was essentially Pitt's policy can be inferred from the Duke of Newcastle's letter to Cumberland of 4th March 1747/8. Add. MSS. 32,714.
[3] Add. MSS. 32,714.   [4] Robertson. *England Under the Hanoverians*, p. 108.

M

But, well- or ill-made, the preliminaries of peace were signed on the 30th of April and matured, on the 18th of October 1748, into the Treaty of Aix-la-Chapelle. Troubled Europe was temporarily at rest. Pitt had already summed up his views on the signing of the preliminaries in a letter to George Grenville: 'I most heartily rejoice with you on this happy event; happy, I call it, because absolutely necessary to our very being.'[1]

[1] Pitt to G. Grenville, April 26th, 1748. Grenville. *Correspondence*, I, 73.

28

QUIET INTERLUDE

The six years from the Treaty of Aix (April 1748) to the death of Pelham (March 1754) were for Pitt a period of rest and expectancy; the interest lies rather in his private than his public life. England's need was peace and recuperation, which Pelham, as an inferior edition of Sir Robert Walpole, proposed to give her. 'Quiet,' he told Marchmont, 'is what we want; economy is necessary.'[1] Pitt, accepting that view, found opposition meaningless, and was content to work unobtrusively for England's convalescence against the time when the struggle with France should be renewed. For renewed it must be, though he hoped and believed in a different fashion from the past. In his eyes, the ancient tussle on the Continent had gone beyond recall. The true rivalry lay now, not in the old but in the new world—in America, in India, in the colonies. Over them there must, if necessary, be another Hundred Years War, and in this new struggle England must and should be triumphant. Until the final solution any peace was but a truce, and the days of the truce, being numbered, must be employed to the utmost in recuperation and refitment. This general belief Pitt expounded to his small circle—the Grenvilles, the Lytteltons, Legge and the like—and they learnt at least the jargon. 'The abilities and good intentions of some honest men I know,' Legge wrote to Pitt in May 1748,[2] 'will, I dare say, in a few years, by the arts of peace and good economy, put England into more substantial health than violent remedies could ever have done; and I know you hold for regimen against physic.' The last words are illuminating, and help to explain Pitt's attitude towards the Government. Nothing could well have been less violent than the so-called Broad-bottomed Administration; nobody could well have been milder than Henry Pelham, or less disposed to force 'physic' down England's throat than Newcastle. Sheer want of imagination would result in a policy of 'dolce far niente.' But its success

---

[1] Pelham to Marchmont, 1st Sept. 1750. [2] Chatham. *Correspondence*, I, 29.

must depend upon the continuance of peace not only abroad but also at home. The jarring elements of the Cabinet must somehow be reconciled. As Pitt reiterated time and again harmony and union between Pelham and Newcastle was 'the only effectual and solid system by which I conceive the King can be served.'[1] The two were 'essentially necessary to each other,' and the two together were essentially necessary to England. The necessity did not arise out of their genius, which was pitifully small, but out of the lack of an alternative government and the solidity of their parliamentary support, both of which gave a promise of strength and tranquillity. 'The promoting this happy union,' therefore, became 'the object of my life,'[2] and Pitt's efforts to that end are at once the story of the next six years and the key to his behaviour. For the time being his personal troubles were solved. There could be no immediate object for his ambition; he must wait till chance or death introduced new factors and gave him a fresh start.

The result was an inward poise and happiness. He became the life and soul of friendly gatherings; he took his place in an intimate social circle, forgetting public oratory in the delights of simple conversation and exchanging thwarted ambitions for the pleasures of gardening. His letters became gay and playful, and he found time to visit friends and tour places of interest.

Chesterfield said of him that 'he was a most agreeable and lively companion in social life and had such a versatility of wit that he could adapt it to all sorts of conversation,' a verdict which Lord Camelford grudgingly endorsed, though he added that Pitt only exerted his social talents when he had a purpose and that he was never natural—which if true was an uncommonly difficult achievement.

His capacity as a spell-binder in Parliament, which did not, of course, necessarily imply any skill as a conversationalist, was such that even today the compulsion of his eloquence is accepted without question, though scarcely two authentic words of any speech have come down to us. We can judge his oratory only by the records of its effect upon his hearers—but that is enough. Friends and enemies alike admitted his pre-eminence, sometimes against their will. 'Mr. Pitt,' Chesterfield told his son in a vain effort to show him how easily he might 'make a figure' in the country if only he would cultivate the art of public speaking,

---

[1] Pitt to Newcastle, 2nd April 1750. Add. MSS. 32,720.
[2] Pitt to Newcastle, 13th July 1750. Add. MSS. 32,721.

'Mr. Pitt has very little Parliamentary knowledge; his matter is generally flimsy, and his arguments often weak; but his eloquence is superior, his action graceful, his enunciation just and harmonious; his periods are well-turned, and every word he makes use of is the very best and most expressive that can be used in that place. This and not his matter made him Paymaster, in spite of both King and Ministers.' His capacity as a spell-binder is beyond doubt. Less known is his capacity for enchanting the world of ordinary men and women. In spite of Chesterfield, in spite of Camelford, he is credited too often with a coldness and reserve which formed no part of his social make-up. The fact is that he enjoyed society, both male and female, and was at once a welcome guest and a charming and thoughtful host.

As for the ladies, he was so long a bachelor that there was plenty of time for many of them to fall in love with him, and his fame was so great that they had plenty of excuse. Not that they were particularly successful. The purity of his life and the loftiness of his ideas were bound to make him a little formidable, so that even in the licentious atmosphere of the eighteenth century and in spite of its freedom of thought and language, the more romantically minded of his lady friends were apt to eat out their hearts in secret rather than set their caps at him openly. Pitt could fascinate but hardly flirt. Many girls sighed for him, but not one of them can have even remotely imagined herself entitled to sue him for breach of promise. It would be tedious, if it were possible, to catalogue his involuntary conquests, but there is ground for thinking that the sisters of more than one of his friends hankered after this gout-ridden cripple. It is certain that the sister of the haughty Grenvilles loved him dearly. It is but too likely that Molly Lyttelton wept her eyes out for him in secret, and it looks as though Molly West burnt her fingers at a forbidden flame. Maybe also in the round of pious duties which erased the memory of her unfortunate marriage, Sarah Robinson thought wistfully of the time when as a debutante she refused to dance at a Bath ball, 'having no inclination to dance with any man but Mr. Pitt, and that I have not acquaintance enough with him to expect, I can only cherish my hopes of future good fortune.'[1]

How he treated his admirers and how they treated him can be gathered from a few hints here and there. When he was three-and-twenty, girls could come 'thundering at the door as if heaven and

[1] Climenson, I, 167.

earth would come together,' and he had to endure and no doubt thoroughly enjoyed their 'gentle impertinences' and 'sportly sollicitations.'[1] Six years later, when he was rising nine-and-twenty, he was still enduring and still enjoying much the same treatment. The girls were no longer romping hoydens, but they chaffed and laughed with him as much as ever and he played up delightedly. 'Your brother,' the Duchess of Queensberry wrote to Ann Pitt, 'has been with us for a moment, in which time, though, he was sufficiently teazed; we did not only tell him of our castles in the air, but insisted on his discerning them on firm ground; he is gone to Lord Bathurst, who will in some measure alleviate our folly.'[2]

He was now some ten years older and a power in the land, and as such not perhaps to be treated so cavalierly even by a duchess. But if the treatment was milder, the affection was no less strong, and perhaps more fully reciprocated. 'I am not a little proud,' he wrote to a cousin whom he had left behind at Bath, 'to be remembered by the agreeable society of tea and bread and butter.'[3]

It was not merely youth or beauty that attracted him. He enjoyed female society as such; it brought out some quality that gave satisfaction to himself and his company. Probably it fed his vanity; certainly it fed that vein of idealism which ran through every portion of his nature and was reflected in almost every action of his life. In short it produced a feeling of confidence and so of elation in a character that was always at bottom defensive and wary.

As a host he was inimitable. Men and women alike were loud in their praises. With his accession to office and the income which it carried, he felt able to purchase a house of his own, and in 1747 bought South Lodge at Enfield Chase. Here he not only indulged his passion for building and landscape gardening, but also entertained his friends royally. The next year Legge, who was at Berlin, wrote to Lyttelton, and therefore one must presume truthfully, 'I feast my imagination frequently with those parties you mention for next winter at Enfield Chase, those noctes coenaeque Deorum, at which we will discourse politics, poetry, and that greatest of all Nepenthes, nonsense.' Gilbert West told Mrs. Montagu how Pitt 'received and entertained us with great

[1] Pitt to Ann, 13th March 1731. Rosebery, p. 63.
[2] Duchess of Queensberry to Ann Pitt, 5th Sept. 1737. H. M. C. 13th Report. Fortescue MSS., I, 98.
[3] Pitt to Thomas Pitt, 15th Nov. 1750.

politeness and something still more pleasing and solid, with every mark of friendship and esteem. He had provided for me a wheeling chair, by the help of which I was enabled to visit every sequestered nook, dingle and bosky bower from side to side in that little paradise opened in the wild'—a touch of forethought and a delicate compliment to an invalid which stuck in West's memory.[1]

The forethought was habitual. His entertainments were always carefully prepared not only in their arrangements but even in their setting. He fancied himself as a landscape gardener, and it was not only for horticultural purposes that he employed his eye for scenery. Mrs. Montagu, telling her husband of a dinner given by Pitt at New Vauxhall, adds 'the view from it is romantic,' and continues, 'we drank tea yesterday in the most beautiful rural scene that can be imagined, which Mr. Pitt had discovered in his morning's ride about half a mile from hence [Tunbridge Wells]; he ordered a tent to be pitched, tea to be prepared, and his French horn to breathe music like the unseen genius of the wood.' No wonder Mrs. Montagu thought that 'Mr. Pitt mixes the elegant with the sublime.'[2]

The fragrant kindliness of this period peeps out in many directions. Pitt was happy and his friends came to warm their hands at his radiance. It was now that Sir Thomas Lyttelton asked Pitt to take his youngest son, William, under his wing, and guide him on the threshold of life. As William's elder brother, George, was readily available, Pitt may well have felt flattered. He wrote gratefully in reply, 'I feel from my heart the great honour you do me,'[3] and he discussed at length the boy's prospects; he had 'very particular talents for the business of the world,' and in Pitt's view 'it would be ten thousand pities they should be stifled for a long time at least, and perhaps entirely lost, in the inglorious and unprofitable labours of Westminster Hall,' by which Pitt meant the Bar. Pitt never had much of an opinion of lawyers; they were hide-bound and pedantic, tied up with precedent and given to splitting hairs. The world was one of action and reaction; it was far wider than the musty files of the law courts, and too uproarious to be tamed by precedent. It was Parliament which must deal with the tangles in which the law bound both itself and the people; it was Parliament which must initiate and guide; it was Parliament,

---

[1] Climenson, II, 9.   [2] Climenson, II, 35.
[3] Pitt to Sir T. Lyttelton, 8th June 1748. Wyndham, II, 2.

above all, which must deal with that vast world of foreign politics which lay outside the realms of English law and was not amenable to the dictates of judges. That was Pitt's view, and that was what he hoped and wished for any bright and promising lad, and not least for his friend's son. Here Pitt could help him, and he promised his aid readily. 'If I can be of any little use to him, at his beginning in our Parliamentary warfare,' he wrote, 'be assured it will be a most sensible pleasure to me,' though he could not forbear adding, 'should he, on any occasion, want direction, he will always find the surest and best in his brother.' None the less Pitt was as good as his word, keeping his eye on young William and writing him many a friendly and encouraging letter.

Sir Thomas Lyttelton was not the only one of Pitt's friends to seek his aid, nor William Lyttelton the only one to receive it. The Grenville family, always ambitious, were more particularly anxious at this period to push their fortunes owing to Lord Cobham's death on the 13th of September 1749. In the usual crablike way of the eighteenth century the eldest brother, Richard, unwilling to ask directly for a peerage which, incidentally, he never deserved either then or thereafter, was scheming to have his mother created a Countess in her own right, with remainder to her children. The problem was how to do it. The family consulted Pitt, who unlike them was opposed to roundabout methods. His instinct was for direct and forthright action and he was 'very strongly of opinion that it ought to be asked without any previous intimation of it, or feeling the ground beforehand.'[1] Whatever the reason, his advice was apparently sound, for the peerage was duly obtained, and the Grenville family pushed one further step up the ladder. Meanwhile Pitt added to his benefits by prescribing, in delightful letters, for George Grenville's wife, who was indulging in the typical eighteenth-century occupation of taking the waters at Bath. Mrs. Grenville wrote coquettishly in reply and Pitt answered in gallant strain that he had not expected to be fee'd so infinitely higher than the most eminent of the medical profession. It was all very gay and inconsequent and friendly. Nothing could be farther from the loud-mouthed impertinence of the Cornet of Horse, nothing less like the stormy turbulence of the Great Commoner, nothing in greater contrast to the awe-inspiring majesty, aloof and darkly flashing, of the unapproachable Lord Chatham.

[1] Geo. Grenville to Temple, 24th Sept. 1749. Grenville. *Correspondence*, I, 81.

It was during this period of warm-hearted benevolence that he came nearest to shedding his dislike and disbelief in the universal system of patronage and nepotism. Very little can be laid to Pitt's account, and that little was in the main justified by the characters and subsequent achievements of the men Pitt preferred. But if there was one time more than another when Pitt seemed to be attracted by the dangerous power of patronage and was more than usually prepared to recommend his protégés, it was this period of six years from the Peace of Aix to the death of Pelham. Pitt was rapidly falling into the eighteenth-century rut. Yet, if he pushed his favourites, he at least did it with a grace that enhanced the service. It was during this period that he secured the Comptroller-ship of Chelsea Hospital for Nathaniel Smith, a Captain of Horse who had been wounded at Dettingen. It was during this period that he went down personally to West Wickham to offer Gilbert West the post of Paymaster to Chelsea Hospital—'the place,' said Mrs. Montagu, 'is called a thousand pounds a year, it is in the gift of Mr. Pitt, and was given with grace that few know how to put into any action.'

The sunny optimism of this period made him for perhaps the only time in his life hopeful and almost contemptuous of his physical infirmities. At other times, though he might overcome or even ignore them, he was profoundly certain of their existence. Now in the glow of this untrammelled life he could even for a moment doubt their reality. 'I returned to Town about an hour ago,' he wrote to Newcastle on the 19th of March 1749, 'not being yet quite well enough to venture to Court. I am, however, much better and hope soon to get the better of my disorder, which seems more bilious than gouty.' Equally he betrayed an unexpected and touching weakness when his infirmities crowded upon him. In the year 1753 insomnia supervened upon gout, and Pitt disappeared to Tunbridge Wells to recover. He took Gilbert West with him, and clung to him for support and comfort. 'I am afraid,' wrote the gentle Gilbert, 'it will be impossible for me to leave him, as he fancies me of the greatest use to him as a friend and a comforter.' There is something infinitely pathetic in this picture of England's greatest War Minister-to-be leaning upon a mild invalid, and the picture is heightened and darkened by the knowledge that this malaise of 1753 was the foretaste of that greater and most disastrous of nervous breakdowns which fell

upon Lord Chatham a dozen years later. In the light of that
greater calamity there is something incongruous, something
touched with both terror and bathos in Gilbert West's foreboding
reflection that Pitt was suffering from a 'distemperature of his
spirits,' much more to be apprehended than the disorder in his
bowels to which the doctors were giving all their attention.[1]

[1] Climenson, II, 31.

29

FRIENDS AND RELATIONS

If this period is remarkable for the pleasure which Pitt gave and received in the society of his friends, it is still more remarkable for the spirit of kindliness and conciliation which he showed to his relations. The Pitt family were notorious for their unruly behaviour, especially to each other. Old Governor Pitt had poured the vials of his wrath on wife and children alike, in letters bubbling over with indignation and a racy flow of invective. His sons and daughters in their several degrees had followed his example and quarrelled violently—sometimes almost insanely—with their kith and kin; and the heritage of turbulence was to descend to later generations. William Pitt was the one shining exception; he was always loyal to his blood relations and always loving to his own wife and children. At this period, wife and children were in the future, but the ties which had bound him to his brother and sisters had been working loose, to his evident distress. He had one brother, Thomas, his senior by some three years, and five sisters, two of whom were older than himself.

Thomas was in most respects the antithesis of his brother. Physically he was fine and upstanding. His illiterate Aunt Essex Cholmondeley, writing of him when he was six, declared that 'he have a fine coller [colour] and groose [grows] fat.'[1] However, he continued on better lines, for as a young man he was well-knit and graceful, an all-round sportsman and a keen rider to hounds, headlong, rampagious and uproarious—in short, an Esau compared with the Jacob of his brother William. Mentally, he cut an altogether different figure. At Eton, according to his masters, he wasted his time, was a duffer at Greek, and was not worth sending to a university. Later in life he proved himself to be a woeful bungler in practical affairs and to be innocent of all financial acumen. Towards the end, if he did not actually become a madman, he presented a very passable imitation of one.

[1] Dalton. *Life of Thomas Pitt*, p. 458.

As the elder son, he inherited the Pitt estates, coming into his property at the unfortunately early age of twenty-two (1727), and the next year signalised his freedom from parental control and his access to wealth by marrying Christian Lyttelton. His fitness for marriage may be judged by the fact that he saw her for the first time one night at the opera, and falling head over heels in love with her face, proposed the next day. She accepted him, which might be thought to reflect on her intelligence but for the fact that she was only seventeen and was no doubt swept off her feet by his impetuosity. It is also possible that she had heard good reports of him from her brother, who had been at Eton with him, and may have fallen in love with tales of his sporting prowess before she had even seen his handsome figure. She was a charming, pretty girl, but too quiet, too accomplished and too refined for her wayward lord, who before long grew tired of her goodness and finally left her for other pleasures. She died in 1750.

His wife, however, was a mere incident in his career. As a landed proprietor and the owner of a number of rotten boroughs, his object was to make a splash in politics. He had barely come to that decision, when he married, and as his wife still held for him the fascination of novelty, and was Lord Cobham's niece, it was only to be expected that he should throw in his lot with the 'brotherhood,' and join the Opposition under the Prince of Wales. In 1734 he secured election at Okehampton and Old Sarum simultaneously—not a difficult feat as both boroughs belonged to him. Having chosen to represent the former, he handed the latter over to William, and so, to use the words of Lord Camelford, 'laid the foundations, at his own expense, for all his brother's fame and greatness.' The expense was not, perhaps, very large.

The Prince, who liked handsome men, especially when they had a number of rotten boroughs in their pockets, made a favourite of Thomas, and as a reward for his services in the general election of 1741 appointed him Warden of the Stanneries, a sinecure in Cornwall carrying a salary of £1,500 a year. But that was Thomas's high-water mark. At the next election (1747) he indulged in an orgy of corruption and bribery, but succeeded only in losing a number of seats and half ruining himself. The Prince, annoyed at his want of success, looked coldly upon him, and on the Prince's death in 1751 he lost his appointment as Warden.

Extravagance led to debts and debts soured him. He became more and more violent, more and more unpredictable, and finally in 1755 evaded his creditors by escaping to the Continent, taking with him his two daughters, Amelia and Christian. He would also have taken his son, Thomas (afterwards the first Lord Camelford), but that William intervened and undertook responsibility for the boy, who was then in his first year at Cambridge.

Thomas, who at one time had possessed sufficient brotherly feeling to contribute to William's expenses at Utrecht, had begun to look askance at his brother as early as 1745, when William resigned his appointment in the Prince's household. The coolness, bred of politics, increased and in the elections of 1747 Thomas did his best to break up the foundations of his brother's future fame and greatness by refusing to bring him in again for Old Sarum. Nor was he mollified by William's advocacy of the young Thomas's claim to remain at Cambridge. The breach between the brothers widened still further when a few years later Thomas conceived the idea that William as Secretary of State ought to appoint him to the post of Minister to the Swiss Cantons and William failed to admit or even observe his qualifications for the job. Thomas by way of revenge spent much time and ingenuity in spreading stories round the Continent to William's detriment. In 1758 he returned secretly to London, and there by working on his son's feelings induced him to break the entail of the Pitt properties in order to pay off his debts. This involved William, who as next in the entail had a reversionary interest, but in spite of the slanders with which Thomas had so plentifully bedaubed him, William behaved with generosity. Thomas, freed from debt and able to look the world once more in the face, succumbed first to the attractions of a Miss Murray, described a little maliciously as 'above forty years of age, without any advantages of mind, or person, or education,' whom he married in 1760, and then succumbed to a stroke which killed him in the spring of 1761.[1]

Pitt could hardly be fond of so difficult an elder brother, but he bore with him patiently, looked after his son, and made a genuine if in the upshot an immaterial contribution to the payment of his debts. Although greatly provoked, he used to speak of him with commendable restraint as 'the unhappy man.'[2]

[1] M. Wyndham's *Chronicles of the Eighteenth Century*, II, 29-30.
[2] Rosebery, p. 18.

Of William's two elder sisters, Harriet and Catherine, very little is known. Harriet, some four years his elder, was said by her nephew, Lord Camelford, to have been 'one of the most beautiful women of her time.' In due course she became engaged to a Mr. Corbett, apparently against the wishes of both families, and being unable to win their consent married him secretly. But the only result was that she worried herself into an early grave. William's feelings for her were expressed in a letter to another sister dated the 5th of June 1733, when he was nearly twenty-five and Harriet about twenty-nine: 'the pleasure you give me in the account of Kitty's recovery, is disagreeably accompanied with that of poor Harriet's relapse into an ill state of health; which I too much fear will never be removed till her mind is made a little easy: I never think of her but with great uneasiness, my tenderness for her begins to turn to sorrow and affliction; I consider her in a great degree lost, and buried almost in an unsuccessful engagement.'[1]

Of Catherine almost less is known. Lord Camelford described her briefly as having 'much goodness, but neither beauty nor wit to boast of. She married Robert Needham, a man of uncommon endowments, but of good Irish family and property, by whom she had several children.'[2] She does not seem to have entered much into her brother's life, and the references to her in his letters are few and colourless, though he seems to have reposed confidence in her, recommending her and a Mrs. Stuart as 'the properest, as well as the most agreeable places' in town for his youngest sister, Mary, to frequent.[3]

His third sister was Elizabeth, and of her, the less said the better. Camelford described her as having 'the face of an angel and the heart of all the furies'; Chesterfield declared that her reputation was 'really too strong, *et sent trop le relais*, to be served up in good company'; Walpole called her 'dangerous,' and had she lived in this less robustious age there would no doubt have been talk of complexes. Everyone agreed that her morals were loose and her conduct outrageous. Most people agreed that her wits were deranged. Wherever she went there was turmoil, and whatever she did was vexatious. The outstanding facts of her life clatter and bump down the pages of social history like the wagons of a noisy goods train. She made trouble between Thomas and his wife; she was virulent against William; she brought a

<hr>

[1] Rosebery, pp. 69-70.   *Ibid.*, p. 49.   [3] *Ibid.*, p. 96.

lawsuit against her trustee, Dr. Ayscough; she published family letters with malicious intent; she outraged Society by living openly with Lord Talbot as his mistress; she pursued men shamelessly at home and abroad, and if thwarted flared up into transports of hate; she changed her names like her dresses, and at one time changed her religion, claiming to be a Roman Catholic, and of course persecuted and misunderstood. In short she betrayed every symptom of mental and moral instability. At first, after her father's death, she lived with Thomas, who found her company extremely distasteful and was glad enough when his means became straitened to make that an excuse for getting rid of her. William then took her in hand, providing her with a house, and trying patiently but in vain to exercise a measure of control. She was utterly irresponsible and England soon became too hot to hold her; whereupon she fled to France and William gave her an allowance of £200, one half of which was to be absolute and the other half subject to good conduct. Needless to say she forfeited this latter half, probably at once, but certainly in no long time, and when at last William, on unimpeachable grounds and for the best of motives, withdrew it, she promptly threatened him with a Bill in Chancery for cheating her out of £100 a year. He must have heaved a sigh of relief when she told him in 1761 that she had married a certain John Hannan, a rich lawyer some years her junior. Thereafter she seems to have settled down, and one may hope that her restless spirit found some peace before her death in 1770.

The youngest sister, Mary, was an afterthought, being born in 1725 when William was seventeen. She never married, but filled to admiration the post of universal aunt to her nephews and nieces. She was in her early twenties when Thomas left his wife and retired to Boconnoc with his family. Mary went with him and did her best, not only to keep house for him, but also to mother his three children. Life in that far-off Cornish village could hardly be exciting, but she made it pleasant and tolerable, and won the affection of the boy and the two girls under her charge. In later life when, as Lord Camelford, the boy indulged his spleen against his various relatives, the worst he could find to say of his Aunt Mary was that 'she had neither the beauty of two of her sisters, nor the wit and talents of her sister Ann, nor the diabolical dispositions of her sister Betty. She meant always, I believe, to do right to the best of her judgment, but that judgment was liable to

be warped by prejudice, and by a peculiar twist in her understanding which made it very dangerous to have transactions with
her.'[1] This last adverse criticism seems to have arisen out of
Mary's claim to some share of the family wealth when the entail
was broken to pay her brother's debts.

William was always and obviously attached to Mary. When she
came to Town from Boconnoc, he guided her steps in the social
world with almost fatherly care. 'Miss Mary Pitt,' wrote Mrs.
Montagu in 1754, 'youngest sister of Mr. Pitt, is come to stay a
few days with me, she is a very sensible, modest, pretty sort of
young woman, and as Mr. Pitt seem'd to take every civility shown
to her as a favour, I thought this mark of respect to her one
manner of returning my obligations to him.'[2] What began as a
compliment to William continued as a mark of affection for Mary.
She can be traced in frequent visits to Mrs. Montagu at Hayes,
to the Wests at West Wickham, and to the Boscawens at Hatch-
lands near Guildford—all William's close friends. When William's
children were being born, she was hovering round—helpful and
unobtrusive—and the feelings of William and his wife can best be
summed up in his own words: 'Our Love follows dear Mary,
whose merits you must, to your great satisfaction, more and
more feel every day.'

There still remains his favourite sister Ann, who was born in
1712 and so in point of age came between Elizabeth and Mary.
The mutual sympathy which bound Ann and William together in
their early years was touching and beautiful, though like most
things in this wicked world it was marred by the passage of time.
Perhaps it was excessive and delayed the flowering of other
normal affections, at least in the case of William, who married
late, and maybe also in the case of Ann, who never married at all.
Otherwise she was not particularly inhibited, and at the age of
eighteen passed through a period of healthy flirtation, when
parties and dancing and conquests occupied much of her time and
no doubt more of her thoughts. She received certainly one proposal
—from Dr. Ayscough, George Lyttelton's tutor at Oxford—and
apparently others, all of which she refused out of hand.

At twenty-one or thereabouts she was appointed Maid of
Honour to Queen Caroline, and turned promptly and a little
tremulously to William for advice. She can hardly have needed it,
for, according to Camelford, 'she equalled her brother in

---

[1] Rosebery, pp. 52-3.   [2] Climenson, II, 53.

quickness of parts, and exceeded him in wit and in those name-
less graces and attentions by which conversation is enlivened and
endeared.' With such qualifications she found her feet quickly
and shone in a circle of beauty and wit. But the death of the
Queen in 1737 and possibly Pitt's firm adherence to the Prince of
Wales cost her the appointment. On leaving the Court she set up
house with William. The two remained together until 1741 when,
apparently for reasons of health, she travelled abroad, first visiting
Spa and then taking up her residence with the Bolingbrokes in
France. The art of living with those who are not related to us is
never easy, least of all in the case of a girl such as Ann, who
possessed to the full the impatience and the venturesome self-
confidence of the Pitts. It is not surprising therefore that she felt
constrained, and after enduring a manner of life which proved
increasingly irksome for a year, she began to think seriously of
setting up an establishment of her own in Paris, in spite of public
opinion and Pitt's urgent entreaties. When she persisted in her
threats to flout his wishes, he remonstrated sharply, telling her
that Paris was a most improper place for a single woman, and that
her whole scheme was unbalanced and unfitting. Ann flounced
off in a rage, declaring that she was old enough to judge for herself, and this seems to have been the origin of a quarrel which was
not only violent but also enduring, lasting a number of years.
The fact that she felt constrained to follow his advice only made
it rankle the more. The breach widened, though the widening was
all on one side. Pitt was always anxious to make it up, though at
times it was clearly difficult for him to keep his unruly tongue in
check. His letters to her breathe an atmosphere of resignation and
restraint. He could not avoid repeating the phrases in her letters
which had wounded him most, but always cut off the retort which
sprang to his lips with some abrupt hope for her happiness,
expressed in terms that had neither the carelessness of untrammelled intercourse nor the flowery eloquence of insincerity, but
only the smouldering truth of a bruised love. 'I can desire nothing
of you but to please yourself and make any use of me that may be
convenient to you. I sincerely wish you may find all the present
relief to your health and spirits and the future comfort and
pleasure you propose to yourself from new foreign objects and
new foreign friendships.' But if his words had the coldness of
constraint, his actions were generous. When Ann lost her
appointment at Court, the diminution of income had been serious,

N

and may have contributed to her wish to live abroad. Pitt had done his best to soften the loss by making her an allowance of £200 a year, which he maintained throughout the period of the quarrel, and which Ann continued to accept, though without relenting.

The exact date of her return to England is not known, but in 1751 she was appointed Privy Purse to the Princess of Wales, and was certainly in the country. Pitt made a great effort at reconciliation. The two met in June—and quarrelled. Pitt, stung by her sharp tongue, was goaded into saying that she had a bad head and a worse heart, and the two flung off in opposite directions. Both were sorry, and Ann went so far as to pen a hasty note promising to write 'in a manner capable of effacing every impression of anything painful.' Pitt waited for it hopefully—and received what is vulgarly known as a snorter. 'I did not expect such a letter as I found late last night, and which I have now before me to answer,' he replied a little haughtily, a little indignantly. He had slept upon it; he had, as he said, 'well weighed your letter, and deeply examined your picture of me, for some years past.' It was a condescension granted to no one else. Grandees, Ministers of State, Kings might rail at him and try to blacken his character, and he flung the abuse back. But this spitfire was different; she was his sister, there had been a time when harmony 'unexampled almost' had existed between them, and the loss of it was a bitter blow. Pitt would bow his head, Pitt would eat humble pie, Pitt would do almost anything to regain it. Certainly he would curb his pen, which he declared he had not had the least desire to sharpen. But he did something that was almost worse—he reasoned with her— a little sadly, but, unluckily for him, also a little portentously, 'Indeed, sister, I still find something within, that firmly assures me I am not that thing which your interpretations of my life (if I can ever be brought to think them all your own) would represent me to be. I have infirmities of temper, blemishes and faults, if you please, of nature, without end; but the Eye that can't be deceived must judge between us, whether that friendship, which was my very existence for so many years, could ever have received the least flaw, but from umbrages and causes that the quickest sensibility and tenderest jealousy of friendship alone, at first, suggested.' And then, still sadly, but a little priggishly, a little like a schoolmaster: '*Absolute deference and blind submission to my will*, you tell me I have often declared to you in the strongest and most mortifying terms could alone satisfy me. I must here beseech you coolly to reconsider these precise terms, with their epithets; and I will venture to make the appeal to the sacred testimony of your breast, whether there be not exaggeration in them.' He had reproached her (he admitted it) because 'I found no longer the same consent of minds and agreement of sentiments'; he had thought that she might pay some attention to his wishes, give some ear to his opinions. But even then there had been a limit to his expectations and 'I was never so drunk with presumption as to expect *absolute* deference and *blind submission to my will.*' A degree of deference, yes, in view of his age, his experience, his position, but 'if what I expected was too much (as perhaps it might be) our former days' friendship had led me into error. That error is now at an end and you may rest assured, that I can never be so unreasonable as to expect from you now anything like deference to me or my opinions.' There was only one other point. Ann had accused him of spreading exaggerated stories of his generosity to her for his own glorification, and she professed a desire to fling the money back in his teeth. Pitt denied the charge most solemnly. He *had* referred to the allowance, but in self-defence. 'I declare, upon my honour, I never gave the least foundation for those exaggerations which you say have been spread concerning it. I also declare as solemnly, before God and man, that no consideration could ever have extorted from my lips the least mention of the trifling assistance you accepted from me, but the cruel reports, industriously propagated, and circulating from various quarters round to me, of the state you was left to live in.' As to repayment, 'allow me, dear Sister, to entreat you to think no more of it. The bare thought of it may surely suffice for your own dignity and for my humiliation, without taxing your present income merely to mortify me.'

This letter was humble enough in all conscience, but hardly wise. Between relations, as between lovers, argument rarely does anything but rasp and annoy. Here the letter merely served to fan the fires of Ann's wrath, and the very next day (20th June 1751) Pitt found another furious epistle from her, in which she accused him of calling her a liar, and covering her with obloquy. If he insisted on raking up the past, she would follow suit and call to his mind old scenes of upbraiding and ancient quarrels. Pitt replied at once, more in sorrow than in hope: 'I believe I may venture to refer you to the whole tenor of my letter to convince yourself that I had no desire to irritate. . . . As to the late conversation you have thought necessary, since your letter of yesterday, to recollect, I am ready to take shame before you and all mankind, if you please, for having lost my temper, upon any provocation, so far as to use expressions as foolish as they are angry.' But argument with a furious woman rarely succeeds and Pitt might have saved himself the trouble. Yet perhaps that is not true. He had sown the seeds of reconciliation and in due course they fructified. How and when are again unknown, but by 1753 the reconciliation was complete. On the 8th of February William wrote to her: 'I can never reflect on things passed (wherein I must have been infinitely in the wrong, if I ever gave you a pain) without the tenderest sorrow; and the highest aggravation of this concern would be to think, that, perhaps, you may not understand the true state of my heart towards you.' Here was a wiser and more sure approach, and Ann responded. Her letter has been lost, but William's reply, dated 27th February, survives: 'I am unable to express the load you have taken off my heart by your affectionate and generous answer to my last letter: I will recur no more to a subject, which your goodness and forgiveness forbid me to mention.' Thereafter, to quote Lord Rosebery, there was 'a complete removal of tension and the restoration of close and friendly relations.'

Two further kinsmen deserve a passing mention for their share in the sunshine of this period of Pitt's life. The one was his nephew, Thomas, afterwards Lord Camelford, who seems to have secured, without altogether deserving it, the affection which Pitt was unable to give his father. It was during this period—in 1751—that Pitt began a series of letters to the boy, then only fourteen years of age, sketching out a course of education. The letters continued, on and off, till 1758, and were subsequently published. They have been called famous, and they have been scanned for hints on Pitt's own upbringing, but in fact they contain little that is of permanent interest, and nothing that can safely be distilled as autobiography. If Pitt had not cut a figure in the political world, it is unlikely that his letters would have appeared in print. They are, none the less, a lasting monument to the affection which he lavished on a subsequently ungrateful nephew and a refutation of the charge sometimes brought against him that he quarrelled with nearly all his relations and intimates. The facts are otherwise—Pitt may have annoyed them, may have lost their love, but the quarrelling was not of his seeking. It is, in any event, far more likely that a nephew on reaching manhood should revolt against the overpowering influence of a famous uncle than that the uncle should turn against a nephew on whom he had lavished care and tenderness. Whatever the truth, it is a fact that Thomas came ultimately to feel deep and lasting rancour against Pitt, but at this period, when he was in sore need of help and encouragement, he received unstinted affection which he probably disliked, and coins of the realm which he certainly took.

The second relation was John Pitt of Encombe, a distant cousin and Pitt's contemporary. Here there was neither the irksome restraint which must be felt between two different generations nor the contempt which too much familiarity is said to breed. Instead there was similarity of outlook and just sufficient kinship to create warmth without compulsion. Pitt enjoyed his cousin's company and sought it eagerly. 'I hope in God this may find you in town,' he wrote in August 1750, 'but let it find you when it will, you cannot do so great a charity as to come and hunt prospects with me, and keep me from hanging myself. I propose to be at Bath by Saturday next, 15th. Come to me, my dear Pitt, if you can, and believe me you will do a real pleasure and infinite good to your ever affectionate W. Pitt.'

It was in these happy years that John Pitt wooed and won his wife. William took a great interest in the course of this somewhat protracted affair. 'Come to Bath,' he reiterated in October 1750, 'the seat of health and pleasure. I have the orders of a young lady, I won't name, to let you know she wishes with impatience to see you; if this won't do, you are really worse than I care to think you.' John was apparently far from well, but the young lady's impatience seems to have been a compelling goad, for five days later Pitt wrote with mixed feelings, 'I am extremely sorry to hear so bad an account of your disorder, but am much satisfied to find your resolution is taken to come directly here.'

Year by year there is the same wish to meet. 'I am forced to renounce all the pleasure I had promised myself in seeing you in Dorsetshire. I have tried to surmount impossibilities to get to you. . . . I come now to the succedaneum, which depends upon you, and therefore, I trust, will not fail me; it is the pleasure of meeting at Bath. . . . Despatch your honest venison and strong-beer friends, and turn your horses' heads to Bath.'[1] It is the same

[1] To John Pitt, 13 Sept. 1751.

story in 1752. 'In disobedience to my dear Pitt's prescription of
sea-water, whey etc, I have taken the liberty to get well, or very
near it, by Bath waters, Raleigh's Cordial etc. . . . I am advised
to a longer course of waters than will make a visit to the dear
unknown, delightful, picturesque Encombe practicable this year;
may the coming year make amends.' But the end of untrammelled
friendship was drawing near; Eve was at last entering this masculine Paradise, and Pitt, who had gone to Bath, showered his
curious and cumbersome wit on his Benedick cousin. 'How many
hours, or rather tedious days was the incomparable Encombe
bearing his amorous lord to Marlborough? Was the tea well
sweetened with celestial smiles? and did the stately tutelary power
divest itself, in your behalf, of one flake of that majestic snow
which her prudeship designs to shower down on the awed
beholder? In a word, has anything passed that may confirm your
humble servant's sagacious confidence upon this otherwise inexplicable enigma?' Apparently something had, for a month later
(23rd December 1752) Pitt is writing congratulations. 'I rejoice at
your account of Dorchester; I rejoice a million of times at that of
London. Sic te, Diva potens Cypri; you are really the best of
friends to find place for the memory of an old piece of Bath
lumber, your humble servant.' The wedding took place the
following month (January 1753), but Pitt alas! was absent.
'Unfortunately disabled from attending your happiness in person,
may I be allowed to address a line to you of the most sincere and
affectionate felicitations? I will keep my word; it shall be but a line;
for I love you too well to take your eyes from Mrs. Pitt, for more
than an instant, to read assurances of friendship, which, after all,
you can never fully read but in the heart of your ever affectionate,
W. Pitt.'

   It is a pleasant picture, showing Pitt at his truest and best,
happy in the happiness of his friends. The survey of his private
life in those glad years of freedom may fitly end here.

'INCOMPARABLE ENCOMBE.'

30

PRIVATE INTERESTS

During these same years (1748 to 1754) Pitt's public life was settled for him by facts, both public and private. Privately he recognised the King's determination to keep him in subordinate posts, and he acquiesced, waiting on death to provide him with other chances. Publicly he was bound to take the mould imposed by European events. When the Peace of Aix was concluded, he had declared that the peace 'was absolutely necessary for our well-being.' What exactly he meant may be a matter of conjecture, but there was truth enough in his remark from many angles, and not least the unseen angle of his own future ministry.

So far as England was concerned, Aix merely closed a period of misdirected endeavour. It gave little to any European power and nothing whatever to England. Frederick the Great acquired Silesia and placed Prussia definitely on the map; the Bourbons extended their hold upon Italy, and both Austria and Holland were weakened. But England, who had originally gone to war with Spain over matters of commerce, secured nothing beyond the restoration of the *status quo ante*. Nothing was gained, nothing was lost, nothing was settled, and but for its aftermath of poverty and affliction, the war was simply expunged.

Yet the war—or perhaps the peace—must have played its part in opening British eyes, since both together led to a surprising denouement. England's foreign policy was shortly to take a new and amazingly successful turn, breaking the sterile legacy bequeathed by William of Orange. It was he who had plunged this country into its course of meddling on the Continent, and his policy had been given a spurious lustre by Marlborough's resounding achievements. Men were too dazzled by the constant victories to grasp that they led to nothing. In the midst of this blaze the Hanoverian dynasty had been founded, and had at once given William's policy a new centre and a very sinister meaning. The safety of Hanover was substituted for the safety of the Netherlands; the boundaries of England were buried deeper in the Continent; her obligations were increased and riveted on her neck. As the implications of Hanover began to be realised, a healthy reaction followed. People began to ask why England should concern herself with such distant lands and for such fruitless ends. The old Tory conception of a colonial and maritime policy began slowly to raise its head and secure a new lease of life. Men looked askance at Hanover, which more than anything else kept green the memory of the Stuarts. It was not unnatural for the Squire Westerns to think at times how far more profitable it might be to import a king from over the water than to export their acres to Hanover. Even the Whigs, when not growing rich on the profits of war contracts, could appreciate the benefits of overseas trade, and both Whig and Tory had concurred in driving Walpole into the Spanish war. That war had been absorbed in the War of the Austrian Succession, not necessarily, not inevitably, but mainly because of Hanover and the country's reluctant interest in the Pragmatic Sanction.

Now, after Aix, the war was over, and England could sit back and lick her wounds ruefully. If she had gained nothing else, she had gained experience, and the question was how she would use it. In one direction at least the results of the war were over-whelmingly evident—the national debt had been doubled. In other directions the lessons were writ large—our military weak-ness had been exposed, our lack of organisation made apparent; and above all our naval system had been found wanting. After the initial fiascos victories had been won at sea, but no effective strategy had been evolved, and no real use made of our naval power. Worse still, the commercial benefits, for the sake of which we had embarked on the war, were as far from realisation as ever. The colonial position in America remained undefined and unsatis-factory; the boundaries of Acadia had been left like ragged edges to produce fresh tears; Louisbourg had been returned to France to remain a menace to the English colonies; the spheres of influence in the Ohio valley and down the Mississippi had not been agreed in principle, much less settled in detail. All the former causes of dispute were alive in the New World, and, in the old, France had acquired a taste for India, which might well prove disastrous to English enterprise in the future. Nor had England's European entanglements been solved; on the contrary her policy had been left in chaos. The Dutch alliance had not proved successful; the

Austrian alliance had been shaken; the Prussian alliance was suspect; and Hanover had neither disappeared nor been rendered harmless. Truly the problems were many and great, on which the experience of the past eight years might work.

The immediate effect of peace, however, was a relaxation of the intolerable tension, and a tendency to forget the Continent and all it implied. Weariness with the war had long been oppressing the country, and with Pitt's uncanny knack of representing public feeling, it was only natural that he too should be inclined to shun foreign politics. Shut his eyes to them entirely he could not. It was his pleasure, as well as his duty, to watch over England's interests abroad. But war-weariness he undoubtedly felt, induced partly by the failure of England's efforts and partly by the tacit veto which had prevented him from taking an effective share in the conduct of the war. He showed his feelings indirectly by displaying for the first and last time a lively interest in debates on purely domestic matters. Pitt's speeches have for the most part been lost. Of some there is no account; of others only notes; and of yet others records of varying merit written by journalists who may or may not have been present in the House. But the subjects on which he spoke are known with some degree of accuracy, and the list repays study, showing very clearly in what direction his interests lay. Foreign affairs, the army, the navy, and constitutional points invariably stirred him. Most of his speeches dealt with these matters in one form or another. But there is a small group of other speeches, all without exception to be found between November 1747 and December 1754, dealing with minor matters—provincial, municipal, individual and even personal. It began with the speech on the Seaford election (20th November 1747) to which reference has already been made—a speech no doubt forced on him owing to the possibility of losing his seat, but a speech which dealt with a personal matter on personal lines and with none of that widening of issues and deepening of interest which was so characteristic of Pitt in his higher and more exalted moods. The following January he plunged into the fray on another election petition. His cousin, John Pitt, had been elected for Wareham—not without opposition and probably not without the usual bribery and violence. Pitt had taken a lively interest in the election, and as might be expected adopted a strongly partisan attitude, which flamed up more particularly when the local factions came to fisticuffs and John's arm was broken. 'It is with the greatest concern and

indignation,' he wrote, 'that I perused your letter of the 20th
[July 1747] from Wareham. . . . The outrage committed against
you and George Pitt is so inhuman, that I feel more resentment at
it than will at present leave me in a proper state of mind to offer
you my advice.' He gave advice none the less; John should
procure as many depositions as possible 'against all persons, the
two Draxes especially, concerned in the riot,' so that he would
have the means to prosecute if, when blood was cooler, that
seemed the wisest course. Meanwhile Pitt assured his cousin that
he would be present when the election petition came before the
House. He was as good as his word and took part in the debate
(26th January 1748). His speech has not been recorded, but one
slight reference to it, written some ten years later, shows something of its temper. It appears that Wilmot, a Parliamentary
pleader, well known and admired in the House and subsequently
to become a judge, took part in the debate—on the wrong side.
Whereupon he was 'reprimanded with great haughtiness by Pitt,
who told him he had brought thither the pertness of his profession.'[1] Wilmot was so chagrined by Pitt's attack that he 'flung
down his brief in a passion, and never would return to plead
there any more.'

Pitt followed up these two family speeches with a third of the
same genre, in which he plunged into the fray on behalf of his
Grenville friends. Cobham and his family had imposed themselves
on North Buckinghamshire like princelings, petty but oppressive,
and being both ambitious and arrogant had raised up a number of
secret enemies. Great therefore and widespread was the excitement
when a proposal was put forward to remove the summer assizes
from Buckingham to Aylesbury. Such a change would indeed be
a smack in the face for the Grenvilles and the open and almost
unholy joy of the anti-Grenville party stirred up a whirlwind of
resentment among the pro-Grenvilles. Feeling ran high and the
debate on the subject (19th February 1748) engendered a deal
more heat than many questions of far greater moment. Pitt was
not backward. The speech which has come down to us as his is
full of raillery and verbal felicity. Pitt enjoyed tying his opponents
into knots, and by a judicious twist making an argument
boomerang back on its author. On this occasion he indulged this
capacity to the full, adding barbs of his own, but following hard
on the rapier play of his quizzing came the bludgeon stroke. He

[1] Walpole. *Memoirs*, II, 273.

ended his speech on another and a different note. The last speaker had claimed to know the county and to be impartial. 'He is acquainted with the county'—echoed Pitt, mounting from banter to high indignation, pulsating with something more than personal abuse, 'he is acquainted with the county some other way than by the map; and it seems he is acquainted likewise with Aylesbury, very well acquainted with it by the character he bestows upon it— "I never got a vote there that I did not pay for." He is a man of honour, Sir, and nobody will doubt the truth of what he says. Perhaps this method of procuring votes may not be altogether out of fashion, but it is to be hoped, for the future, that private interests will be supported by private purses; for I dare say, Sir, even he will not think it reasonable to exchange that method for public privileges.' So with the dark hint of bribery and corruption and the villainy that buys personal gain with public money, Pitt ended his harangue.

The effort lasted him a long time, for he does not seem to have taken part in any further debate for over a year. On the 21st of April 1749, however, the House debated a petition from Glasgow. During the '45, the Pretender had levied a large sum from the city, and now that the rebellion was over and done, the canny Scots thought they might ask to be reimbursed. Pitt spoke on their behalf. He put forward two arguments. Glasgow, he said, had been accused of yielding without effort to the rebels and only showing their loyalty when the danger had passed. That, Pitt retorted, was not a true representation of the case. The fact was that before the rebels had entered England, Glasgow had no power to show their loyalty; they had no time to provide for their defence, and, being an open town, no hope of defending themselves if they had been given time. They were without arms, ammunition or military training. Besides, added Pitt, what of England? 'The rebels marched up through one half of England without any opposition from the militia, and even in their retreat back again, though pursued by the Duke [of Cumberland] and the regular forces, they met with no obstruction from the militia.' If the English countryside could do nothing, can we blame Glasgow for being unprepared? More important was their subsequent behaviour; and here the facts were beyond dispute. 'They honestly and bravely resolved not to be idle spectators of the confusions of their country. They resolved to be active in putting an end to them as soon as possible; and with this view, as soon as they had an opportunity, they put themselves to a very great expence.' So much for the one, and the more pedestrian, side of the argument. On the other side Pitt maintained that the ruin of Glasgow could only be a disaster for the country as a whole—'if we think of the justice due to the public creditors, or of relieving our poor labourers and manufacturers, we must agree to this motion, because the public revenue will suffer a great deal more by the ruin of such a trading town as Glasgow than it can suffer by granting the relief desired by the petitioners for preventing that ruin.'

The speech is full of interest for the future. It shows that Pitt realised the lack of preparation for future wars and the inefficiency of the militia. The speech gains in significance when one looks forward to his remodelling of the militia and the explosive energy which he brought into the eighteenth-century equivalent of the Ministry of Munitions. It foreshadows in its kindliness towards the Scots the great and beneficent change which Pitt brought about in Anglo-Scottish relations, and which he tried desperately and vainly to promote in Anglo-American relations. And lastly in its financial and economic argument it shows that Pitt was very near reaching the hidden source of our quarrel with the colonies. The scarcity of money in America and the illiberality of the trading regulations imposed upon her were at least two of the main causes of the trouble, and Pitt was groping towards a solution. In this speech he showed clearly enough his conviction that the body politic, like the body corporeal, was a single entity, and the whole was bound to suffer from the ill-health of the part. This sense of brotherhood with all portions of the empire; this conviction that the richer parts should help the poorer; this belief that loyalty would be the offspring of love; this certainty that kindness was the natural extension of kinship, were all ingrained in Pitt and formed the teeming soil out of which the British Empire grew. The speech on the Glasgow petition was the first public hint of a new policy, and contained almost all the ingredients of Pitt's future tonic for the nations which were the partners in the empire—trustfulness, generosity, encouragement, an open hand and an open heart.

Pitt showed the same spirit of wide tolerance and understanding in his support of Pelham's Bill to naturalise foreign Protestants in April 1751, and the more hotly debated Bill for the naturalisation of Jews in 1753. In both these cases he was flouting popular opinion. The fact is worth recording, because the title of Great Commoner obscures the fact that Pitt was far from being a demagogue. He was essentially a leader, and as such many of his measures ran counter to popular feeling and popular prejudice. If he relied on the people, it was the reliance of a general, sure of the loyalty of his men, not the gamble of a demagogue, tossed hither and thither on the credulity of his dupes. As a leader Pitt could adopt unpopular measures and play unpopular rôles. He could do more than that; he could recant and change his mind; he could recover from false steps; he could, even, lower his own prestige and fall from his high estate and yet in some degree win back his influence and his following. He has been twitted for his inconsistencies, which were many and obvious, but it is only fair to note that those inconsistencies were of two sorts. Where there was an honest change of opinion, Pitt had no hesitation in proclaiming his conversion. There were, however, other cases where expediency had more of a voice than conviction. In those cases Pitt spoke haltingly. Never was a man in high public station less glib when his heart was not engaged. There were such occasions —it cannot be denied—and one of them was in connection with the Jewish Naturalisation Act. The Bill had been unpopular, and its passage was the signal for a panic-stricken and unseemly outburst of anti-Semitism. The Jews have a knack of stirring up resentment; they are not a lovable people, and their undoubted abilities and outstanding success make them the more hated and feared. It is a thousand pities, since, like all human beings, they are to be won by kindness. But England in the eighteenth century was not much farther advanced than Central Europe in the twentieth century. The Act caused a hue and cry, in which the Church was as violent and vocal as any. Riots and rowdiness flourished, and at last the Government, with one eye on the approaching elections, felt constrained to repeal the obnoxious enactment. A Bill was introduced for the purpose, and Pitt with his usual courage, but with a heavy heart and a confused tongue, spoke in its favour (23rd November 1753). The Act had raised discontents and disquiets in the minds of many of His Majesty's subjects; that was the only ground on which the repeal could be justified. The talk of religion was nonsense. 'I am fully convinced, I believe most gentlemen that hear me are fully convinced, that religion has really nothing to do in the dispute; but the people without doors have been made to believe it has; and upon this the old High Church persecuting spirit has begun to take hold of them. We are too wise,' Pitt continued sadly, 'to dispute the matter with them; as we may upon this occasion evade it without doing any notable injury to the public. But at the same time we ought to let them know, that we think they have been misled; and that the spirit they are at present possessed with, is not a true Christian spirit. If we do not do this, we do not deal honestly or candidly by them.' The repeal of the Act would plunge the Jews once more into a position which in point of strict law was quite impossible, and proved tolerable only because 'neither our ridiculous laws against aliens, nor our persecuting unchristian laws relating to religion, have of late years been carried into execution.' There was nothing to be gained by the repeal and much that might be lost. 'Therefore I must still think that the law passed last Session in favour of the Jews was in itself right; and I shall now agree to the repeal of it merely out of complaisance to that enthusiastic spirit that has taken hold of the people'—a poor excuse for a bad action.

And so this period of quiescence and personal interests drew to its inglorious end.

31

CHANGING EUROPE

The war weariness which impelled Pitt towards minor domestic matters was bound to fade, and in fact side by side with his apparent absorption in trivialities there can be traced in him throughout these six years (1748-1754) a renaissance of interest in the broader issues of foreign policy. It was as well for England, since great matters were pending and there was little time for preparation. Now that the old policy had gone beyond recall there was need for a new beginning, and the foundations were being laid by two men, neither of whom was fit for the job. There was the King, not without shrewdness, not without statecraft, but an old man wedded to Hanover and warped by prejudice—a European by birth, upbringing and predilection. Then there was Newcastle—another man not altogether without shrewdness, and certainly well versed in the political jobbery which seemed to be inseparable from Whig statecraft, but a man of narrow mind and narrower vision, set firmly in the mould of the past. Both were tenacious and in their curiously contrasted styles at once extremely overbearing and ungraciously pliant. The King had been bred in the traditions of a German princeling, which gave him an autocratic or, to use the modern jargon, totalitarian outlook. Like Louis XIV he believed in his heart of hearts that he was, or at least should be, the state. But he had learnt in the painful school of experience the limits of an English constitutional monarch. He chafed at the restraints, he swore roundly, he growled and muttered, but he was able to recognise when he had been driven into a corner, and he had given way more than once. The experience was unpleasant and increased his relish for Hanover, where he could still strut and preen himself among the fat ladies of Herrenhausen and issue commands that would be obeyed instantly with a click of the heels. It increased also his taste for Hanoverian politics and that shady course of action which forced, or attempted to force, the hands of Parliament by confusing the functions of

207

King and Elector. Newcastle was of somewhat the same mould. He believed intensely in the merits of birth, and while he supposed himself to be slightly inferior to the King, knew himself to be well above the common herd: he had to the full the aristocratic intolerance of the eighteenth century. Newcastle expected to have his own way, and he became querulous and agitated when anything or anybody appeared to thwart him. Politics were for him the most natural and the most exasperating of pursuits. As a Whig magnate he regarded them as at once his occupation and his duty, his pleasure and his penchant. He did not question his own ability to run the country; it was not a thing to discuss; it was axiomatic and as little to be thought of as the body when one is in good health. What he did question was the right of anyone less exalted to disagree with him. This curious psychological trait explains his constant state of nerves, his incredible fussiness. All criticism was for him a personal attack. He does not seem to have grasped the possibility of honest difference of opinion. Those who disagreed with him were either Jacobites and Tories—wrong-headed fellows whose views were automatically stupid, if not traitorous—or Whigs eaten up with faction and bent on the downfall of the Duke of Newcastle. The background of his mind in short was a subconscious belief that all opponents were either unscrupulous or envious. It followed that no advice was likely to be good, unless it confirmed his own opinions, and that all opposition must be unkind. Flowing from the same psychological fount was the constant irritation of holding a position subordinate to his younger brother. Newcastle was continually, if unconsciously, affronted at being merely Secretary of State when Pelham was First Lord of the Treasury, and retaliated by absorbing as much business into his own hands as possible and picking quarrels with his brother on the slightest provocation. Had he been of the same rough mould as the King he would have ranted and roared, but being of quite another mould he whined and snivelled.

Such were the two men who partly out of preference, partly ex officio and partly for their own prestige, conducted England's foreign policy in these pregnant years. They were insensible to what was happening on the Continent, but their blindness did not prevent them from meddling. The Continent was an absorbing study for those who had eyes to see. On any view the peace of Aix left two great rivalries unresolved—the struggle between

Prussia and Austria for pre-eminence in Germany, and the duel for world empire between England and France. And against this tremendous background of divergent forces which were to tear the world for two generations and more the King could see nothing but a possible threat to Hanover, and Newcastle nothing but an opportunity to peddle the German principalities. The broad outline of Newcastle's policy was what he called the 'old system'— the system of William III and Marlborough—in which Austria, England and Holland were firmly allied against France. The rise of Prussia had no part in this policy, and Newcastle tended to ignore it. Prussia, in so far as its existence had to be accepted, was to be regarded as a subsidiary of France, rather unreliable, rather troublesome, distasteful to the King and on the whole better forgotten.

Whatever might have been said for the 'old system' in earlier times, it was now outworn. Facts had altered and were altering from day to day, and the basis of Newcastle's policy was crumbling. The one outstanding fact on the Continent after the Treaty of Aix was the transference of Silesia from Austria to Prussia. It was symbolical, and posed the insistent question of German hegemony. Was Prussia, under its young and ruthless King, to seize the overlordship of the German states from Maria Theresa's feeble, if unfaltering hands? The rivalry was more than latent; it was a fact, not even properly disguised by the recurring alliances between Prussia and France. Frederick had not been acting as a friend of France; nor did he follow the French custom of restoring conquests at the Peace. He had struck for himself, and what his claws had grasped he had every intention of keeping. Here was a fact to be reckoned with, and whilst Newcastle ignored it, a new man was rising in Austria, who not only saw it but understood its implications. These six years coincide with the rise of Kaunitz. To him it was evident that the 'old system' was becoming useless for Austria, whatever it might be for England. Under that system Austria was continually called upon to fight France in the Netherlands, for no specific purpose but the humiliation of France and the aggrandisement of England. No Austrian interest worth the name was served; on the contrary Austrian power and wealth were being sapped, and her powers of resistance against the rising star of Prussia weakened. It would be better by far that Austria should lay less insistence upon the alliance with England, without perhaps dropping it for the

o

moment, though ultimately slipping out of the obligations it involved. And meanwhile, in place of the sterile English alliance, a darker and deeper scheme might be evolved for the destruction of Prussia. The times were favourable but would not remain so. Russia was governed at the moment by the Empress Elizabeth, who loathed Frederick personally and for that reason might well be disposed to join in humbling Prussia, whilst her successor, the Grand Duke Peter, who was an ardent and even fanatical admirer of Frederick, would undoubtedly refuse. And Elizabeth's health was precarious. France, again, was not too well pleased with Frederick as an ally. He had a disagreeable knack of changing course; and he had been too successful. It was irritating to think that he alone had come out of the war with tangible spoils. France could not be sure of him as an ally and was not altogether pleased with the turn of events; she might well be weaned away from Prussia, and instead of fighting endless and unmeaning battles with England and Austria, join in a conspiracy to crush Frederick. Such a policy, in Kaunitz's eyes, had the twofold advantage of relieving Austria from profitless endeavours and opening up the possibility of regaining her lost provinces and her diminished prestige.

Over against Kaunitz was the Argus-eyed Frederick, following the various moves on the European chessboard with a flippant cynicism that frequently damaged his personal relations with foreign potentates, but never for one moment blinded him to realities. Frederick had the good fortune to possess the German qualities by birth and the French qualities by adoption. Though passionately true to his calling as the King of Prussia, a devoted ruler and a far-seeing statesman, he despised the German people, detesting their culture and even their language. For him civilisation began and ended in France, and the brutalities of his own father had driven him faster and more determinedly along his self-chosen road of Gallic sentiment. It was consequently in a very real sense that he assimilated the qualities of both nations— the Prussia of his patriotism and the France which was his spiritual home. But the clash of divergent cultures and the stress of facts made him curiously shallow and cynical. He was not a great poet or musician, though he wrote French verses both in season and out of it, and practised the flute with an equal disregard of time, place and inspiration. Nor was he by nature a great general, though he inherited a magnificent army and prided himself upon the height of his grenadiers. But on the other hand he combined in a startling and highly successful manner the gambling instinct of the Frenchman with the perseverance of the German, the Gallic flashes of insight with the ruthlessness of the Prussian. Time and again he staked all on a gambler's throw and lost, only to recover, now by a stroke of genius due to himself alone, now by a stroke of luck following a refusal to accept defeat. No one, perhaps not Frederick himself, could predict what this unpredictable character would do. All that could be said was that it would be no easy task to find him off his guard, and desperately difficult to overreach him. At this point of time he was not fully appreciated by anyone, but he had managed to stir up Maria Theresa's undying hatred and to irritate Elizabeth of Russia. Also he had managed to acquire Silesia. Frederick the man was indifferent whether or not he stood in the good graces of the two Empresses; but Frederick the King was fully aware of the dangers which their enmity threatened. He was on his guard before Kaunitz started, and he meant to extend his sway over Germany rather than restore her lost province to Austria.

This antagonism between the two branches of German sovereignty—the Hapsburgs and the Hohenzollerns—was in no sense anti-British. England did not come into the question unless she chose to interfere. But in its effects on the two protagonists it ran counter to all the currents of the 'old system' as interpreted in England, and because of its growing urgency and insistence should obviously have been taken into the reckoning when foreign policy was to be settled. Instead it was ignored by Newcastle, or, perhaps more truly, not observed. Newcastle was not the man to take long views or understand trends. It was enough for him to be busy, without much thought of what he was being busy about. At this precise moment he was very much distracted, being torn between an instinctive belief in enmity with France and a feeling that peace was essential.

For Newcastle, and indeed for Pitt, and for practically every English statesman, the one eternal enemy of Great Britain was France. It would have puzzled Newcastle, if he had posed the question, to understand why he felt so certain on this point, because the simplicities and directness of England's foreign policy had been beclouded by Orange and Hanoverian interests. But the certainty sprang from the old colonial and maritime policy of the Tories. France and England were rivals for world empire

—half-consciously in America and unconsciously as yet in India—
just as they were later to become rivals in Africa. The world outside Europe was to be conquered and given a mould—English or
Latin—and the eighteenth century was the temporal setting of the
struggle. All this had nothing to do with European politics as
such. It might be necessary, as Carteret had said, to fight France
everywhere, but only with a view to conquest overseas. Once that
rivalry had gone, there was nothing beyond wounded feelings to
prevent an *entente cordiale*. But the rivalry had not gone; it was in
one sense barely starting, since Newcastle and his like had no
conception of the issue at stake. England must therefore continue
her battle with France, and the trend of events on the Continent
made it the more imperative to see that the battle took place overseas and not in Europe. It had been difficult enough for Marlborough to win his victories with the Grand Alliance at least
nominally at his back. It would be quite impossible now with no
Marlborough to lead the troops, with a weakened Holland and an
Austria intent on making peace with France in order to recover
Silesia. A continental war was madness for England; yet war with
France there must be, till the question of world empire was
settled.

George II and Newcastle were wholly unaware of the trend of
world movements and blind to the new orientation on the
Continent. They saw only Hanover in the near foreground,
standing out insistently against the background of the 'old
system'! Austria must be bolstered up and kept true to the latest
version of the Grand Alliance. On the other hand Prussia must
not be annoyed, because Prussia was a prickly customer and
uncomfortably near Hanover. Nor must France be attacked; she
must be encircled, but not deliberately attacked. War would no
doubt come sooner or later—it was a perennial—but France must
be made to seem the aggressor, so that England could claim the
assistance of Austria under the arrangements of the 'old system.'
Everything which England did was likely to annoy France and so
conduce to war, and the counter preparations inevitably presupposed and prearranged a struggle on the Continent. Yet peace
was what Newcastle wanted and what he genuinely believed he
was promoting.

If his policy was bad his methods were even more confused and
foolish. Somehow he persuaded himself that Austria would gain
in power and become more beholden to England if the Archduke

Joseph, Maria Theresa's eldest son, were elected King of the Romans. The title meant nothing in itself, but should—if anyone paid attention to such formal legalities—ensure that the ten-year-old Archduke would succeed his father as Emperor. The scheme was fantastic. It made no difference to England who was Emperor, and the election would either do nothing or create another Pragmatic Sanction to confuse the world in general and the German principalities in particular, when the existing Emperor died.

As the crowning proof of its imbecility, Newcastle could not even secure the wholehearted assent of the boy's parents. Neither Maria Theresa nor her husband was enamoured of the prospect. None the less Newcastle, during visits to Hanover in 1749 and 1750, worked busily at bribing the electors. They were ready enough to accept good English money; their only interest was to see how high Newcastle would bid. So the months passed, and Newcastle's letters were filled with details of his fussy negotiations. In the end he succeeded in persuading them to accept subsidies, but in nothing else. Austria obtained a subsidy of £100,000; the Bavarian Elector sold his vote for £20,000, and the Saxon for £32,000. There were other Electors on Newcastle's list into whose gaping pockets he was anxious to pour money, but he was prevented almost, one might say, to his chagrin, for he seems to have measured the value of his diplomacy by the amount of money he spent.

In this policy Newcastle received very little support from Pelham. In the Cabinet Pelham had acquiesced, not, as he afterwards said, out of conviction, but because he was 'overruled by numbers and by power.'[1] He feared the results, both financially and still more politically, and being almost weaker than Newcastle, though more balanced, he found it difficult to pursue a consistent course. On the one hand he urged Newcastle to secure the election of the King of the Romans 'for the sake of gilding the pill'[2]— whatever the pill might be—and grudgingly admitted, as each new subsidy was proposed, that the sum was trifling in itself and might not matter if it were not that many a mickle makes a muckle—'this sum is a trifle, but I hear of more and more every day.'[3] On the other hand he could not conceal his disbelief in the

---

[1] Pelham to Newcastle, 29th Sept. 1752. Add. MSS. 32,729.
[2] Pelham to Newcastle, 2nd July 1750. Add. MSS. 32,721.
[3] Pelham to Newcastle, 26th June 1750. Add. MSS. 32,721.

project, his dislike of subsidies as mere extravagance, and his fear that Parliament would react unfavourably. He kept complaining: 'we have been great dupes during the whole course of the war';[1] and again, 'I am unwilling to run the Civil List more and more in debt for nothing but moonshine.'[2] Being full of doubts, he could not co-operate wholeheartedly nor could he refrain from making suggestions that he was neither strong enough to insist upon, nor clever enough to make attractive. 'I agree with you,' Newcastle wrote regarding one of them, 'a substantial connection with the House of Austria is preferable to any expensive management with the inferior princes. But this substantial work for the House of Austria [i.e. the election of the Archduke] cannot be done without those inferior princes. Neither is the House of Austria alone of that weight and use for preventing a war that it is when it is supported and joined with the Princes of the Empire.'[3] Pelham was too weary of continual squabbles and too buffeted by the cares of office to expose the question-begging and *non sequitur* of Newcastle's letter. 'That I am tired is certain,' he replied, 'if labouring in a shop, which neither by nature or circumstances suits my temper, for near thirty years should tire me, I must be so.'[4]

These quotations, which could be multiplied almost indefinitely, show clearly enough the grit in the machinery. Newcastle, fussy, fearful and arrogant all at the same time, forced a reluctant consent to his schemes, and thereafter used that consent not only to shed responsibility on to others but also to brush aside any attempt at advice or control. Foreign affairs were in his department, and except for the King he would brook no interference. Pelham chafed, but in the upshot accepted the position of younger brother. Newcastle once described, with querulous fidelity, a meeting between himself and Pelham, at which all grievances were to be settled: 'the meeting was opened with oblique reflections; ill-natured constructions upon the conduct of foreign affairs for this last year; and direct complaints of the manner in which the Bavarian negotiation had been begun. This necessarily drew from me a justification of myself. . . . After these very useless and very disagreeable altercations about foreign affairs had taken up about two hours . . . I thought it honest and necessary to

---

[1] To Newcastle, 26th June 1750.
[2] To Newcastle, 2nd July 1750.
[3] Newcastle to Pelham, June 17/23, 1750. Add. MSS. 32,721.
[4] Pelham to Newcastle, 6th July 1750. Add. MSS. 32,721.

consider the situation of things at home. . . . This laid me under a necessity of making a *declaration* . . . to which I had the answer I had reason from the former part of our conference to expect, viz. "That I might do as I pleased; that my brother would neither *assist* nor *obstruct*." '[1] Nothing could show more plainly the relations between the brothers—the elder indignant and authoritarian, the younger half overawed but wholly unconvinced. If they had still been boys in the nursery, the one would have been openly bullying and the other patently sulky.

The two brothers were, in fact, at variance with one another on practically every point. Inevitably they found the position well nigh intolerable. Both wanted comfort; both needed advice; both turned in their need to Pitt. Their spontaneous bid for his support was an amazing proof of his worth, a first-class 'reference.' It was also an opportunity. Pitt could side with one or the other; he could make his own terms; he could intrigue and push himself; he could in short make himself the power behind the throne and when occasion served come into the limelight to seize the throne. Instead, he gained the confidence and earned the thanks of both. 'Go on in your correspondence with him,' Pelham wrote to Newcastle in August 1750, 'with all the frankness and cordiality you can; I do so in all my conversations with him; I think him besides, the most able and useful man we have among us; truly honourable, and strictly honest. He is as firm a friend to us, as we can wish for, and a more useful one there does not exist.'[2] In a similar strain Newcastle wrote to a friend in January 1751, 'As you can be no stranger to the able and affectionate manner in which Mr. Pitt has taken upon himself to defend me, and the measures which have been solely carried on by me, when both have been openly attacked with violence, and when no other person in the House opened his lips in defence of either but Mr. Pitt, I think myself obliged in honour and gratitude to shew my sense of it, in the best manner I am able.'[3]

Pitt was so successful in winning the approval and gratitude of both, that historians have been divided ever since as to which of the two Pitt really supported. Almon, with the arrogance of the idolater, will not allow that Pitt bowed the knee to either. Pitt, according to Almon, 'was not ignorant of the clandestine projects

---

[1] Newcastle to Pitt, 31st March 1750. Add. MSS. 32,720.
[2] Coxe's *Pelham Administration*, II, 370.
[3] Add. MSS. 32,724.

of both parties; but he despised them. In one conference he had
with the Duke of Newcastle, he treated that nobleman in such a
manner, that if he had not dreaded him he would have dismissed
him.'[1] Almon describes the conference. 'Mr. Pitt told his Grace
that he engaged for subsidies without knowing the extent of the
sums, and for alliances without knowing the terms.' Put like that,
one may well believe that Pitt was riding a very high horse, and
one cannot be surprised that 'the Duke complained of Mr. Pitt's
hauteur to his confidential friend, Mr. Stone.' But the storm
begins to take on the appearance of a breeze at most, when we
read of Mr. Stone's reaction. That long-suffering gentleman,
Newcastle's secretary and henchman and very much under the
Duke's thumb, 'advised his Grace to overlook it, saying it would
be most prudent.' Stone would have given no such advice if Pitt
had been really obstreperous or the Duke more than usually
querulous. Lord Rosebery[2] declares that 'Fox had sided with
Pelham, and Pitt with Newcastle'; and Professor Williams[3]
maintains that 'in foreign politics Pitt was less in sympathy with
the Duke of Newcastle, who had charge of them, than with his
brother in domestic affairs.'

The confusion arises out of the position in which Pitt found
himself and the constraint which it imposed upon him. In one
sense Almon comes nearest the mark, since it is probable that
fundamentally he was out of sympathy with both. But there is,
and must be, such a thing as making the best of a bad job. Pitt
had declared immediately after Aix that peace was essential, and
he had averred more than once, by inference if not in so many
words, that there was no alternative to the Pelham administration.
Given these two premises, he could not oppose either, but as
they were generally at variance he must incline one way or the
other, and it is not difficult to gather from his letters which
brother attracted him most—or perhaps repelled him least. As
the mediator between them, he had to keep in with both; but small
signs show clearly that he felt more at ease and more in sympathy
with Pelham. A few hints must suffice. When writing to Newcastle, Pitt was always on his best behaviour, which like so much
best behaviour was unnatural and insincere. His letters to Pelham,
if he wrote any, have not been preserved, and cannot therefore be
compared; but a postscript which Pitt wrote to his cousin is very
significant. 'Be so good,' he wrote from Bath on the 16th of

---

[1] Almon, I, 254.   [2] Rosebery, p. 293.   [3] Williams, I, 176.

October 1750, 'as to let Mr. Pelham know when you set out, and ask if he has any commands for me.' This suggests an ease of intercourse and a degree of confidence which are nowhere apparent in the correspondence with Newcastle, and indeed are out of keeping with Pitt's obsequious flattery and Newcastle's pompous condescension. Perhaps even more enlightening is Pitt's knack of escaping interviews with Newcastle. 'If your Grace had been in town I shou'd have had the honour to wait on you,' wrote Pitt on the 2nd of April 1750; and on the 10th of November of the same year he lamented that 'I am most unlucky to have an engagement I can't put off for a dinner Tuesday; when I should otherwise have had the honour of waiting on your Grace.' And on the 10th of March 1753, when the mountain was proposing to come to Mahomet, Mahomet did his best to cut short the interview: 'whenever your Grace can have leisure to do me the great honour you are so good to think of, I shou'd be glad to be apprised before. I trust you will pardon a sick man for mentioning an hour that suits him. I will therefore venture to desire, it may be any evening, between the hours of seven and nine.' And a few days later (24th March 1753) Pitt writes a letter of congratulations on the issue of a parliamentary question 'not being able to do myself the honour to wait on your Grace to do it in person.' But there were times when he was simply naughty, promising to pay his duty when he came up to Town from the country,[1] and then, when he had come and gone, writing that he was 'extremely mortify'd to have been obliged to leave town without having the honour and pleasure of receiving your Grace's commands.'[2]

It was different with Pelham. Pitt was in frequent touch with him, often visiting him when he avoided the elder brother. In the same letter of the 12th of August 1753, for instance, while lamenting his inability to see the Duke of Newcastle, he let out that he had visited Pelham at Carlton House.

If he sympathised most with Pelham in the eternal squabbles between the two brothers, he none the less spent a great deal of soft soap on Newcastle. His real feelings however peeped out in a few pregnant sentences of a letter written on the 13th of July 1750. Pitt had received a long whining complaint of Pelham's behaviour, and replied with a slab of condolences, flattery and

---

[1] Pitt to Newcastle, 9th August 1753. Add. MSS. 32,732.
[2] Pitt to Newcastle, 12th Aug. 1753. Add. MSS. 32,732.

advice. He was sorry at all this misunderstanding and hoped that at least an appearance of unanimity would be kept up because appearances were so important. The trouble would vanish—must vanish between two Ministers so essentially necessary to each other; and when fair weather returned, 'let me most earnestly entreat your Grace to bid it welcome.' Then, after disclaiming any desire to advise, he begs leave to suggest a doubt: 'may not frequent reproaches upon one subject gall and irritate a mind not conscious, intentionally at least, of giving cause; nay perhaps at that very moment as weary as the rest of the world is, of many occurrences in business which every day and hour furnishes in a celebrated department, and consequently (if not ruffled and indisposed by upbraidings) open, may be, to be led and carry'd by the course and stream of conjunctures where it may not be driven.' This for all its tortuosity was a very direct hint, and Pitt was sufficiently frightened of his daring to apologise properly: 'Pardon, my Lord Duke, the great freedom I use; your Grace has ordered me to write freely; and I do it with the less fear, because I know how truly and warmly I am yours.'[1]

In the uneasy position which he held, Pitt was remarkably consistent and all things considered remarkably frank. Pelham's policy in home affairs had Pitt's support though not his enthusiasm. Like Pelham he believed that England needed peace and quiet, and an opportunity to recuperate both spiritually and financially. Recuperation is always slow, and convalescents have to be humoured more than the doctor would like. So Pitt found it necessary to acquiesce in certain actions with which he disagreed —and to hint at, rather than press on, measures which might be unpopular. The most striking example of the former was his assent to the repeal of the Jewish Naturalisation Act; of the latter, his speech on the Bavarian subsidy, mentioned in Stone's report to Newcastle (22nd February 1751). He there expressed the hope that the happy prospect abroad 'would be attended with measures of economy at home—perhaps by a different manner of collecting the revenue—and he was not afraid to mention the odious word *excise*—(and then he mentioned Sir Robert Walpole with honour) —that the reduction of interest was a great point gained for the public—and that the whole together made him hope that England would make as great a figure in a few years as it had done in any age.'[2]

---

[1] Pitt to Newcastle, 13th July 1750. Add. MSS. 32,721.   [2] Add. MSS. 32,724.

This reference to excise and the accompanying praise of Walpole are sometimes pointed at as one of Pitt's most flagrant inconsistencies—a complete and brazen eating of his words. 'The middle-aged Pitt seemed never to tire of trampling savagely on the young Pitt, even wantonly, as on this occasion,' says Lord Rosebery, and adds rather primly that 'Pitt deliberately chose this method of public atonement for past recklessness, and as an avowal that he had learned and ripened by experience.' One may perhaps doubt if Pitt was quite so concerned with educating the public. Inconsistency was common in the eighteenth century, and Pitt had no need of any justification beyond the fact that he had now passed from the sterile ranks of mere Opposition to the Cabinet, where a positive policy had to be evolved. No one would have cared much at any changes in his opinion; and Pitt was not concerned particularly to explain, emphasise or justify them; he spoke as the spirit moved him, and his candour in drawing attention, as he did on this occasion, to his altered views, shows merely that he was in earnest. That, however, is a digression.

In foreign affairs Pitt was undoubtedly serving an apprenticeship and gaining experience of real value, though it is impossible to believe that he looked up to his master with any sort of reverence. Newcastle, like Pelham, had to be endured for want of an alternative, and perhaps the endurance was not too hard. For if his foreign policy was short-sighted, silly and expensive, it did aim at preserving peace and it had the negative merit of being on the whole harmless. It was far better that Newcastle and the King should busy themselves about such balderdash as the King of the Romans than touch upon vital questions which might blow up into a flame before England was ready. For the sake of peace and quiet, Pitt undoubtedly encouraged Newcastle's efforts abroad. He knew that the Secretary of State was a meddler, and preferred that he should meddle with trifles. There can be little doubt that Pitt assessed Newcastle's futilities at their true worth, and that he urged Pelham to endure the subsidies mainly in order to keep Newcastle out of other mischief. It is impossible to read Pitt's letters to Newcastle and fail to realise the irony that lurks beneath the fulsome compliments. Great and glorious as Newcastle's work was, magnificent as were the results, the true and crowning glory was the smallness of the subsidies. His highest satisfaction, he told Newcastle in a burst of candour which betrayed him, was that Newcastle looked like achieving his aims 'still confining new subsidiary engagements to Bavaria only.' 'If no contretems happens,' he continued, 'your Grace will have done really great things in a very short time indeed, and the glory of doing them will be truely great, because the expense that is to attend them will not be at all immoderate';[1] and again, 'the object all must applaud, and the greatest oeconomists can't complain of the expense.'[2] In all the correspondence of these years two points stand out clearly, first Pitt's real fear that the want of harmony between the brothers might lead to the downfall of the Government, and secondly, his anxiety to keep Newcastle happily occupied over trivialities.

[1] Pitt to Newcastle, 13th July 1750. Add. MSS. 32,721.
[2] Pitt to Newcastle, 24th August 1750. Add. MSS. 32,722.

32

PREPARATIONS

Pitt's efforts to preserve the peace between the brothers was the negative side of the picture. More positively, he worked, as opportunity arose, for the strengthening of England against the struggle that was bound to come, and, particularly as his war weariness passed, he explored the position overseas where the struggle, in his eyes, must be fought to a finish. The tale of his real interests can be traced like a scarlet thread through the tangle of his correspondence. He was very jealous of England's rights and England's honour, and whenever points arose which he regarded as vital, he reacted at once, dropping the fulsome insincerities of his letters to Newcastle for a forceful style more in keeping with his subject. Not that there were many occasions. For the most part these years were comparatively barren.

Foremost among vital matters were bound to be all efforts to improve the fighting forces. The navy came first. With the end of the war, the navy was reduced from 40,000 to 10,000 men, but with this reduction in strength went an effort to secure better administration. The effort was fortuitous rather than planned, but was none the less welcome to Pitt. It arose out of the fact that the Duke of Bedford resigned the post of First Lord of the Admiralty in February 1748 and was succeeded by his protégé, Lord Sandwich. The new First Lord was at the time an arrogant young rake of thirty, and what was more had for the past two years been playing an important, though by no means successful, rôle in the negotiations which ultimately led to the Treaty of Aix. He was much too satisfied with himself and much too occupied with his work as a plenipotentiary to think of coming home or to find time to attend to his new official business. When therefore Anson, who was also on the Board of Admiralty, wrote to 'explain to you the disagreeable situation your absence places me in,' Sandwich replied hastily but helpfully: 'I would not lose a moment to desire that you would consider yourself as in effect at the head of the

Admiralty. . . . I must beg you will suffer everything I do to go through your hands, as it is my meaning to throw my share of the power and the direction of the whole as much as possible into your hands.'[1]

Anson, like so many other great admirals, was a poor administrator and a poorer parliamentarian. He knew the many evils rampant in the navy, and wished to do away with them, but though he had now been given *carte blanche* he had neither the ability to devise lasting remedies nor the art to carry them through the House. He was silent, taciturn and unbending in manner, while he was bewildered and confused in action. None the less he was well-meaning and more than a trifle dogged; and he managed at least to bring some scandals to light and to introduce some measures of reform. In all such cases he had Pitt's sympathy, and wherever possible his support. Much had to be done by internal reorganisation, and here Anson's foes were the indifference and incapacity of his colleagues, the conservatism of the navy and the ramparts of vested interests. Pitt could not help him there. Matters which came before the House were on a different footing, and Pitt made his views known, pressing them at times even against the Government. But here, as in other matters, he realised that the preservation of a stable administration was the essential foundation of reform and as such more important than the rectification of individual abuses. So it came about that the measure of support which he gave to Anson varied. He approved the revision of the Navy Discipline Act, containing a clause about cowardice and desertion which, whatever its justification, was afterwards to cause him much heartburning. So, too, he supported the proposal to make half-pay officers amenable to martial law; but this latter proposal had to be dropped, not because of its ineffectiveness but because of the opposition shown by the senior officers. In Pitt's eyes spirit meant more than discipline, and a contented navy was a better weapon of war than a listless automaton. He approved of discipline, but only where it was animated by patriotism and based upon loyalty. More startling than either of these cases was the line which Pitt took in 1751 when Pelham proposed, in the interests of economy, to cut the navy from its normal peace-time strength of 10,000 to the unmeaning figure of 8,000 men. Pitt could not agree. The navy was, in his strikingly paradoxical phrase, England's standing

[1] Barrow's *Anson*, p. 203.

army, and there was a point below which it should not and must not be reduced. Accordingly, though he was a Minister in the Government which proposed the measure, he spoke and even voted against it. He lost at the moment, but won in the long run, as the numbers were raised once more to 10,000 men in the following year.

With the army, Pitt, as Paymaster, was more officially concerned, and as an ex-officer he might have been expected to feel a lively interest in it. So within limits he did, though hardly more than he felt in the navy. It was his self-appointed job during these years to build the army into an effective force, and here again his method was to raise the spirit rather than insist too strongly on discipline. There must be loyalty, there must be *esprit de corps*; politics must be eschewed; outside interference must be quashed. Cumberland, as Captain General, had found the army lax and inefficient: the officers, chosen by the usual eighteenth-century methods of favouritism, too often incompetent, and the men given over to riot and licence. He proposed to introduce a new strictness into the Mutiny Act. His suggestions were opposed by the followers of Leicester House, not on merits but because the Prince of Wales looked with a suspicious eye on any increase in the power and dignity of his younger brother. Pitt wished to keep a footing in the Prince's camp, expecting as he did that his own accession to power might coincide with the beginning of a new reign, but here was a point where conviction fought with interest and conviction won. Yet, to be honest, it must be added that the breach with the Prince was perhaps the less important and the less likely to be enduring, in that Pitt was, after all, merely supporting prerogative; the army was the instrument of the executive, and while the executive must, of course, use it under the control of Parliament, it must have a free hand in all questions of discipline and establishment. 'Our business,' said Pitt, 'is to consider what number of regular forces may be necessary for the defence of the nation and to grant money for maintaining that number; but we have no business with the conduct of the army, or with their complaints against one another, which belongs to the King alone or such as shall be commissioned by him.'[1] It would be a bad day when the army could appeal direct to the House, and it was unnecessary: 'the only danger,' he declared, 'of oppression under martial law is when the direction of the army becomes wicked or

[1] Speech, 7th February 1750. *Parliamentary History*, Vol. XIV.

the army itself loses its virtue.' If left unmolested, the army must
keep itself pure, for 'I believe that as a colonel's life as well as
character very often in time of war depends upon the behaviour
of his regiment, every colonel will choose to have a regiment
of brave and well-disciplined soldiers, rather than a regiment of
voters at an election.' The struggle over the Mutiny Act lasted
until the Prince's death in 1751, and formed the main bone of
parliamentary contention during these years of legislative inac-
tivity. 'The Mutiny Bill,' Pitt confided to Grenville in January
1750, 'at present employs all our time, and all our rhetoric on all
sides.'[1]

Besides working to improve the fighting services, Pitt was
worried at this period about England's finances. Pelham was not
a financial genius, but he was an orthodox and careful Chancellor
of the Exchequer. He realised to the full the burden which the
war had imposed on the country, and he was striving with all his
might to reduce that burden and restore the finances. Striking
measures were not to be expected from this mild bourgeois,
and striking measures were conspicuous by their absence. But
orthodoxy was to be expected, and some degree of competence.
Pelham was economical and hard-working, and his efforts met
with a large measure of success. He secured a reduction of interest
on the national debt; he cut down expenses as rapidly as possible.
Beyond that he was not able to go. Whether Pitt's reference to
excise was an effort to spur Pelham on, or a kite flown at Pelham's
request, will never be known, but it is certain that no scheme for
reforming the basis of taxation was produced—everything went
slowly, desperately slowly, along the usual lines of retrenchment
and orthodox finance.

Meanwhile Pitt watched and waited with exemplary patience.
Hardest of all, he curbed his national pride. In February 1750 Lord
Egmont moved in the House that we should insist on France
completing the demolition of Dunkirk. The destruction of the
harbour was one of the conditions of the peace and no steps had
been taken to carry it out. We ought now, so it was urged, to
demand compliance. Such a motion, said Pitt, was not only
unwise and dangerous but wicked, because it involved the risk of
war. And war we could not face at the moment, nor until time
had freed us from 'a great part of that load of debt we groan
under at present,' and had established 'our public credit upon a

---

[1] Pitt to Grenville, 20 Jan. 1749-50. Grenville. *Correspondence*, I, 94.

basis which it will be hardly possible to shake.' The wiseacres of Parliament seized upon his humility to twit him with inconsistency; this truckling to the enemy was something new and something disgraceful. 'I must confess,' Pitt retorted mildly, 'that I have upon some former occasions, by the heat of youth and the warmth of a debate, been hurried into expressions, which upon cool recollection I have heartily repented.' Others had done the same—not least Lord Egmont himself. What, Pitt suggested, they ought to consider was not his personal inconsistencies but 'whether in the present circumstances of Europe, it would be wise in us to hurry ourselves into a new war with France.' A few years might make all the difference, and in the meantime, we must wait with patience.[1]

All this watching and waiting, all this preparation had a definite end in view, however vaguely it might as yet be formulated in Pitt's mind. There can be no reasonable doubt that somewhere in the background of his consciousness lurked a conviction that England and France must come to grips again, and that the prize, if not the venue, must lie in America. His speeches and his letters continually look forward to the future, to the time when England's glory would revive, when the days of waiting would be past and the days of fulfilment would have arrived; and the predominant characteristic of this period was a riper and more mature form of that prudence which Pitt had shown in the first flush of youth. This capacity for waiting and watching has been overlooked in the suddenness and brilliance of Pitt's later achievements, yet it was the essential complement of his daring and reappears throughout his life—sometimes with disastrous effects. It was this caution which made him prop up the Pelham administration, and governed much of his advice to them. It was this caution which settled, *inter alia*, his attitude towards the other Whig factions, the most important of which was the 'Bloomsbury gang.' Its chief, the Duke of Bedford, that evil genius of the eighteenth century, was Newcastle's colleague, the other Secretary of State. There had been a time when Newcastle and Bedford had been on good terms; but that was when Bedford was Lord Lieutenant of Ireland, a virtual exile and without influence in home affairs. Now that Bedford was his colleague, Newcastle began to reflect that he was *persona grata* with the Duke of Cumberland and Princess Amelia, that he was a powerful magnate

[1] Speech, 5th February 1750. *Parliamentary History*, Vol. XIV.

with devoted followers and interested retainers. Fox, that unknown quantity, was his man; so was Lord Sandwich at the Admiralty; so were other and smaller fry. Newcastle felt the stirrings of jealousy and began to look around for someone to take his place, someone who would be a nonentity and devoted to Newcastle. He began also to prepare the ground, sowing seeds of dislike in the King's heart and pouring embittered reflections down Pelham's ear. The whispering campaign was on—Bedford must go. Pelham was distressed at the thought; he wanted to keep Bedford in office not because he fancied either his person or his abilities, but for precisely the reason which made Newcastle anxious to get rid of him. Bedford was a man of substance, and while this fact grated upon Newcastle, it made Pelham chary of annoying him. Why make unnecessary enemies? Especially as Bedford was remarkable for doing nothing? 'The Duke of Bedford,' Pelham assured Newcastle, 'is scarce ever in town but on a Regency day, and then there is so much to do, and so little done, that I cannot pretend to answer for consequences.'[1] If this was how Bedford worked when the King and Newcastle were abroad and the regency gave him at least a share in the royal power, how much less would his indolence perform when the King and Newcastle were at home and busy doing their own jobs? On the other hand, to turn him out was to make an enemy: 'I take for granted any proposed change [in the Ministry] will end in a breach; but, if not, where do we stand then? The Duke of Bedford will, it is true, be out of an office, in which he makes a bad figure; but he, his family, and friends, will be nearer court than ever. He will come there with the grace of obliging the King; and if intrigues are what we fear, and nothing else do I see that is to be feared, how many more opportunities will they have for that purpose.'[2] This was an extremely cautious attitude, showing a preference for King Log over any possible King Stork, and, fully in keeping with his 'prudence,' it was an attitude approved by Pitt. He had no opinion of Bedford, or at least not sufficient to cultivate him—'the noble Duke, your Grace's colleague,' he confided to Newcastle, 'I have not the honour to talk with upon business';[3] yet he, like Pelham, held back from Newcastle's proposal to drive him from office. 'Your Grace's object,' he wrote

---

[1] Pelham to Newcastle, 2nd July 1750. Add. MSS. 32,721.
[2] Bedford. *Correspondence*, II, 85.
[3] Pitt to Newcastle, 19 June 1750. Add. MSS. 32,721.

in July 1750, 'I confess appears to me to be of a nature that it must ripen naturally and will not so well be forced. The numbers which may come to be concern'd in the event (shou'd it take place) and above all the spirit and very great talents, as your Grace admits, of *one*, renders the step arduous enough, shou'd it become ever so necessary. What I mean therefore is, be prepared, my dear Lord Duke, be arm'd every way, particularly with Parliament,'[1] or in other words, move slowly, move cautiously, test each step and be prudent. Newcastle followed this advice, at least to the extent of waiting the best part of a year, and then instead of dismissing Bedford, manœuvred him into resigning by the simple expedient of persuading the King to remove Sandwich from the Admiralty, whereupon, as Newcastle expected, Bedford at once resigned in high dudgeon.

[1] Pitt to Newcastle, 13th July 1750.   Add. MSS. 32,721.

Side by side with his streak of caution and prudence there ran in Pitt's make-up a suddenness, electrifying in its vigour and certainty. Let any matter of vital import arise, and the seeming lethargy, the very real patience, the hesitating caution were thrown to the winds. Pitt's whole nature changed and his letters took on a terseness and vigour that are as remarkable as the verbosity and circumlocution of his more 'prudent' epistles. An occasion for vigour arose in the midst of these barren years.

While Newcastle, in 1750, was with the King in Hanover, busying himself with the election of the King of the Romans, an alarming despatch came from Edward Cornwallis, Governor of Acadia (Nova Scotia) reporting that the French had invaded the province and burnt a town. Even Newcastle, disturbed in the calculation of his German subsidies, was forced to give it a momentary attention—he characterised the whole episode as 'extraordinary proceedings,'[1] and ordered the Ambassador in Paris to make a protest. 'As to foreign politics,' he wrote to Pelham, with the report in front of him, 'I really think things look well everywhere but in the West Indies . . . the news from America shews the necessity of making ourselves as strong in Europe as possible.' He thought that Pelham should take a firm line, though 'if you do, you may run a risk of rupture with France; but I think that is to be run; for if we lose our American possessions, or the influence and weight of them in time of peace, France will with great ease make war with us whenever they please.'[2] But a few days later he had practically forgotten America in the absorbing jig-saw puzzle of Austria and the Princes of the Empire.[3]

Not so Pitt. His correspondence with Newcastle was difficult.

[1] Newcastle to Bedford, June 9/20, 1750. Add. MSS. 32,721.
[2] Newcastle to Pelham, 9/20 June 1750. Add. MSS. 32,721.
[3] Newcastle to Pelham, 17/23 June 1750. Add. MSS. 32,721.

No letters so laboured, so fulsome, so contorted, could be written with ease, and Pitt wrote only when constrained by necessity. But the news from America was a spur not to be escaped, and Pitt wrote quickly, emphatically and without restraint. He was driven on by the 'difficulties that seem to threaten. I mean the affair of Nova Scotia, and very alarming, I confess, it is to me. Your Grace will soon see, perhaps you already do, if France be in earnest to maintain that act of violence; if she be, I can't figure to myself a more unhappy event; for His Majesty's right to the country in question, and the infinite importance to all North America of asserting that right, I find are equally undeniable. . . . This step being taken under orders of a Governour sent out by France since the Peace has an ugly aspect and looks like a measure not slightly undertaken. . . . I shall for myself remain in the utmost anxiety about the turn this affair will take and in the meantime most heartily condole with your Grace upon it. If France can be brought to reason at all, it imports infinitely that she shou'd be so speedily.'[1]

The affair in question was the burning of Beaubassin on the Acadian frontier and was more symptomatic than dangerous. The interest which France took in her colonies differed fundamentally from the interest which England took in hers. The French were logical and full of ideas. The English were hardly ever logical; they left the colonies to grow. The result in each case was surprising. France conceived a grand strategy by which the American continent would become wholly French except for a small strip on the eastern border where the English would eke out a precarious existence, hemmed in by the sea on one side and by mountains and enemies on the other. The difficulty which in the end brought down the schemes of France was the lack of men and consequently the lack of vitality. For men she substituted logic and leaden plaques, the former deciding where she should assert sovereignty and the latter proclaiming it. Céleron de Bienville, under orders from the Marquis de la Galissonière, the Governor of Canada, had travelled precariously down the Ohio Valley in 1749, proclaiming French sovereignty to the primeval woods by hanging coats of arms on the trees, and burying lead notices in the soil. It was all very impressive to the intrepid company of his adherents, but it meant less than nothing to the Indians who had decamped before his approach and could not

[1] Pitt to Newcastle, 19 June 1750. Add. MSS. 32,721.

read the notices on their return; it meant less than nothing to the English traders, who were not concerned with the feudal claims of overlordship, but only with the tangible and very modern profits of trading. The English swarmed over the mountain frontiers of the Alleghanies and down into the forests and valleys beyond to trade and barter and grow rich. They were bold and enterprising; they were rough and lawless; they were pulsing with life and licence, dealing with the Indians as man to man, on a friendly or at least a human footing.

The French methods were different. When they moved, they came in ordered companies, not to barter or trade, but to proclaim an overlordship that meant nothing to the natives. When they returned, they left behind not a depot or a merchant, but a priest who very ably confused in the simple Indian mind the persons of the King of France and the Founder of Christianity. If the English trader gave the natives drink, the French priest gave them superstitions.

In Acadia, or Nova Scotia, the priests were particularly active under the leadership of Le Loutre, a burning and fanatical patriot, somewhat underestimated by Cornwallis, who called him 'a good-for-nothing scoundrel.' The results of his efforts were more than usually atrocious. By the threat of damnation he prevented the inhabitants, both French and Indian, from taking an oath of allegiance to the English King after Acadia had been ceded and kept them in a state of restless perplexity. His activities were carried on from over the border, and in order to keep a check upon him Cornwallis sent an English force under Major Lawrence to Beaubassin in April 1750. Le Loutre got wind of their approach and promptly set fire to the church and huts of the small town and compelled the inhabitants to cross over into French territory. It was this act of violence which caused such heart-searching to Pitt when the news arrived in England. Here was something which pointed the difference between the foreign policies of Pitt and Newcastle. To Pitt this incendiarism in a far-away corner of the wild new world was of infinitely more moment than the diplomatic quadrilles of Vienna. It had a touch of reality about it. Hence the urgency of his letter to Newcastle. The Duke tried to soothe him; 'The affair of Nova Scotia gave me the same concern, at first, that it did you; and I am not yet quite easy as to the final event of it,'[1] but a promise of redress and satisfaction

[1] Newcastle to Pitt, June 26/July 7, 1750. Add. MSS. 32,721.

had been given, and so 'the present disposition of the French
Ministry enables us to do these things, and talk this language,
without running the risk of a rupture; and this therefore is the
time, when a King of the Romans should be elected.'[1] And so,
with a sigh of relief, Newcastle had shuffled back from America
to his favourite auction room. Pitt, however, could not feel so
complacent. 'I am eased,' he admitted, 'of a part of my pain on
account of Nova Scotia by the civil turn of M. Puysieux's answer
to the complaint upon it: yet, I confess, I am far from being quite
at ease about the issue of the matter. . . . I will however hope the
best till you see further what turn this thing takes.'[2] And so,
having made his protest and offered his warning, Pitt relapsed
into a smouldering and uneasy silence, only broken when
Newcastle wrote to complain of Pelham's behaviour or to recount
his successes in persuading German princes to accept subsidies.
After all, from Newcastle's point of view, his diplomacy was
highly successful, even if it was not crowned by the election of
Joseph as King of the Romans; the American scare died down;
commissioners were appointed to settle the exact boundaries of
Nova Scotia; a treaty was concluded between Holland, England
and Bavaria; and Bedford left the Cabinet. All was very nearly for
the best in very nearly the best of Newcastellian worlds.

In February 1751 Newcastle's activities came before Parliament
when Pelham moved the ratification of the Bavarian subsidy. Pitt
spoke, and after defending the subsidy referred approvingly to
the alliances with Holland, Austria, Russia and the German states,
and the conclusion of the Spanish treaty. All this should lead to a
firm and lasting peace, during which measures of economy might
lead to recuperation in this country, so that 'England would
make as great a figure in a few years as it had done in any age.'[3]
But underneath there was a current of doubt. It was all very well
to keep Newcastle quiet by allowing him to be busy with trifles,
but the minnows must not be allowed to grow into Tritons. By
February 1752 Pitt was a little alarmed; the liabilities were
mounting too fast. 'If your endeavours,' he wrote to Newcastle,
'contribute to the honest end you aim at, namely, to check
foreign expenses and prevent entanglements abroad, under a
situation burdened and exhausted at present, and liable to many

[1] Newcastle to Pitt, July 4/15, 1750. Add. MSS. 32,721.
[2] Pitt to Newcastle, 6th July 1750. Add. MSS. 32,721.
[3] Stone to Newcastle, 22 Feb. 1751. Add. MSS. 32,724.

alarming apprehensions in futurity, you deserve the thanks of this generation, and will have those of the next.'

Pitt's interest however was waning—in modern parlance he was feeling 'browned off'—because nothing appeared to be moving in Parliament or out of it beyond Newcastle's petty intrigues. The only ripple was caused by the death of the Prince of Wales on the 22nd of March 1751. Nobody missed 'Poor Fred,' but his demise left a boy of twelve as the heir to the throne, and some arrangement had to be made for a possible regency. As ever, in those days of Whig jealousies, the Regency Bill was the signal for covert manœuvres. The King, disliking his daughter-in-law, favoured the selection of his second son, the Duke of Cumberland, but was too well versed in constitutional matters to interfere directly. Newcastle took exception to the Duke, because his appointment would give too much influence to his adherent the Duke of Bedford. Pelham was also frightened of the Duke, but hardly dared to ignore him altogether. So as a compromise they decided that the Princess of Wales should be made the sole regent with a council to assist her, on which the Duke of Cumberland would have a place. The Bill was one of no particular interest or importance, but it led to one of the first serious clashes between Pitt and Fox. The latter, a friend of Bedford and the Duke, opposed the Bill with some persistence and not a little ingenuity. He was answered by Pitt.

But, besides finding little to do in these barren years, Pitt was forced to withdraw himself more and more from public life because his health was going from bad to worse. In the middle of 1750 he had been restless and nervy. 'If I am an irregular correspondent,' he told his protégé, William Lyttelton, now travelling on the Continent, 'you must impute it to my rambling about; for I lead so vagabond a life that no letter scarcely reaches me as soon as it might,'[1] and the reason of his vagabondage was disclosed to his cousin John Pitt: 'I am a good deal out of order, and shall set out tomorrow for Bath' (11th August 1750). The journey, however, was postponed by 'an ugly quartan ague,' which laid him so low that he was quite incapable of writing,[2] let alone travelling. It was not until October that he reached Bath, where he remained

---

[1] Letter of 14th July 1750. Phillimore, II, 436.
[2] To George Lyttelton, 20th Sept. Phillimore, II, 437. To Newcastle, 28th Sept. 1750. Add. MSS. 32,723.

for a month or more, taking the waters and gradually recovering health.

He was sufficiently well to return to London when Parliament met and take a reasonable share in the session. He spoke in favour of Newcastle's activities, and also took a prominent part in the case of General Anstruther, against whom had been brought complaints of oppressive conduct while Governor of Minorca. Pitt, against the wishes of Pelham, ventilated the charges in the House, during the debates on the Mutiny Bill, though at the same time insisting that the House should not exercise the executive power by taking action against him. The following year his health was worse. In August he was at Bath 'much disordered in my spirits, and otherwise a good deal out of order,'[1] and remained there till the end of the year 'an old piece of Bath lumber.'[2] Though he then returned to the Pay Office, and was generally supposed to be much recovered,[3] he was in fact working up for one of the most serious of his attacks. The old restlessness returned, and after touring round Kent and Sussex, he took up his abode at Tunbridge Wells, where he told his cousin his stay would have to be long 'as my sleep continues very broken, and the irritation not yet off my nerves and out of my blood.'[4] So bad did he become that for a time he lost all hope, and his friends became seriously alarmed.[5] However, he began slowly to mend, and by October was sufficiently himself to be interested in the coming elections. His relations with his brother had been deteriorating for some time, and as a consequence Old Sarum was no longer available for him. He was consequently forced to apply to the Duke of Newcastle: 'I feel it is so anxious to my mind to rely on Old Sarum, and so great an honour and pleasure to owe obligations to your Grace, that if it does not break too much into arrangements you may have made, I shall esteem myself most highly honour'd by this additional mark of your Grace's favour.'[6] Newcastle replied at once, promising to nominate him for Aldborough (Yorks). Matters being thus satisfactorily settled, Pitt retired to Bath, where he divided his time between nursing his gout and building a house in the Circus. The cloud over his spirits seems in part at least to have been dissipated, but in its place came

---

[1] To John Pitt, 24 August 1752. [2] To John Pitt, 23rd Dec. 1752.
[3] See Pelham to Newcastle, 24th July 1753. Add. MSS. 32,732.
[4] To John Pitt, 31st July 1753.
[5] Temple to Newcastle, 2nd August 1753. Add. MSS. 32,732.
[6] To Newcastle, 6th October 1753. Add. MSS. 32,733.

violent attacks of gout. 'I am extremely sensible,' he wrote to
Lyttelton on the 16th of February 1754, 'of your friendly and kind
remembrance of your faithful servant, now under the wholesome
but painful discipline of fit the second of gout in both feet; I was
just beginning to use my feet when I lost them again, and have
been for this week in much pain, and nailed fast to my great chair.'[1]

He was 'still at Bath, under the third fit of the gout in both my
feet, or rather a continuation of the same fit, with some remis-
sions' when on the 6th of March 1754 he received alarming news
of Pelham's health. He immediately wrote a few lines to Newcastle,
and indulged in hyperbole which for once was true: 'I cannot
express the mortification it is to me not to be near your Grace,
and attend you on this melancholy occasion. Let me assure you
that every adverse and unhappy event which threatens you and
yours, makes me feel with the warmer sensibility and affection the
unalterable attachment with which I am ever yours.'[2] His anxiety
was real enough; it was maddening to be tied to his great chair
at Bath when Cabinets were to be made; and he expressed heart-
felt hopes for Pelham's recovery. But it was too late; as he wrote,
Pelham was dead.

[1] Phillimore, II, 448.
[2] To Newcastle, 6th March 1754. Add. MSS. 32,734.

34

FRUSTRATION

Pelham's death was sudden and unexpected. A three days' fever carried him off and everyone was taken unawares. Even Newcastle had barely time to hurry back to London before his brother was gone. As for Pitt, the news found him utterly unprepared and chained to Bath. But the suddenness was not the only disturbing element, and the physical disability of gout not the most vexatious. The fact is that wherever Pitt had been, and however well prepared, he would have found Pelham's death little short of disastrous, because it shattered every one of his plans—those deep-laid, undiscovered plans which he cherished in the secret places of his heart.

Pitt first heard of Pelham's illness from Grenville, who laid no stress on the fact, for no one thought it serious. Yet Pitt at once took fright. 'The post of this day,' he wrote on the 6th of March, 'has brought a much worse account of Mr. Pelham than your letter which had given me much uneasiness. I am infinitely concerned at the state of his health.' At the end of the letter he reverts to the same subject in almost the same words: 'Mr. Pelham's illness fills me with infinite concern.'[1] Having vented his anxiety to Grenville, he vented it again to Newcastle: 'I write,' he assured Newcastle, 'in great pain under the third fit of gout in both my feet,' but 'the uneasiness of mind I feel upon the alarming news this day's post brought me of Mr. Pelham's illness is infinitely more sensible to me.'[2]

The next day brought news of the death, and Pitt sank into something like despair. He wrote again to Newcastle, a letter of condolence in which he declared that he was overwhelmed with the fatal news; that the Duke's grief must be inconsolable as the cause was irreparable; that the death was a fatal calamity and the most deplorable loss the King and the public could sustain.

Much may no doubt be written off in a letter of condolence,

---

[1] Grenville. *Correspondence*, I, 105.   [2] Add. MSS. 32,734.

especially coming from a master of hyperbole. But the interesting fact is that the letter is short and rings true. This harping on the magnitude of the loss and its irreparable character was more than was necessary or usual; moreover the same tone pervades the first letter written to the Cousinhood, when there was no need of pretence and no object in exaggeration. In writing to them he was writing a letter of advice on the attitude they should adopt when Newcastle set about Cabinet-making. Yet his letter plunges straight into the same apparent hyperbole: 'the shock of Mr. Pelham's death has affected me so powerfully as not to leave me in a proper condition to write'—a manifest untruth when the number and contents of his letters at this period are considered. And he emphasises that the shock is political rather than personal by adding the tepid words 'I am sensibly touched with his loss, as a man, upon the whole, of a most amiable composition.' The shock, it is clear, was not the reaction of deep friendship: those damning words 'upon the whole' give Pitt away. His reference to Pelham the man was calm, almost cold. It was the death, not of the man, but of the Minister, which so shook Pitt; 'His loss as a minister is utterly irreparable, in such circumstances as constitute the present dangerous conjuncture for this country, both at home and abroad.' What, in good truth, did he mean? Did he really consider Pelham a heaven-sent leader? Did he really believe that there was no possible successor? And what was the present dangerous conjuncture for England both at home and abroad? Taken at their face value, these words are so hyperbolic as to be ridiculous. The country lay in a profound peace both here and in the colonies. Under Pelham's administration the war with France had been ended, and the peace of Aix, however uneasy, still subsisted and was to continue to subsist, in spite of rumblings in America, for a couple of years; the Jacobite peril was dead; the finances were restored; trade was flourishing. It was nonsensical to speak so urgently of the present dangerous conjuncture, if Pitt was looking merely at the facts in which the country found itself. But Pitt was looking at the facts not primarily as a patriot but mainly as a politician. Pelham's death had shaken, if it had not demolished, the edifice of Pitt's ambition. Pitt had clearly hoped, and probably assumed, that the robust Pelham would outlive the old King. When George II was dead, Pelham might die or resign as soon as he liked and a successor would easily be found—would, in fact, be waiting. No sense can be made of Pitt's early career unless it is realised that he aimed at coming in with the new reign; at the outset he was to be Frederick's Minister, and later on when Frederick died, George III's Minister. And now this death shattered his schemes—this death which in other circumstances might have been so opportune, creating, as it did, a vacancy at the very top and starting a whole series of promotions. It might have been so opportune! Instead it merely presented him with the horns of a dilemma, and that at an awkward moment. Should he try to come in to place and power at the fag-end of George II's reign, with the possibility of losing caste with Leicester House and declining in power and position when the new King ascended the throne; or should he stand down and see someone—Fox, maybe, or Murray—a man of his own age, firmly ensconced in power and definitely put over his head? Pitt did not know what to wish—and to make matters worse, he was not on the spot. This absence from London was the other burden of his letters; he could not express his 'unspeakable mortification,' as he repeated over and over again, at being tied down to Bath.

His absence from London left him very much in the dark. He was unable to sound anyone; he had no method of judging how matters were moving. It was irritating, it was exasperating—but perhaps it had a useful side. At first sight one would assume—and indeed it has been generally assumed—that his 'intense mortification' sprang from the inability to conduct negotiations for himself, if not for the Cousinhood. He was forced to act through others, and even his advice had to be given by letter instead of by word of mouth. But a closer examination suggests another line of thought. Perhaps the irritation arose not only or so much from the inability to present his own case as from the inability to study the actions of others. As he himself put it, 'I am sorry to be forced to answer in writing, because not seeing the party, it is not possible to throw in necessary qualifications and additions or retractations, according to the impression things make.'[1] It is arguable that at heart Pitt was not altogether sorry at having to speak through another's mouth, because he was very uncertain what he wanted to say.

Wilkes once declared that Pitt was the worst letter-writer in Europe, and the judgment has been widely accepted. Yet it is by no means true, and in one important sense might even be called wholly untrue. Pitt's epistolary style is often turgid, often

[1] To Lyttelton, 10th March 1754. Phillimore, II, 451.

obscure, often involved; but on occasions it can be amazingly direct and vigorous. The fact is that when he was deeply concerned Pitt was lucidity itself, and on such occasions he found it excessively difficult to hide his thoughts. Yet in much of his correspondence, hide them he must; and where the necessity fell upon him, he wallowed in involutions as laboured as they are unreal.

His letters at this juncture afford excellent examples of both his styles. For over a month after Pelham's death, he was bombarding Newcastle ,Hardwicke, Lyttelton, Temple and Grenville with letters full of comments on the political situation. The letters to Newcastle and Hardwicke were diplomatic and should not be accepted too confidingly in their literal sense. Even in the letters to the Cousinhood there were reservations, and what he told one was not always intended for the others. He warned Temple against Lyttelton's want of discretion, and in so many words told him that some observations in a postscript were 'not for Sir George.' He also besought both Temple and Lyttelton to burn or lock up his letters, and on no account to leave them in their pockets. When there was no actual reservation, he could indulge in deliberate obscurities, and seems often enough to have preferred hints to plain statements. To arrive at his true thoughts must therefore be a matter of some difficulty, but not perhaps an impossible task, owing to his moments of complete and obvious sincerity.

These letters[1] fall naturally into two series, those written before the new Cabinet had been completed, and those written when Pitt was aware of its composition. They should not be treated as a single whole, not only because the first series was written before and the second after the event and were therefore charged each with a different emphasis, but also because in the second series Pitt was dealing, as will appear, with an entirely new subject.

In the first series, however obscure he might be on other points, there was at least one point on which he was clear and consistent. Whether he came into power now or waited till the new reign, he must walk circumspectly, annoying neither the old,

---

[1] A full list of the correspondence relating to the negotiations after Pelham's death—from the 6th March to the 20th May 1754—together with the sources, is given in Vol. I, p. 249, of Professor Williams' Life of Pitt. It should, however, be borne in mind that, so far as Pitt is concerned, the first series ends with his letter of the 14th March to George Grenville. The second series begins with his letter of the 24th March to the Duke of Newcastle.

upon whom his immediate bread and butter depended, nor the new, under whom he hoped to attain power and glory. Hence in letter after letter he reiterated his main object—'to support the King in quiet as long as he may have to live; and to strengthen the hands of the Princess of Wales, as much as may be, in order to maintain her power in the Government, in case of the misfortune of the King's demise.'[1] This tight-rope walk was significant not only in its positive but also in its negative aspect. It referred to the King and the Princess of Wales; but it made no mention of the third faction in that faction-ridden age. There was a party which looked up to the Duke of Cumberland as its head, apparently cherishing hopes that on George II's death the new King's uncle would become the guiding power in any period of regency. There was watchful suspicion between Leicester House and the Duke's entourage. Pitt had been connected with Leicester House from the first, though the degree of intimacy had waxed and waned; but of leanings towards the Duke of Cumberland he never showed the least sign. And now at this juncture his decision never wavered on this particular point. It is therefore of special interest to note that from the first moment Pitt supported the pretensions of Fox to promotion as Chancellor of the Exchequer and Leader of the House of Commons, pressing the Cousinhood to acquiesce and evidently hoping they would use any influence they might possess in that direction; 'as to the nomination of a Chancellor of the Exchequer, Mr. Fox in point of party, seniority in the Corps, and I think ability for Treasury and House of Commons business, stands, upon the whole, first of any.'[2] Now Fox was the lieutenant and follower of the Duke of Cumberland, and at first glance it might be assumed that by this stroke Pitt was hoping to placate the third faction and get a footing in every camp. But it was not so. Fox's promotion involved danger. Pitt recognised the fact and indeed referred to it in a postscript: 'nothing is so delicate and dangerous as every word uttered upon the present *unexplained* state of things, I mean *unexplained* as to the King's inclinations towards Mr. Fox, and his real desire to have his own act of Regency as it is called maintained in the hands of the Princess.' Fox, in a word, must not become Chancellor, at least not with their acquiescence, if the Regent was to be the Duke of

[1] To Lyttleton and the Grenvilles, 7th March 1754. Grenville. *Correspondence*, I, 106.
[2] To Lyttelton and the Grenvilles, 7th March 1754.

Cumberland; but apart from this contingency, Fox was eminently suited to Pitt's plans.

Why was Fox so suitable? It is not difficult to guess, and indeed Pitt makes it plain in his other letters. As a candidate Fox had excellent qualifications; he was in the prime of life; he was capable enough—an experienced parliamentarian, a skilful debater and well versed in the intricacies of finance. No one therefore would be surprised at his choice and no one would have a legitimate grievance. But there were other less obvious qualifications which appealed more strongly to Pitt. Fox did not hold a very high place in the good books of Newcastle and Hardwicke, and so would not be entrusted with too much power or allowed to exercise too much influence—a very important point for, as Pitt told Lyttelton three days after his first letter, 'as a necessary consequence of this system, I wish to see as little power in Fox's hands as possible.'[1] Best of all, the very fact that he was so closely identified with Cumberland's interests made it all the more likely that he would fall on the King's death; 'the strongest argument of all,' Pitt declared cynically, 'is that Fox is too odious to last for ever.'[2] Here then was a candidate who filled the bill to perfection—a stop-gap until the new reign, not likely to raise awkward questions now, not likely to work easily with the rest of the Cabinet, not likely to last when the real struggle for power began under the new King.

All this was clear enough to Pitt's mind, but only on the assumption that Pelham's death did not alter the general plan of waiting until the new reign. Should that plan still hold good? It was this that worried Pitt, this which needed his presence in London. There he could get so much clearer an insight into men and matters. At a distance, he could only conjecture, and there were so many possibilities. The easiest and simplest way of resolving all his perplexities would be for all the contending parties to enter into a truce pending the King's death; or at least for a union of all those opposed to the Duke of Cumberland. This latter, Pitt declared, 'might easily be effected, but it is my opinion, it will certainly not be done.'[3] Then there was the mystery of the King's own attitude. If he really meant the Princess of Wales to have the regency, he might turn his eyes, however reluctantly,

---

[1] To Lyttelton, 10th March. Phillimore, II, 449.
[2] To Lyttelton, 10th March. Phillimore, II, 452.
[3] To Lyttelton and the Grenvilles, 7th March.

towards the Cousinhood as a bulwark against Cumberland's faction. If so, there was a prospect of bargaining, of demanding marks of royal favour, of securing a seat for at least one of the connection in the Cabinet, where he could be called to a real participation of councils and business, and could pave the way for a further accession of power in the new reign. Without real support from the King, it was far better to wait. The trouble was that Pitt in Bath could not sound people, could not weigh up facts, could not collect evidence for himself. He must rely on the judgment of others, and unfortunately he had no high opinion of their judgment. Actually he entrusted Lyttelton with such negotiations as he thought fit to make, from which one must assume that he thought Lyttelton the best, or at least the most conversant with his own mind. In either event, it is some indication of the unfortunate position in which he found himself that he was obliged to warn Temple of 'my apprehensions of Sir George's want of discretion and address' and recommended him 'to preach prudence and reserve to our friend Sir George.'[1] It is perhaps even more significant that in spite of his apprehensions he preferred to have Temple as a watchdog on Lyttelton rather than *vice versa*.

After the first hesitation, however, Pitt seems to have made up his mind to pursue the waiting game. By the 10th of March he was much less forthcoming. Three days earlier (in the letter of the 7th of March) he had warned the Cousinhood that 'too much caution, reserve and silence cannot be observed towards any who come to fish or sound your dispositions, without authority to make direct propositions.' Three days later he had passed beyond mere coldness towards underlings. 'The conjuncture itself,' he told Lyttelton, 'and more especially our peculiar situation, require much caution and measure in all our answers.' He did not wish to recommend 'a sullen, dark, much less a double conduct,' but he did mean to lay down a plan and not only stick to it, but keep others guessing. He would indulge in empty platitudes 'this and the like which may be vary'd for ever, is answer enough to any *sounder*.' If Principals came on the scene, 'professions of personal regard cannot be made too strongly; but as to matter, generals are to be answered with generals; particulars, if you are led into them, need not at all be shunn'd; and if treated with common prudence

[1] To Temple, 7th March. Grenville. *Correspondence*. I, 111.

and presence of mind, cannot be greatly used to a man's prejudice.'[1] All this is well in Pitt's more obscure style; it seems to say
much, but in fact says nothing. What was he really advising
Lyttelton to do? Suppose Lyttelton were offered a post—as in
fact he was—what did Pitt mean him to do? One would have
expected something far more concrete, some hint at least of the
posts which Pitt thought appropriate, some hint of the terms he
was prepared to accept or suggest for the Cousinhood. But of
this there is not a sign. All is vague; the only point on which Pitt
insists, and then with clearness and compactness, is that the
Cousinhood should not go into opposition; they should stay in
office, support the King and strengthen the Princess. Beyond this,
if they kept aloof and mysterious 'the mutual fears in Court open
to our connection some room for importance and weight, in the
course of affairs.' Looking at these letters in the light of history,
it becomes reasonably clear that Pitt meant to keep in the lower
ranks so long as the old King survived, but in those lower ranks
to build up a reputation which should serve him in good stead
when the time came. So, after the first shock, he reverted to his
prudent waiting game. The last step he wished the Cousinhood to
take was to push their claims to high office unduly. Pitt himself
put forward no claim either directly or indirectly, and when at a
very early stage he was sounded by Hardwicke wrote a blank
refusal—through Lyttelton. 'I am so truly and deeply conscious of
so many of my wants in Parliament and out of it, to supply in the
smallest degree this irreparable loss, that I can say with much
truth, were my health restored and His Majesty brought from the
dearth of subjects to hear of my name for so great a charge, I
should wish to decline the honour, even though accompany'd
with the attribution of all the weight and strength which the good
opinion and confidence of the master cannot fail to add to a
servant.' The nature of the feelers thrown out by Hardwicke is
not known for certain (see p. 246 below), but what does emerge
from the whole correspondence is that Pitt was very unwilling at
this juncture to press his own claims, and apparently not anxious
that his friends should press theirs.

Having reached his decision, Pitt's mind was set at rest. He
could now turn his thoughts to the future and mature his plans
quietly. And accordingly, after a night's rest, he wrote more
openly to Temple, though still with a measure of reserve. His

[1] To Lyttelton, 10th March.

advice was to preserve an air of moderation, almost of detach-
ment; to keep their own counsels and to spread an atmosphere of
apprehension 'by what we avoid saying,' and so 'to wait the
working of all these things in office, the best we can have, but in
office. My judgment tells me that this simple plan steadily pursued
will once again, before it be long, give some weight to a connection, long depressed and yet still not annihilated.' The important
words are the forward-looking phrase 'before it be long.' In the
meanwhile Temple should begin collecting a party: 'give me leave
to recommend to your Lordship a little gathering of friends about
you at dinners, without ostentation . . . in short *liez commerce*
with as many members of Parliament, who may be open to our
purposes, as your Lordship can . . . the conjuncture is made to
awaken men, and there is room for action. I have no doubt
George Grenville's turn must come. Fox is odious, and will have
difficulty to stand in a future time.'[1] Those last two words are the
keynote; Pitt was waiting, and his letters ceased. For the best part
of a fortnight there was an interregnum and Pitt used the lull to
study Bolingbroke's *Essay on Human Knowledge* which had been
published on the day of Pelham's death; incidentally Pitt thought
very little of it. 'The work contains a vast compass of reading;
it is writ with much clearness, great eloquence, as much wit
and still more arrogance; but I find it in some parts, not a few,
filled with repetitions, from my Lord's fondness of the matter.
The arrogance is so excessive, that great as the performance is, it
becomes often even ridiculous.'[2]

[1] To Temple, 11th March. Grenville. *Correspondence*, I, 112.
[2] To Lyttelton, 20th March.

35

THE DARKEST HOUR

Meanwhile matters had been moving in London. Newcastle was at first prostrated with grief—a little unexpectedly, as he had usually been at loggerheads with his brother. But, to do him justice, for all his nonsensical ways, Newcastle was a good family man, and the death of a kinsman never failed to have a strong, if fleeting, effect upon him. On this occasion he was genuinely overcome—perhaps partly because a younger brother's death threw some doubt on his own immortality—but in a day or two he had plucked up heart again, and was ready to accept Hardwicke's plans for filling his brother's place. What that long-winded but hard-working and by-no-means-incapable lawyer suggested was that there should be two, or perhaps more accurately three, successors. My Lord of Newcastle was obviously destined to become First Lord of the Treasury. The Chancellor of the Exchequer, however, must be in the Commons, and so it was incumbent upon Newcastle to select an obedient satellite who could introduce the budget. Further, Newcastle's promotion to the Treasury had best be accompanied by his resignation from the office of Secretary of State. Another obedient satellite should therefore be chosen to fill that post and act as Leader of the House.

Newcastle, now fully recovered, was more than happy to step into his brother's shoes. He expanded like a turkeycock at the thought that he was now head of the Government, and overwhelmed Hardwicke with thanks for the perspicacity with which he had picked out exactly the right person.

But, the first flush over, there inevitably followed a searching of heart, for the new dignity heaped upon him could not disguise the fact that Newcastle was timid. How best could he carry his burden of responsibility? And who were to be his obedient satellites?

The choice for the post of Chancellor of the Exchequer was

comparatively easy. The lot fell upon Henry Bilson Legge, a younger son of the Earl of Dartmouth, and at the moment Treasurer of the Navy. His life seems to have been reasonably blameless, but unfortunately for his reputation he incurred Horace Walpole's wrath by making love to his sister—unsuccessfully, perhaps because the lady disapproved of 'the meanness of his appearance and the quaintness of his dialect.'[1] His crime, however, in looking so high was heinous, and Walpole felt obliged to describe—with some relish—the less agreeable traits of Legge's character, proving to his own satisfaction that Legge's ambitions outran his abilities and so reduced him in his intercourse with the great to a lower level of flattery than Walpole considered decent.[2] He was certainly unfitted by nature for great affairs, but was useful in minor posts, and he had the possibly doubtful advantage of Pitt's friendship. From Newcastle's point of view he was unlikely to cause trouble, and if his appointment could be construed into a compliment to Pitt, he might even become an asset.

A far more serious matter was the choice of the new Leader of the House. There were three obvious candidates—William Murray, the Solicitor-General; Henry Fox, the Secretary at War; and William Pitt, the Paymaster of the Forces. All three had outstanding abilities, and for that very reason were unfit to be Newcastle's satellites. Accordingly the problem to which Newcastle and Hardwicke set themselves, no doubt with the best of intentions, was how to deny the post to any of the three. If one must be chosen, Murray would have suited Newcastle best, for Murray was a man of mild manners and mellifluous oratory, whose faint-heartedness made him a natural subordinate, and whose forensic skill might have controlled the House. But Murray had no stomach for the rough and tumble of parliamentary debate, and besides, was frightened of Pitt, before whose invective he cowered like a scolded child. He preferred the law and was more than content to forgo the leadership of the House in return for the post of Attorney-General. And so the first candidate disappeared.

Pitt was a man of very different calibre. The conspirators never had the least intention of choosing him, and they knew that they had an invincible weapon to their hand in the King's animosity, which they were determined to use as an absolute bar. But they had to avoid the insult of merely ignoring him. Their method was not without a measure of cunning, sly but undoubtedly skilful. Hardwicke set the plot in train by approaching Pitt at once with the most disarming friendliness. His message, sent through Sir George Lyttelton, arrived in Bath within three days of Pelham's death. What Hardwicke said is unknown but may be inferred with some degree of assurance from Pitt's reply (see p. 242 above). He expressed his own admiration of Pitt's abilities, and 'sounded his disposition,' apparently throwing out the suggestion that Pitt should lead the House. But to make quite sure that Pitt would refuse, Hardwicke offered only his own 'protection' and such help as he could give in trying to overcome the King's animosity—a help which alas! had not been effective in the past and was not in the least likely to be so now. Pitt fell into the trap. In his reply he deplored at some length the prejudices against him in the royal mind, prejudices 'so successfully suggested and hitherto so unsuccessfully attempted to be removed.' There may have been an undercurrent of complaint or even of sarcasm in those words, though the latter seems unlikely, but that did not prevent Pitt from reflecting that consideration and weight in the House needed 'the protection and countenance of the Crown, visibly manifested by marks of royal favour at Court.' The reflection forced him to admit, sadly but quite definitely, that in the absence of such marks he could not assume 'anything like the lead, even though encouraged to it by as animating a consideration as my Lord Chancellor's protection.' He made his refusal the more final by hinting that Fox should be the Chancellor of the Exchequer, and expressing the hope that one of his own friends might succeed to Fox's present office.[1] Hardwicke must have smiled a little contemptuously as he read the letter. It had been too easy to outmanœuvre Pitt. He was now, of his own free will, out of the running.

There remained Fox. As a candidate for the leadership of the House he was the most formidable of the three. He was the oldest of them; he had knowledge and experience; he possessed the ear of the House; he stood well with the King and had other powerful friends; and, for his own peace of mind, he had Pitt's suffrage. But the higher his qualifications the less desirable he seemed. Newcastle dreaded him both as the King's choice, as Cumberland's henchman, and perhaps most of all as Newcastle's superior

---

[1] Letter of 10th March to Lyttelton to be shown to Hardwicke. Phillimore's *Lyttelton*, II, 453.

in every branch of learning and ability. Newcastle had no intention of living like Damocles under a sword, and if for any or every reason Fox must be offered the post, he must also be jockeyed into a refusal.

It seemed an impossible task, for Fox, unlike Pitt, was evidently bent on obtaining the office, and, being as dead to feeling as he was alive to opportunity, had lost no time in pushing his claims. Pelham had died at six o'clock in the morning. Before eight on the same day, Fox was closeted with his friend and patron, Lord Hartington, discussing his prospects, and shortly afterwards called at Pitt's door, presumably to come to terms with him, not knowing that Pitt was at Bath. Then—still on the same day—he approached Newcastle and sickened Hardwicke with grovelling apologies for the opposition he had given the year before to that darling of the Chancellor's brain, his Marriage Act. He was clearly hoping to step into Pelham's shoes. But that was altogether too much. As Hardwicke pointed out, Fox would then 'be the Treasury, the House of Commons, and the Sword joined together,' the last named through his connection with the Duke of Cumberland. The most he could reasonably expect was something much more restricted, and Pelham's immediate functions were distributed without further ado between Newcastle and Legge.

There still remained, however, the office of Secretary of State vacated by Newcastle, and the job of leading the House. It would have been difficult enough to ignore Fox's claims to either or both of these offices even if he had stood by himself—unconnected, in the jargon of the day. It became impossible when the King expressed a preference for him. Hence the necessity for a further dose of chicanery and intrigue. Hardwicke and Newcastle had a twofold problem; first, and preferably, to get rid of Fox altogether, or rather to leave him in his present position of Secretary at War; secondly, if that were impossible and he had to be promoted, then to tie his hands and restrict his influence in every conceivable way.

As a preliminary step they decided to transfer Lord Holdernesse, the other Secretary of State, from the Southern to the more weighty Northern Province. It could be argued that such a promotion was natural and right; it was unnecessary to add that Holdernesse was a nonentity unlikely to challenge Newcastle, or to remark outside a very select circle that Fox would by that means obtain a post which 'will carry very little efficient power along with it,' as Hardwicke confided to the Archbishop of Canterbury.[1] So much could be done by way of insurance, but the primary object still remained, the object of circumventing Fox altogether.

The conspirators went about their congenial task like masters. Through the Marquis of Hartington they offered Fox the post of Secretary of State with 'the management of the House of Commons,'[2] or in other words a free hand in dispensing the 'gratifications' which made a parliamentary career so attractive and cemented the power of the Government. Fox accepted cheerfully; a reconciliation took place with Hardwicke and a meeting with the Duke of Newcastle. At the meeting the Duke quietly withdrew all promise of 'management'; 'he endeavoured,' as Waldegrave says,[3] 'to palliate, explain and excuse himself; that his anxiety of mind, the affliction of his family, and grief for the loss of his brother, had quite disordered his memory; that possibly he might have expressed his meaning in improper words; but certainly it could never have been his intention to give Fox that share of power which he now claimed.' Fox argued and Hartington remonstrated, but Newcastle's anxieties of mind and griefs were proof against all arguments and all remonstrances. It was not part of his design, as he subsequently informed Hartington, that 'Mr. Fox should have any power whatever out of his own office.'[4] There was nothing more to be said, and Fox promptly—and a little precipitately—wrote a letter of resignation which Newcastle as promptly accepted. Once more he had outmanœuvred a rival whom he feared, and put him into a false position. The post had been offered, accepted and resigned—all in two days. Who would think further of so irresolute a man? And lest the King, in a misguided moment, should give him another chance, Newcastle and Hardwicke made haste to put forward the nominee whom they had had in mind all the time—Sir Thomas Robinson, an ex-Ambassador from Vienna turned Master of the Great Wardrobe—a platitudinous and impeccable man, void of all parliamentary experience—an unwieldy figurehead of large physique and oratorical flatulence. The King accepted him, indeed rather welcomed him because of his links with Germany. By the 18th

[1] Hardwicke to the Archbishop of Canterbury, *Harris*, II, 515.
[2] Fox to Marlborough, quoted in Ilchester's *Fox*, I, 203.
[3] *Memoirs*, p. 19.   [4] Ilchester, *Henry Fox*, I, 205.

of March Newcastle had completed his Ministry to his entire satisfaction.

He and Hardwicke had every reason to congratulate themselves. They were the more content because they had not only gained their way, but had, as they thought, made doubly sure of Pitt, the one man who could be a thorn in their side. There had, of course, been the earlier correspondence in which he had acquiesced, however grudgingly, in the King's veto. But that was not all. They had since been in touch with Sir George Lyttelton. He had been negotiating for the Cousinhood; and he had accepted the sop which Newcastle offered—the post of Cofferer of the Household for himself and the post of Treasurer of the Navy for George Grenville, both lucrative jobs. More than that, he had actually and specifically accepted Robinson in Pitt's name. Walpole says that the acceptance was unauthorised,[1] and later historians have noted, as confirming this view, that Lyttelton paused for several days before telling Pitt the news. Even if that were so, Newcastle had no reason to doubt him. It may be, however, that Walpole jumped to conclusions. Pitt had certainly, in the first series of letters, voiced his apprehensions of Lyttelton's 'want of discretion and address,' and had urged Temple to preach prudence and reserve to him, but in the second series, after the mischief had been done, he seemed to have forgotten his misgivings and wrote with no trace of anger or bitterness; on the contrary, he displayed almost greater affection than before and by inference gave Lyttelton very wide powers of attorney by asking him specifically to 'say all you suppose I feel towards the Chancellor.'

None the less, when the news of Robinson's selection arrived on the evening of the 23rd March, it came as a blow. The next morning Pitt wrote a long letter of remonstrance to Newcastle,[2] in which he is supposed to have vented his fury at being excluded from office. Certainly that was the burden of the letter and certainly the letter was vigorous. Perhaps it merits Rosebery's description as 'the greatest Pitt ever wrote, full of scornful humility, suppressed passion, and pointed insinuation.' But possibly Rosebery was not so right in saying that 'unlike most of his letters it needs no interpretation, it speaks for itself'; for if it speaks for itself, it does not speak the same language as the covering letter to Lyttelton, nor as Pitt's previous letters, nor does it tally with many of his actions.

[1] *Memoirs*, I, 387.   [2] Add. MSS. 32,734.

To see into the mind of another at a given point of time is always difficult, especially when the picture is blurred by the lapse of two centuries, and confused by the knowledge of subsequent events. It is, however, reasonable to assume that Pitt did not foresee Hardwicke's plans, and on Pelham's death expected two results; first that Newcastle would automatically become head of the Government, without resigning his post as Secretary of State; and secondly that Fox would be appointed Chancellor of the Exchequer and Leader of the House of Commons. Pitt's first letters to the Cousinhood are sufficient evidence, and are confirmed by his conversation with Newcastle in the following June when, on being pressed for his views on the political appointments, he told Newcastle bluntly, 'Your Grace will be surprised, but I think Mr. Fox should have been at the head of the House of Commons.'[1] Fox's appointment would have made an opening for some minor promotions, in which Pitt hoped the Cousinhood would share. For himself, there was nothing he coveted; his eyes were on the future. On that assumption, it is easy to understand why he declined Hardwicke's suggestion of leadership; and even if that refusal is to be regarded as a mere move in a game, it is noticeable that he never mentioned any office for himself in any of the private letters to the Cousinhood. In contradistinction, the letter to Newcastle of the 24th of March dilated at some length on his exclusion from office, and dilated with much appearance of indignation. The contrast is made the more notable by the fact that the covering letter to Lyttelton was comparatively tranquil. All he thought it needful to say to Lyttelton was: 'I judge it upon the whole necessary to remonstrate as fully as I have done.' Moreover, in one vital respect, the covering letter was completely at variance with the remonstrance. In the latter, he warned Newcastle that after such painful and visible humiliations he could not be expected to take an active part in Parliament, and declared that 'my mind carries me more strongly towards retreat than towards Courts and business.' Yet to Lyttelton he confided that 'my plan continues fixt'; he would not quit office; he would not oppose Government; he would not even make trouble, which 'must at this time be faction; and faction for others' benefit, not our own.'[2] As a final commentary on his threat to retire, it is to be noted that before Newcastle had answered the remonstrance, Pitt had written him another letter which, so far from suggesting retreat, reminded

[1] Walpole. *Memoirs*, I, 392.   [2] Phillimore's *Lyttelton*, II, 461.

Newcastle of his promise to bring him in for Aldborough at the coming election.

What did it all mean? What were his real views? No one can doubt that Pitt's letter of the 24th of March was genuine in its anger and resentment—but not perhaps for the reasons usually ascribed. He was, of course, bitterly chagrined at having a man like Robinson put over his head, and to that extent at least bitterly chagrined at his exclusion from office; but neither the exclusion nor the mere indignity was the sole or the most galling barb. If, as suggested, Pitt had made up his mind that he did not want office at this particular point of time, it must in one sense have been immaterial to him whether Fox or Robinson or someone else secured the office. What Pitt was considering was not so much the individual chosen as the effect the choice would have upon his own future chances. He had convinced himself that Fox was innocuous because he could not last. With the death of the King, Fox must disappear as obnoxious to Leicester House, making way for Pitt. He had banked on Fox's appointment; he had been so ready to acquiesce that Lyttelton may well have felt no qualms in accepting Robinson in Pitt's name. If Pitt could accept Fox the dangerous, *a fortiori*, he could accept Robinson the nonentity. But Pitt, looking at matters from a distance, saw in Robinson's very vacuity a greater danger than in Fox's ability. There were two aspects, and in neither did Pitt see any comfort to himself. Robinson was not necessarily obnoxious to Leicester House; he might therefore be kept on when the new reign started. And secondly, his selection would appear to the world as a direct snub for Pitt, pushing him down in public respect. Pitt had meant to consolidate his position, so as to step normally and inevitably into power when Fox was driven out. But could he be certain of doing so, if Robinson were preferred to him? Might he not appear in the eyes of the public as a man of no importance? Anyone could be put over his head; his claim was not worth considering. Moreover it left Fox as a strong possibility later on instead of a discarded failure. Fox himself undoubtedly thought that he had improved his own prospects.[1] It was this fear that worried Pitt and sharpened his pen. The burden of his letter to Newcastle is not so much the failure to obtain office as the humiliation inflicted on him by the choice first of Legge and then of Robinson—particularly Robinson. It was not merely one

[1] Riker, I, 166.

humiliation, but humiliations repeated and multiplied so that 'my small share of prudence suggests no longer to me any means of colouring them to the world,' humiliations which made him doubt whether he could continue in office 'without losing myself in the opinion of the world.' And without the opinion of the world, where were his prospects? Here was the rub; let him lay his plans as he might, one scheme after another came crashing about his ears—first the death of Pelham, then Fox's refusal to accept office, and now this double humiliation in the eyes of the public. The doubt must have assailed him whether it might not have been better if he had thrown aside his prudence and his plans for the new reign, and had staked out a claim for the present, climbing into office and trusting to chance for the future. As it was, he could only hope for the coming of a time that seemed infinitely remote. 'When the day will dawn,' he told Grenville on this same 24th of March, '(for to my poor eyes it is not even twilight at present) I cannot guess; when it comes, may it show us a view men will see with pleasure, and not wish to change!'— i.e. the Cousinhood in power on a basis of popular support![1] Meantime his only solace was to read Bolingbroke's *Essay on Human Knowledge*, and pretend to be a philosopher.

Newcastle received Pitt's letter with perturbation, and he and Hardwicke spent a harassed week wondering how best they could reply. During that week there was a report of Pitt's death. 'The Newspapers,' wrote Sir George Lyttelton, 'have killed our friend Mr. Pitt, but, God be thank't, he is better than he has been for a long time'; and his brother, Sir Richard, added that 'the report of his death was a horrid lie to make the world uneasy.' It is an interesting speculation whether the report was put about by Newcastle to justify Pitt's exclusion or by Pitt to explain it. If the report was mere chance, it was remarkably apt for either purpose.

By the 2nd of April Newcastle and Hardwicke had both composed long letters[2] to soothe Pitt, but their effusions, which incidentally crossed Pitt's letter about Aldborough, merely served to reawake in his mind the pangs of wounded vanity. He answered promptly in much the same strain as before; he had been humiliated, and let the explanation be what it will 'what reasonable wish can remain for a man so circumstanced (under a fixt resolution on no account to disturb government) but that of a decent retreat; a retreat of respect, not resentment; of despair

---

[1] Grenville. *Correspondence*, I, 117.   [2] Chatham. *Correspondence*, I, 89-100.

of being ever accepted to equal terms with others, be his poor endeavours ever so zealous. Very few have been the advantages and honours of my life; but among the first of them I shall ever esteem the honour of your Grace's good opinion. To that good opinion and protection I recommend myself; and hope from it, that some retreat, neither disagreable nor dishonourable may (when practicable) be open'd to me.'[1] But he betrayed himself first by the halting words 'when practicable,' and still more by the postscript of his letter: 'I wrote to your Grace by the post ye 2nd instant, which I hope came to your hands.' Now the letter of ye 2nd instant was the letter asking for the Aldborough seat!

Yet if Pitt did not seriously intend to resign, he had been shaken out of complacency. He knew now that high office under George II was not something which he disdained to accept but something which he could not secure for himself and no one would give him. Moreover, he was hurt and dispirited. He began to think that if the labourer was not worthy of his hire, the labourer might as well take things easily. Why should he toil for others? Why play so strenuous a part in Parliament? Why not relax? The idea appealed to him in this moment of frustration, and he began to formulate it to himself and even to his friends. He was prepared to sit in the House—indeed, that was essential; he was prepared to continue in office—for financial reasons and as a jumping-off ground when the hour struck; he was even prepared 'to be called out into action when the Duke of Newcastle's personal interests might require'—but he was not going to weary himself. 'I desire to be released from the oar of Parliamentary drudgery,' was how he described it to Lyttelton, and added, half apologetically, half in explanation, and altogether surprisingly: 'I am not fond of making speeches (though some may think I am). I never cultivated the talent but as an instrument of action in a country like ours.'[2]

So much he told them; so much he thought for himself; but there was a deeper psychological change which perhaps none of them realised, and which yet was destined to result in the break-up of the Cousinhood.

Hitherto the Cousinhood had marched forward as a phalanx; the good fortune of one had been the joy of all, and the failure of one, a scurvy trick of fate to be deplored by all. They were

[1] Add. MSS. 32,735.
[2] To Lyttelton, 4th April 1754. Phillimore's *Lyttelton*, II, 467.

equals in standing, however different in abilities; and this sense of equality, though more apparent than real, had sustained Pitt in his struggle for royal recognition. It was notorious that if the King had consistently snubbed him, he had shown no leaning towards the others. The Cousinhood, in short, were all equally misunderstood—a band of brothers in misfortune.

But now for the first time there was a difference, springing out of that mighty solvent, success. The King had accepted Lyttelton and Grenville without demur and with none of the resistance which he had shown against Pitt's first entrance into office. And while accepting them he had remained adamant against Pitt, in spite of his admitted capability, in spite of eight years of obsequious service, in spite of the dearth of able men, in spite of the country's need—or, as Pitt put it, 'be the want of subjects ever so great and the force of the conjuncture ever so cogent.' Pitt had to face the fact that the King looked upon him as an impertinent upstart against whose name 'an indelible negative is fixt.' He recognised that the prejudice against him was different in kind as well as implacable—and he acquiesced.

Whilst Pitt thus accepted defeat, the others were feeling more jubilant. They had no reason to suppose that the King looked down on them; they felt that they were placing their feet on the first rungs of the ladder, and that they would in due course take their rightful position in the hierarchy. Pitt could still congratulate them sincerely, and they could still commiserate with him, but the parting of the ways had come. With success there was to emerge into the light of day the conviction, latent in both Lyttelton and Grenville, that they were of a finer clay and that Pitt, after all, was not one of them by right but only by sufferance. It was his ability which had raised him to their level, and perhaps they had thought too highly of it.

There was no break at the moment, only the beginning of constraint, only the first hair-line crack, but the damage had been done; the value had gone. The old happy intercourse came to a stop. Lyttelton was slow to inform Pitt of the news, and Pitt drew in his horns. He repeated the fiction of his wish to retire, and he slid out of expressing opinions on matters political. To Grenville he wrote briefly, 'you know so thoroughly my heart about public matters, that not even one word is necessary on that subject.'[1]

[1] To Grenville, 6th April 1754. Grenville. *Correspondence*, I, 119.

Of all the Cousinhood, only Temple seemed to retain his full sympathy, only in Temple did he seem inclined to confide, perhaps in part because Temple, like himself, had been ignored; and no doubt Temple, as head of the Grenville family, felt somewhere in his gawky body a touch of resentment at his younger brother attaining office while he himself was still unsatisfied. The Cousinhood was in danger. There was a slight rift between George Grenville and Temple as there was between George Grenville and Pitt, and there was a slight uneasiness between Pitt and Lyttelton. At the moment it was the tiniest of rifts, but it was destined to widen.

36

CONVALESCENCE

The feeling of frustration, the soreness, the depression, lingered on through the spring and summer, fading away insensibly as such feelings do. The gradual return to normality can be traced in small trifles and slight changes of emphasis.

For a few weeks Pitt continued to toy with the idea of retirement, but it had never been serious and became steadily more faint-hearted. He was first shaken out of his fanciful self-pity by a letter from Newcastle, confirming his nomination for Aldborough and telling him that in his present poor state of health there was no need for him to visit the constituency; Newcastle would do all that was necessary. Pitt was stimulated. The Duke's condescension touched him sensibly. He was gratified by the kindness; he was proud of the honour. Only one thought abated his satisfaction—'that your Grace has been so good to nominate a very useless person, and who, I fear, fills the place of a better man. I consider my political life, as some way or other drawing to a conclusion, or rather as arrived at its period.'[1] It was a nice-sounding phrase, and fortunately there was no one at his elbow to ask him what he meant.

A day or two later the Duke informed him of his election. Pitt was pleased in spite of himself. To have been the Duke's nominee rendered the seat 'most agreeable,' and differentiated it from all the other seats which, according to his letter, he had declined. He wished the Duke joy of the good turn the elections had taken and was impatient to wait upon his Grace. But his heart was still sore and so on all other accounts he was 'not in haste to see London, as a scene that administers no kind of satisfaction.' It was however significant of returning ease that he could not conclude his letter of thanks without commenting on foreign affairs. The Spanish Prime Minister Don José Carvajal y Lancaster, a descendant of John of Gaunt and well disposed

---

[1] To Newcastle, 20th April 1754. Add. MSS. 32,735.

towards England, had recently died. As France and England were both courting Spain, the question of his successor was a matter of some moment. The choice had fallen on General Richard Wall, an Irishman in the Spanish service, an acquaintance of Pitt, and at the moment Spanish Ambassador at the Court of St. James. 'I am extremely sorry for the death of Mr. Carvajal,' wrote Pitt. 'His dispositions were try'd and known; those of General Wall I expect everything that is right from; but the thing is yet to be try'd.' He weighed up the possibilities in a few pregnant sentences.[1]

Though, with the curiously human itch to reopen half-closed sores, he had disclaimed any desire to hasten to London, the fact is that there was no particular reason why he should hurry there at all. Parliament was not sitting, and when it did meet on the 31st of May after the elections it was only for a short formal session of a week—to give itself essence, in Walpole's phrase. Members, otherwise, were in the country, and Town was 'empty, dusty and disagreeable.'[2] 'Mr. Pelham's death,' Walpole summed up, 'has scarce produced a change. . . . I, who love to ride in the whirlwind, cannot record the yawns of such an age.'[3]

Even the Cousinhood did not think London attractive, and the Temples and Grenville paid a visit to Bath at the beginning of May. Their coming helped Pitt further along the road to recovery. 'I think,' he wrote, 'the cheering countenances and sweet converse I have enjoyed for two days, will go a great way, both literally and figuratively, to set me upon my legs again.' He used his returning mobility to visit William Hoare and have his portrait painted.

Meanwhile his sulky and slightly mysterious attitude, his reiterated intention to retire, and his professed distaste for London, were having their effect on Newcastle and Hardwicke. That precious couple were not quite sure whether Pitt's disappointment would make him more tractable or more troublesome when he had settled down again into harness. They hoped the former, but whatever their hopes, in the middle of May, about a fortnight before Parliament met, they thought it as well to make fresh overtures. Hardwicke approached him through Lyttelton, expressing a wish that Pitt would come to Town and take the lead,

---

[1] To Newcastle, 22nd April 1754. Add. MSS. 32,735.
[2] Horace Walpole to Chute, 14th May 1754.
[3] Walpole to Bentley, 18th May 1754.

and then, with misplaced and eminently lawyer-like caution, reminding him, by way of a cold douche, of ' the King's alienation of mind.' Lyttelton passed on the message, probably without much tact. It served a purpose different from that expected by either Hardwicke or Lyttelton. It made Pitt angry, and anger is a wonderful restorative for a wounded mind.

Pitt sent his answer under cover of a letter to Lyttelton which he intended to be merely polite. He talked about the delights of the country and his taste for it, which 'every hour takes deeper root in my mind'; it was the home of indolence and innocence, and he proposed to yield himself up to it. London he dismissed with a Latin tag, office with the wry grimace of sour grapes, patriotism with a surly resolve to do his country no harm. Then with a brief request to be told how long Parliament was to sit, he cut short his letter with the excuse of a gouty hand.

But he could not really stop there, and so in a sudden post-script, twice the length of the main letter, he plunged head over heels into a sea of politics. He declared that his reply to the Chancellor set out 'my poor plan in the exactest limits and extent of it,' though in fact he had deliberately given Hardwicke no intimation whatever of 'what consideration I might expect for myself'; offers must come from the Ministers. To Lyttelton, however, he was ready to confide his belief that if the Ministers were in earnest they would call him to the Cabinet. More than that, their wants were so great and would infallibly grow so fast upon them that 'if God grants us all health, our poor, depressed, betrayed, persecuted band, will have its weight.' All they need do for the moment was to work, as he had so often urged them to do, for 'the present security and quiet of Government, and the maintenance of the future Government under the Princess.' Then, when he seemed to have finished, he flared into sudden wrath at the cat-and-mouse tactics of his superiors. How dare the Chancellor, in one and the same breath, ask him to take the lead and 'claim to plead the King's alienation of mind'? Whom did his Lordship think he was talking to? Finally, a word of warning— no careless talk, no letters left lying about; 'pardon all these cautions; but we are beset with snares and dangers.'[1] It had not as yet occurred to Pitt that Lyttelton, and George Grenville for that matter, were no longer poor, depressed, betrayed and persecuted,

---

[1] To Lyttelton, 20th May 1754. Phillimore, II, 468.

or that Lyttleton at least was within an ace of becoming a chiel amongst them taking notes.

The end of May found him still ostensibly 'the same indolent, inactive thing,' living 'the vernal day on verdant hills or sequestered valleys where . . . Health gushes from a thousand springs.' But Health was doing something more than gush; it was stirring his blood and raising in his mind familiar images full of insidious charm. He could say that he heard unmoved of 'Parliaments assembling and Speakers choosing,' but that was because he knew the session was to be short and the Speaker unlikely to be changed. He could pretend that he enjoyed 'the absence of that thing called Ambition, with no small philosophic delight,' but that was because Ambition had no scope for her wings during the parliamentary recess.[1]

His real feelings were betrayed early in June when he returned to London, and returned, if Walpole is to be trusted,[2] 'much in discontent.' He snapped at Newcastle more in anger than in sorrow, and developed his political disgusts to George Grenville, who in turn retailed them to Bubb Dodington. What Pitt's soul panted for was not money, but power, and recent events had filled him full of uneasy doubts. He had not only received no promotion, but had not even been consulted; he had not only been passed over, but he had been kept in the dark; his health had been bandied about as an excuse, but he was the best judge of that, and his views had not been sought; his so-called friends shook their heads over the King's inveteracy, but they made no effort to allay it; and last but not least, those of his intimates who had been promoted were not being treated with the confidence and consideration they had a right to expect. Truly much ground for dissatisfaction.[3]

Having vented his disgust and despatched whatever business was to be done, he returned to the country, to brood a little longer over his wrongs. He was interrupted in this occupation by a letter from Fox, dated 20th August 1754, on a matter pertaining to his office as Paymaster of the Forces. A J.P. in Dorset had sent the Duke of Cumberland a heart-rending description of the hardships suffered by the Chelsea out-pensioners owing to the system of paying them their pensions (see p. 157 above). He had gone further, and out of the fullness of his heart had produced a scheme

---

[1] To Temple, 23rd May 1754. Grenville. *Correspondence*, I, 122.
[2] *Memoirs*, I, 392.   [3] Dodington's *Diary*, p. 304.

for putting all to rights. But alas! hearts and heads have a habit of differing, and the accountants, those hard-headed realists, had dubbed it impracticable. As the Duke was distressed Fox had reminded him that Pitt had once had it in mind to deal with the scandal, and the Duke had thereupon declared that he would be much obliged if Pitt would 'resume his thoughts of contriving some method that might relieve them.' Pitt answered at once that he had long been interested, and though hitherto nothing had come of his efforts, he would now, in obedience to the Duke's command, take the matter up again. As already recorded, he soon found the solution to the problem.

Was the J.P.'s letter just chance? And if so, was it chance that roused the Duke's interest and reminded Fox of Pitt's previous concern? Or was the whole thing—contrived or otherwise— a feeler thrown out by Fox? Pitt and Fox had been acquaintances for many years, but never so far either friends or associates. They had been at Eton together, but as Fox was the elder by four years it is improbable that their paths had often crossed; they had both been to Oxford, but Fox had left three years before Pitt arrived; they had both travelled abroad in early manhood, though there is no evidence that they had met on the Continent. In February 1735 both were elected to Parliament for the first time, Pitt as Member for Old Sarum, and Fox as Member for Hindon in Wiltshire, but Fox was at the time abroad and did not actually take his seat till January 1736. Pitt had consequently been the first to make his maiden speech, but Fox, who had taken the precaution to enlist under Walpole's banner, had made more rapid progress up the ministerial ladder. Both had soon become marked men, but on opposite sides, and were notorious for their sparring with one another. By 1751 Walpole was writing to Mann of their 'smothered rivalship,' and in 1754 Bubb Dodington spoke of their most inveterate enmity. But if they were opponents, they had perhaps for that very reason a wholesome respect for each other's ability. Fox had long ago admitted that Pitt was the better speaker, though he had claimed better judgment for himself;[1] and Pitt had within the last few days openly admitted Fox's claim to the leadership of the House, even if in private he had disparaged his character. Now for the first time they had something which might be called a common bond; both had been passed over in favour of a man who was infinitely their inferior

[1] Walpole. *Memoirs*, I, 62.

in every respect—in experience, in merits, in deserts. Both were angry; their discontents were notorious, and what attitude they would adopt to Sir Thomas Robinson when Parliament met was becoming a matter of profound concern to Newcastle, and amused anticipation to the rest of the world. It was not at all impossible that the two should come to an understanding, and almost inevitable that the first move should be made by Fox— if for no other reason, then because Fox was by nature shameless whilst Pitt was aloof and reserved. The letter of the 20th of August may well have been deliberate, and if so, it was in due course to secure some return. For the moment, however, the Chelsea out-pensioners were the only people to profit; the letter was pure gain to them.

Fox's approach came only just in time. In spite of the health which he had found gushing from a thousand springs, Pitt was not really partial to water. The late summer was rainy, and the continual rains had a bad effect upon his physique. Towards the end of August he 'began to want a little repairs,'[1] so much so that he retired to Astrop Wells—a fashionable spa, whose waters were reputed to have 'restored several that have been melancholly or maniac from Hyppo or Hysteria.'[2] Pitt's complaint was more physical than mental, but certainly included a measure of depression. Whatever it was, the waters, aided by plentiful exercise, provided a cure. 'I am now,' Pitt wrote to his cousin on the 10th of September, 'perfectly well, that is cobbled up by Astrop waters and the life of a post-boy, always in the saddle.'

[1] To John Pitt, 10th Sept. 1754.
[2] Dr. Short's account of the Spa in 1740, quoted in the *Purefoy Letters*, II, 290.

37

HESTER

Pitt's plans for the summer of 1754 had been subject to many mischances. In May he had told Temple that on leaving Town he was coming to Stowe 'where the charms, so seldom found, of true taste, and the more rare joys and comforts of true friendship have fixed their happy residence.' Whether he went or not is a little doubtful, but in any event his next move was frustrated. From Stowe he intended to visit his cousin John at Encombe. John was now a proud father. In May William had congratulated him in the quaint language of the age—or at least in his own quaint language: 'I began to wait for an account of Mrs. Pitt with great impatience, which she has been pleased to put an end to in the most obliging and agreeable manner'[1]—surely a particularly masculine and egotistic description of a purely feminine and altruistic accomplishment! Now he wanted to offer his felicitations in person. But John and the obliging Mrs. Pitt and the 'pretty boy' were in London and were not proposing to leave until after the summer had ended. Before they had returned home, William had been driven by ill-health to Astrop Wells. He still hoped, however, not to be done out of his visit. Encombe had much to attract him; it lay in the beautiful Purbeck district near Swanage and St. Alban's Head; it was green and pleasant and opened on to the 'dashing waves'; it was in the county of his forbears, and it was the home of his agreeable cousins. He laid his plans anew. When Astrop had set him up again, he would first go to London for a few days on business; then, towards the end of September, he would visit Legge at Holte. From Holte he would return to Bath, and in the course of October, come what might, he would pay a flying visit to Encombe.[2] Such were his plans, but they went awry. Instead of going to Holte he went, for some reason unknown, to George Grenville at Wotton, arriving there about the middle of September, and spending what was to

[1] To John Pitt, 18th May 1754.   [2] To John Pitt, 10th Sept. 1754.

prove the most momentous fortnight of his life. In the course of it he became engaged to Hester Grenville.

Very little is known of Pitt's wooing. To all appearance, it was sudden and short. Certainly it took the world by surprise, as well it might. Pitt was forty-six and his lady thirty-three; they had known one another for the past nineteen years, and no one had connected their names. Moreover, he had scarcely seen the lady, if he had seen her at all, between December 1753 when he had retired to Bath, and this visit to Wotton—this unexpected and unpredicted visit—nine months later. But expected or not, Hester was there, and whether by design or accident the two met one morning in late September on the banks of a 'Pond.' They returned to the house betrothed.[1]

The engagement may well have been unexpected by the couple as well as by the world, but in spite of the evidence there are some reasons for doubting if it was in any true sense of the word sudden. The first reason is Pitt's own character. If he acted that September morning on a sudden impulse, it was the only sudden impulse of his life. In his youth when the heart was quicker and the head softer, his love-making had been a sorry affair—slow and cautious. Northampton had produced its Dollies and France her passing flames, but Pitt, after a glance and a sigh, had weighed up the consequences and steered a prudent course away from the sirens! If Pitt had hankered after Hester Grenville, he had had opportunities enough through a period of nineteen years to succumb to a sudden impulse, to make violent love to the girl and to sweep her off her feet. But either she had never stirred his blood, or had been proof against his impulses. And now, if the argument is sound, he was to show that gout and the rebuffs of thwarted ambition are a tonic to make premature middle age more dashing than youth; and not only more dashing but more successful, so that, starting with the dead weight of nineteen wasted years, this shattered wreck of a politician, passed over in the race for honours, downtrodden and depressed, found himself in a bare fortnight inspired to conquer and willing to be conquered. The suggestion of a sudden flare-up of love between this almost elderly couple, long acquainted and eminently sober, does not carry conviction.

If Pitt was prudent, his caution was matched by Hester's. She possessed her share of the virtues and defects of her family,

[1] To Hester, 3rd Oct. 1754. Chatham Papers, G.D. 8/v.

but in a softened and more feminine form. Where her brothers were haughty and proud, she tended to be dignified and reserved; but if she smoothed the asperities, she did not and could not alter their character. Hester was not in the more ordinary sense of the words either attractive or lovable. She was neither strikingly beautiful, nor obviously witty, nor softly appealing. There was something hard and practical about her that smacked of the great lady, and a calmness that might be mistaken for indifference. The appearances were largely deceptive, since the reserve sprang more from diffidence than pride, and the calmness was the off-spring of courage rather than coldness. But it is not given to everyone to see beneath the surface, and Hester had little aid from nature or from her environment. Growing up among five brothers, she had, for her comfort, managed to avoid the two major tragedies of an only sister—that of being either crushed or over-masculine. She had acquired a protective armour of reserve which enabled her to hide wounds and face a hostile world without flinching; and if she had also acquired some of the more practical masculine traits, she had kept them within bounds. The final result was that she lacked the soft femininity which sometimes appeals to strong men, and the glamour which generally dazzles young men, but made up for both by an extra portion of protective love and the power of a self-effacing admiration of others. She was wholesome and calm, dependable and loyal—a pleasant companion rather than a disturbing influence; a support as opposed to an incentive. Her qualities—the unruffled common sense, the courage, the reserve—were the complements of Pitt's qualities—his flam-boyance, his flights of imagination, his rhetoric—but were not calculated to produce sudden starts or impulsive love-making.

If Hester was unlikely to kindle a sudden flame in Pitt, she was even more unlikely to throw her cap at him. Such conduct would have been in keeping neither with her character nor with her position. Nor was she likely to yield to him in a moment of caprice or heightened feeling; not even the fact that she was thirty-three would have jolted her out of her ladylike decorum. Though, equally, she would not have dallied or drawn back affectedly, if her love had been genuinely won. She was not without experience; for after all, she had had her suitors. They are somewhat vague and shadowy figures, but they had existed, and Hester had either frightened them off or rejected their advances.

Perhaps her attitude towards them had been influenced by her

LADY HESTER GRENVILLE

from the portrait by THOMAS HUDSON
Reproduced by kind permission of the Right Hon. Earl Stanhope

feelings for Pitt, which there is some reason for thinking had been of long and genuine growth. She had treasured up small notes from him—notes of no intrinsic worth—an invitation to South Lodge, one or two polite letters of thanks. For us, the real point of interest in them is not their contents or their language but the reasons which had moved Pitt to write them. In each case they had their origin in something that Hester had said or done. She had enquired after his health, and he is 'infinitely sensible of the great honour she does him.' She had suggested that he should break his journey at her house and he 'is infinitely honoured by her Ladyship's very polite attention.' In other notes he is full of 'grateful acknowledgment,' and marvels at 'Her Ladyship's extreme goodness' or her 'most obliging offer.' He accepts her invitation, but while doing so is 'ashamed to be so troublesome.' They are all very stilted and all very trifling, so trifling that their preservation is hard to explain except as an indication that Hester had long been interested in Pitt and that her interest was heightened by something more than friendship.

One is driven to believe that this love match—for love match it undoubtedly was—had been a long, slow, tedious affair. Pitt must have laid respectful siege to his lady with as complicated an outlay of 'batteries, saps, ditches and palisadoes' as would have satisfied Uncle Toby, and crept month by long month insensibly nearer, while Hester, to change the metaphor, was all the while a fruit waiting to be plucked. Beyond doubt they had long been mutually attracted, but the attraction had to thrust its way through layers of conventional reserve and snobbish humility, and surely, if the impediments added to the frustration of Pitt's youth and early manhood, and maybe distilled themselves at times in a flood of tears in Hester's room, their overthrow must have given a deeper and a more glorious colour to the flower of love when at last its petals expanded.

At last they did, and Pitt was engaged—only to find himself faced with another and the greatest barrier to his suit—the family. Their consent had to be won; and at the thought Pitt's courage sank. The idea of marrying into the great Grenville family was almost overwhelming. It nearly swamped his natural delight in being an accepted lover. Judging by his letters, the outstanding marvel of his engagement was the honour done to him. Happy, of course, he was; 'the happiest man that lives'—but he never mentioned his happiness without hastening to add an awed reference

to the honour done to him. That, of course, was when the engagement had been made public. As yet it was a secret. For a week or
thereabouts the two said nothing—not even to their host and
hostess—enjoying a short spell of private rapture before they
tempted the possible storms of family opinion. It was a little
difficult, because Pitt was eager as well as anxious, and Hester
was forced at times to elude him. But her calmness and skill
saved the situation—so evidently that Pitt in his first love letter
recalled, with a lover's unbalanced emotion, the thought of her
'kind absence,' when she had failed to keep a dangerous tryst.

The grounds of their apprehension were serious enough. Pitt
had two—his own unworthiness and his comparative poverty.
Hester with a proud consciousness of his worth refused to have
more than one; but that one troubled her. When the family had
consented, she wrote to her brother, Temple, with evident relief:
'your declared friendship for Mr. Pitt and his own superior
merit secured me from any apprehensions, but such as arose from
what prudential views might suggest to you.'[1]

Prudential views might suggest a great deal to a family intent
not only on wealth but on power, influence and dignities. To
Pitt it seemed incredible that the great and pushing family of the
Grenvilles would welcome so poor an alliance—so incredible
that one half wonders if he had consciously delayed his proposal
until Hester's chances in other directions had vanished. Now that
she had reached an age of some maturity, it might be reasonably
supposed that her value in the marriage market was reduced.
She was no longer likely to bring much power or influence to the
family store, nor perhaps much wealth to their coffers. Maybe
now was the time when friendship might come by its own.

None the less Pitt felt that friendship was being put to a severe
strain. 'Stowe,' he confided to Hester, 'still holds me in most
sensible sollicitudes. But I would fain not augur anything gloomy.
Can Friendship, which I have received so much from, that I might
almost hope for everything, fail me, when Love and you, where
I had nothing to pretend, have consented to give me happiness?
Yes, I already fear it may; nay, feel that perhaps it ought, when
I think what your establishment calls for. I am then, I cannot but
be, in infinite disquietudes for Stowe.'[2] Like Hester he betrayed
his real feelings in his letter of thanks, when he lauded Temple's

---

[1] Hester to Temple, October 1754. Grenville. *Correspondence*, I, 123.
[2] To Hester, 3rd Oct. 1754.

goodness and partiality in raising him up to the level of the 'kind, noble and generous fraternity,' before mentioning money matters and the 'infinitely too great a sacrifice of her [Hester's] establishment.'[1]

The financial side, which was all that Hester saw, did not loom so large in Pitt's eyes—though it was large enough. After all he had some resources, and he meant to make the most of them. The reversionary rights left to him by the Duchess of Marlborough and John Spencer gave a lustre to his patrimony which time had not yet proved to be spurious. He could put up a façade and must hope that the emptiness behind would be overlooked.

Perhaps both Hester and Pitt were unduly alarmed. In money matters Temple was not mean; on the contrary, he might even be called generous. It pleased him to fling largesse in a lordly fashion, and he did it rather indiscriminately, relying more upon the gratification of his feelings than upon the merits of the recipients. He dismissed the financial side with a wave of his hand, allowed friendship full scope, and gave the couple his blessing.

It was left to Hester's second brother, the meticulous George, to look into the question of money, and with him Pitt ventured to have an opinion of his own. It is curious and noteworthy that Pitt never felt either the same affection or the same veneration for George as for his elder brother. George was clever enough, and in his way much superior to his brother; but he lacked the patent of nobility; he was nearer Pitt's own standing. Pitt could therefore urge and insist on his own views. He had little enough to put into the marriage settlement compared with Hester's £14,000 in the Reduced Bank Annuities. All he could offer was his reversionary rights—dazzling in one respect but delusive and never to be realised. Such as they were George Grenville wanted them all tied up on his sister, and with his usual officious zeal undertook the business of drafting the settlement with Pitt's solicitor, Mr. Nuthall. Pitt, barely recovered from the delight of being accepted by Hester and her family, was grateful to George for his 'kind attention.' George, with that pedantic and pig-headed diplomacy which subsequently lost the American colonies by its mixture of lies and obstinacy, was offering to 'expedite' what Pitt called 'the most interesting work of Mr. Nuthall.' But Pitt found only five days later that George had used his opportunities

---

[1] To Temple, Oct. 1754. Grenville. *Correspondence*, I, 124.

to mould the draft to his own wishes. Pitt acted promptly and
firmly. He was full of gratitude for what George had done;
he was desolated at the thought of giving further trouble—but
'I conceive there may have been some want of sufficient explanation of my wishes with regard to the estates in reversion. Give me
leave to state in a few words how I understand it.'[1] The magnificent Sunderland estate was to be 'settled in the strictest manner';
but the estates to which he had a reversion under the Duchess of
Marlborough's will were to be left at his disposal, and that for
three good reasons. In the first place, if he succeeded to the
Sunderland estates, he might need money to pay Mr. Spencer's
debts—Mr. Spencer being the sickly youth who stood between
Pitt and the estate. In the second place, if he came in for all that
money he proposed to live as a gentleman should, and would
need 'elbow-room for a town house of some expense,' and perhaps
a country house as well. Thirdly, he would in those happily
affluent circumstances like to buy Old Sarum and be thenceforth
independent of his brother or the Duke of Newcastle or any
other owner of rotten boroughs. It was only if his expectations
of the Sunderland estate fell through that he would agree to
the Marlborough estates being tied up. In a word, he was beginning to expand under the strange and rather malign influence of
being accepted by a great and noble family. He meant, given the
chance, to stand on their level.

This attitude of haughty independence, still very much in
embryo, was one side of a striking result of his engagement.
Hester, in accepting him, gave rebirth to his ambitions. He found
to his joy and surprise that 'every taste of my mind, and more
serious purposes of my life, correspond to those of Lady Hester
Grenville.'[2] It was not for him, as yet, to realise that she was
merely reflecting his inmost wishes. Sufficient the fact that she
did reflect, and by so doing presented to him once more the
glowing ambitions which had been hidden under a veil of
disappointment.

With the revival of ambition Pitt began to live in a tornado of
impatience. From the indolent admirer of nature, he changed in
a moment to the busy man of affairs, from the introspective
valetudinarian to the ardent and impetuous lover. Barely seven
weeks elapsed between his secret engagement and his marriage,

---

[1] Pitt to George Grenville, 2nd Nov. 1754. Grenville. *Correspondence*, I, 131.
[2] To Lyttelton, 31st Oct. 1754. Phillimore, II, 475.

but into them he crowded not only a vast spiritual upheaval but a very considerable degree of bodily travelling. Within a week of his acceptance he left Wotton for London, to storm through a week's business in a day or two. Thence full of gnawing doubts he posted down to Stowe in order to divulge his secret and win Lord Temple's consent. Having won it, he dashed back in transports of delight to Wotton for five days of open and acknowledged bliss. Then the two parted; Hester had her preparations to make, and Pitt felt obliged to visit Bath for the last time as a bachelor—perhaps was despatched there by Hester, who took charge of his health from the first. But Bath was not so peaceful now as it had been; the 'society of tea and bread and butter' was not quite so agreeable. He sought for distraction in sight-seeing and visits, even going so far as Badminton, only to find the weather bad, the palace vast, the day tedious, and none of it to be compared with the sunshine of Hester's letters.

The journey to Bath had, however, one great benefit for posterity. Pitt and Hester exchanged a series of love letters, which, dull as they are, do yet depict their individual characteristics to a nicety, showing the qualities which each was to bring to the common lot. Though she lacked his brilliance, there were many respects in which she displayed a stronger, firmer and more orderly mind. Her letters were full of news, while his were full of words. She had a penchant for arrangements; she made plans; she noted the times of the posts and how letters could be sent or fetched to avoid delays. It was she who reminded Pitt of duties to be performed, or even deliberately omitted to remind him because she knew he would have no time. It was she who refrained from writing because she happened to be in the dumps and was afraid her letter might depress him! There was a calmness and deliberation in her attitude, a sense of confident watchfulness. At times she treated him almost like a child—'my prudence tells me I should reprove you,' she wrote, because he had been out in a storm. But perhaps it was the maternal instinct, springing from a very real and deep pride in his genius—a pride so deep and real that she told him with complete conviction that he was her fame, her pride, her glory, and anybody or anything that protected him from injury was doing a service not only to her but to England.[1]

Pitt, by contrast, was humility itself. Most young lovers find a

[1] Hester to Pitt, Tuesday night, Oct. 15, 1754.

pleasure in comparing their worthlessness with their lady's merits; but Pitt was not young, and his language was more than usually full of hyperbole, sometimes delightful, sometimes pure bathos. Two examples must suffice: 'The tender warmth of your feeling, loving heart,' he assured Hester, 'has almost sweetly robbed me of the only superiority I gave myself, that of loving you more than you could love.'[1] And again: 'I told you truth when I said, to me you turn'd Poetry to Prose, that is to reality.'[2] Throughout the letters he stuck to a curious crescendo of 'esteem, respect, gratitude, passion, adoration,' as though recounting the history of his feelings. Yet originally the esteem had been founded mainly if not solely on Hester's birth; now it began to be founded on fresh merits which he discovered in her to his amazement and delight. He began to appreciate her common sense and precision: 'it belongs to you alone,' he wrote—meaning to her and not himself—'to discern and pursue what is correctly right, in all the fine degrees and delicate shadings';[3] and with a disregard for the more pedantic rules of grammarians he assured her that his letter 'by Wednesday's Post you have with most endearing attention provided for the care of.'[4] He revelled in the thought that she was planning for him and accepted all her views: 'Your own first thought,' he told her, 'I, for that dear reason, and for every other, wish the most,' and so, as the thought happened to be one for a quiet wedding, 'the less Preparation, the less spectacle, the less of everything but of your lovely tender Self, is surely best' —which from a master of display and lover of profusion was surely a touching proof of devotion.

Meanwhile he was impatient for the wedding to take place. The only reasons for delay were Hester's own wishes and the time taken in drawing up the marriage settlement. Pitt chafed at both. 'May I most respectfully implore that small niceties of the Law may be waived?'[5] and 'you seem to make me feel, and to wish to do it, without giving me pain, that my impatience gos faster than your Delicacy and Dignity can allow.'[6] He had hoped that the settlement would be completed by the 4th or 5th of November, and that the marriage might consequently take place on the 6th or 7th. But Hester was not to be so hurried; the earliest day she would concede to his 'most ardent and respectful

---

[1] Bath—Monday, 21st Oct. 1754.   [2] Bath—Sunday, 20th, 1754.
[3] Wed. 16 Oct. 1754. Chatham Papers. Record Office G.D. 8/v.
[4] *Ibid.*   [5] Letter dated Bath 30th Oct. 1754.
[6] Letter dated Marlborough Thursday night.

GILBERT WEST'S HOUSE, WEST WICKHAM

supplications' was the 15th of November. It was not a propitious day, being a Friday and the day after Parliament was due to meet. Fridays have a knack of daunting the superstitious, and the day after Parliament met was difficult for a Minister who was due to introduce the Chelsea Pensioners' Bill on the first day of the session. Perhaps it was for those reasons that in fact the marriage was—not accelerated, but postponed. Whatever the reason, it was not until Saturday, the 16th of November, that Pitt and Hester—Solomon and Esther as Lady Townshend dubbed them—were married by special licence at a private house in Argyle Street. The service was conducted by Dr. Ayscough, a friend of both families, a brother-in-law of George Lyttelton, and at the moment tutor of the young prince destined to become George III. Immediately after the ceremony the happy couple left for a short honeymoon in Gilbert West's house at West Wickham. It had been lent to them for the purpose, and became very dear to them, no doubt for its memories. Pitt had designed a path in the grounds; Hester referred to it as 'loved Wickham' and some years later Dr. Johnson was to describe it as 'a very pleasant house.'[1] It was crammed with provisions by the hospitable Wests before they left, and overcrammed by Pitt's chef (Mr. Campion) who not only brought large supplies himself, but ordered still more to be sent from Croydon. So far as food was concerned, the couple must have had a royal welcome.[2]

Marriage is always a matter of moment and always a speculation. In general the momentousness and speculation do not affect the lives of many beyond the two persons immediately concerned. This marriage, which opened at West Wickham, helped to change the world. It was eminently successful; it was exceedingly happy; it was in many points ideal. In all those respects it affected only Pitt and Hester and their children. But in quite another respect it affected the world in general and the British Empire in particular, by giving Pitt at this precise moment of time the ballast and confidence, the spur and ambition, essential to his famous Ministry. He could not have chosen more happily for England. The combination of person and time was perfect. It might have been possible—though unlikely—for some other woman to have given him all that Hester Grenville gave—but no woman, not even Hester, could have achieved so much if the marriage had taken place earlier or later. It came at a psychological moment.

---

[1] *Life of Gilbert West*. Lives of the Poets.   [2] Climenson, II, 64.

Pitt had swept and garnished his soul, not so much of his own free will, as at the dictates of fate. Until this year he had trodden a path which had wavered to and fro but had always been of his own choosing. At the outset he had deliberately joined Opposition, and had overthrown first Walpole and then Carteret; at the same time he had played fast and loose with the King, first flouting and then wooing him; then he had attached himself equally deliberately to Pelham and Newcastle, and in the hope of breaking down the King's antagonism had long eaten humble-pie and done menial service; at long last he had recognised the impossibility of placating the irascible old King and had acquiesced, looking forward to and working for the prize in the future. And now in this year he had passed through a crisis, when his plans had been rudely shattered by the unforeseen death of the younger and more robustious Pelham before the older and more doddering George II. The crisis had checked him and for a time he had been at a loss, dispirited and unnerved. He was disposed to believe that the chapter of accidents had begun, and that it must continue; self-help was at a discount: fate and fortune had put him into his quandary; they must provide the way out. For himself, he would rest on his oars—he would retire—he would sit back and do nothing—he was one of a poor, depressed, betrayed and persecuted band. In a word his soul was swept and garnished but not inhabited. And the vacuum was dangerous. Indolence, indifference, perhaps despair might enter, and Pitt might be lost. Instead love came in, and with it an extraordinary outburst of bloom and fruition.

38

OPENING SHOTS

The ambition renewed by his engagement lost no time in displaying itself. Even on his way to Stowe to ask for Temple's
blessing and whilst still uncertain of the event, he found time to
visit Newcastle and discuss not merely the Chelsea Pensioners'
Bill but also the trend of affairs in America. The latter was very
significant; though it must be added that according to Bubb
Dodington it was Newcastle who introduced the subject, only to
be snubbed by Pitt's haughty reply: 'Your Grace, I suppose,
knows I have no capacity for these things, and therefore I do not
desire to be informed about them'—a story which is much too
good to carry conviction:[1] certainly American affairs were discussed.

Dodington added that Pitt was likely to resign but not to go
into Opposition—a forecast which might have come true if
Hester had proved unwilling, but was very far from the truth
at the time it was uttered. From the moment Pitt was accepted
he became a new man. Two ideas possessed him to the exclusion
of all others—the need to hurry on his marriage, and the imperative necessity of girding himself for the political fray. Automatically he assumed the leadership of the Cousinhood and began
issuing orders. Temple, Grenville, Lyttelton—all his friends and
adherents must be goaded into action, immediately and urgently.
He told Grenville that his marriage must be hastened, not only
because of his impatience to possess Hester, but because of 'the
approaching opening of Parliament, and variety of other calls
upon my time and necessary attentions.'[2] 'I trust,' he added,
'Lord Temple will have an ear for arguments of such weight.'
To Temple himself he wrote in the same strain: 'Reason of
State says, Lord Temple can hardly be in town too early.'[3]
Then he turned to the Lytteltons. William Lyttelton had been

[1] Dodington, pp. 317-18.
[2] To Grenville, Sunday, Oct. 27th, 1754. Grenville. *Correspondence*, I, 128.
[3] To Temple, 1st Nov. 1754.

angling for the governorship of an American colony. Pitt
had long taken an interest in the young man—ever since his father
had put him under Pitt's care (see p. 183)—but he had not hitherto
moved in this matter of the governorship. Now, however, he was
galvanised into action, and took the matter up in all its rami-
fications. He wrote to Halifax, the First Commissioner of the
Board of Trade and Plantations, in whose province the colonies
lay, supporting the young man's pretensions. Then he began
sketching out the arrangements which should follow. On his
appointment William should, of course, resign his seat at Bewdley,
and his obvious successor—highly acceptable to both Pitt and
Temple—would be Henry Grenville who, as chance would have
it, had himself just returned from an American governorship.
Pitt 'ventured to intimate' these arrangements to both William
and George Lyttelton; then he broke the news to Henry Grenville,
persuaded him to write about it to Temple, and followed up
Henry's letter by one from himself urging Temple to give the
idea proper attention.

More important still, Pitt was scouting round for the policy
which he was to pursue when Parliament met. He found what he
wanted at Reading. It is worth recalling that after the double
shock of Pelham's death and Robinson's appointment Pitt had
determined to pursue a negative policy. He would wait for the
new reign, and in the meantime his general attitude would be
one of passive acquiescence in office and personal loyalty to
Newcastle. With the revival of hope which Hester brought, his
views entirely altered. He would no longer be passive. He would
rebuild the reputation which had been overlaid by his long years
of subservience to the King and now had been shattered by the
contemptuous passing over of his claims to promotion. That reputation had been gained by opposition to Government and the
overthrow of Ministers, and could be regained by the same
methods. He had long since lost caste with the King, and his
unavailing efforts to regain it had tended to estrange him from
the rising sun of Leicester House. Why should he bother about
the moribund King any more? And as for the toil and sweat which
he had lavished on Newcastle, they had been repaid by nothing
but condescending praise in words and humiliations in fact.
What claim had he on Pitt's personal loyalty? He was nothing
now but the relic of an outworn creed; he could be attacked with
impunity.

So Pitt laid his plans, and returning from a nine days' honey-moon plunged into a short campaign which was in some ways the most brilliant of his career. It was entirely successful, and showed him to be a past master in the art of parliamentary jockeying. It was perhaps more interesting than edifying, but it was very typical of the times.

Pitt reappeared on the 25th of November (1754). The House in which he found himself had been elected on plans prepared by Pelham, and carried through by Newcastle, so successfully that the new Parliament could be described by Walpole as 'chosen in the very spirit of the Pelhams.'[1] It was solidly Whig and very amenable to Newcastle's system of 'management.' He purred over it; 'we have as good a body of friends in the House of Commons as ever men had.' He had every reason to feel elated; only forty-two seats had been contested. In fourteen of those forty-two petitions were pending.[2]

The early days of each new Parliament were usually taken up with election petitions, and this was to be no exception; the deliberations involved were to last the best part of six months. Generally speaking the business was dull. Parliament sat as a judge in its own cause, and it was hardly to be expected that a newly elected majority, still jubilant from the polls, would pronounce in favour of any of its opponents. Consequently the debates were mere face-savers, dull and unmeaning. None the less, Pitt was so determined to begin his campaign at the earliest moment that he meant to use the unpromising material of an election petition as a peg for his opening gambit.

Lord Fane had been elected for Reading by one vote, and a petition had been presented against him. Fane was an old friend. Pitt had known him since he was a boy, and for old times' sake intended to support him. On the 1st of November, as he was returning from Bath, Pitt stopped at Reading to visit Fane and discuss the case. They talked long and deeply and Pitt found to his delight that it offered a greater opportunity than he had dared to hope. 'I foresee,' he told Temple, 'an event growing out of that petition,'[3] and it was in order to be present when the Reading petition came on that he had cut short his honeymoon. When he entered the House, the Berwick election was being

---

[1] *Memoirs*, I, 391.
[2] R. J. Robson, *The Oxfordshire Election of 1754*, p. 137.
[3] Grenville. *Correspondence*, I, 130.

discussed, and the unsuccessful candidate, John Wilkes, who had
promoted the petition, was sitting in the gallery listening to
the debate. Wilkes was destined to play an important part in
Pitt's career and in English constitutional history, but at this
precise moment of time was little more than a witty young rake.
He lived at Aylesbury, not far from Stowe, and taking an interest
in county affairs, had come into touch with Temple. The two
quickly struck up an acquaintance which ripened into real
friendship. Pitt had met him at Stowe and had undoubtedly
found him both amusing and attractive. Seeing him in the gallery
Pitt went up to sit beside him.

Meanwhile the successful candidate, John Delaval, tried to
relieve the tedium by a jocose speech, which the bored House
received with joy, laughing loud and long at his sallies. Pitt
realised that this attitude gave him an excellent opportunity to
begin his attack even earlier than he had intended. He descended
to the floor and directly Delaval sat down he rose to make one
of his best known speeches. He was astonished, he said, to find
the House making a joke of bribery, to find them quite uncon-
cerned at their own loss of dignity, to find them degenerating
fast into 'a little assembly, serving no other purpose than to
register the arbitrary edicts of *one* too powerful *subject*.' Pitt's
invective was always overwhelming, and was the more so at this
moment because it flashed up suddenly and unexpectedly after
many years of tameness and acquiescence. Here was something
unusual in itself, excellent of its kind, and founded on powerful
constitutional grounds. More than that, it raised a banner of
revolt. The Commons were, after all, the elected representatives
of the country; as such they had in times past fought kings and
peers. It was for them to legislate, and as the supreme legislative
assembly to maintain their own dignity, their own freedom and
their own sense of propriety. If they did not respect themselves,
no one would; but if they held their heads high they would
become as powerful again as they had been in olden days. Pitt,
in a word, raised the debate to a high level, and in doing so, not
only threw down the gage to Newcastle, the 'one too powerful
subject,' but laid the foundations of an Opposition—the Commons as opposed to the Whig magnates. It is little wonder that
his speech struck everyone silent and left the Members disturbed
and uneasy.

Whether Pitt had originally intended to take this high line of constitutional dignity when he came to support Lord Fane will never be known; it is perhaps unlikely, as he had no reason to expect the ribald laughter provoked by Delaval. What is clear, however, beyond reasonable doubt is that the gibe at Newcastle as overweening and overtopping was premeditated. Its introduction into the speech on Wilkes's petition was due to Pitt's burning desire to begin the attack at the earliest moment. And, as ever, fortune favoured the brave. If he had exhausted the main argument before Lord Fane's case came up for hearing, Sir Thomas Robinson that very evening supplied him with another, by being silly enough—perhaps honest enough—to say that the Reading petition would not take long as Lord Fane had a poor case. Here was an opening to delight the soul of any anti-bureaucrat. Pitt made haste to take it. Who was Robinson to prejudge a cause in that off-hand manner? If Ministers could settle election petitions by a mere *obiter dictum*, where was the liberty accorded to the voters, where the rights and duties of the Commons? It was a sad and sorry day for the House, such as he had never thought to see. Fox joined in the chase, following up Pitt's attack from a different angle and damning Robinson with sarcastic excuses; if his expressions had been irregular and blameable, the House must remember that he had been twenty years abroad, and in the circumstances could not help being wholly inexperienced in such matters. Robinson, as Fox afterwards wrote to Lord Hartington, did not like the baiting.

Of course, Fox had his own reasons for wishing to put Robinson out of countenance, but the occasion chosen was significant. His action was another, and more direct, bid for Pitt's alliance. He told Hartington the next day that while the occasion of Pitt's outbreak might have been accidental, he had been certain that sooner or later it must come. It had been a masterly performance —'the finest speech that Pitt ever spoke, and perhaps, the most remarkable'—the effect had been instantaneous, and 'thus we are already got to a point which I hardly thought a whole session would have brought us to.'[1] He meant to make the most of the opportunity Pitt had created, and his overtures, whatever they may have been, resulted in a meeting with Pitt on the morning of the 27th of November. At that meeting the two agreed that, at all events in the opinion of the world, Newcastle's effort to run

[1] Fox to Hartington, 26th Nov. Waldegrave's *Memoirs*, p. 146.

the House of Commons without a leader could not continue, and that Newcastle would undoubtedly make offers either to Pitt or Fox. What further took place is not known beyond the bare fact that the conversation lasted two hours, and that Fox found it 'difficult,' though he thought he had managed it as well as such a conversation could be managed.[1] They were in fact oil and vinegar, and were being drawn together, not out of any affection or real community of interest, but as a result of their own mortifications. Their approach was based on a mixture of pique and selfishness; each was thinking of his own advantage, but there was one great difference between them—Fox was taking the short, Pitt the long view. No definite alliance took place, but they seem to have reached some sort of understanding, especially on the question of tactics. Fox, as a more work-a-day, humdrum debater, was to concentrate on the discomfiture of the pompous and not-very-formidable Robinson, while Pitt, as the brilliant orator, was to turn his attention to Murray, who could always outshine and outargue Fox, but wilted beneath Pitt's vehemence and sarcasm.

That same evening (27th November) Pitt carried out his part of the bargain, and with contemptuous ease reduced Murray to a mass of quivering nerves. The army estimates were being discussed, and the younger Beckford moved to reduce the numbers from 18,000 to 15,000 men. He was well answered by Lord Barrington, who twitted him on his old-fashioned prejudice against standing armies; they were no longer dangerous, and indeed were necessary to police the country: 'the licentiousness of the capital, the mutinous miners and colliers, the smugglers, the destroyers of turnpikes, all the outlaws that increase of riches and licence produces and encourages, all were to be kept in awe. And so far from soldiers being a burthen, the country rejoices in being under their protection.'[2] All might have passed off quietly, if Nugent had not seen fit to intervene. Nugent was an Irishman, a patron of Goldsmith, a man of some capacity and a ready tongue, but unstable and liable to bouts of absurdity. On this occasion he took it into his head to irritate Pitt by fulsome flattery of Newcastle, 'not without allusion to Pitt's Monday speech,' and followed that up by declaring somewhat irrelevantly that there were no Jacobites in the country, and that many who

[1] To Hartington, 28th Nov. Waldegrave, p. 153.
[2] Walpole. *Memoirs*, I, 411.

thought they had nursed them up were extremely surprised, when the trial came, to find they were no such thing—much as a hen which has hatched out duck's eggs is surprised when the ducklings desert her for the water. Pitt saw his opportunity. After dealing shortly and soberly with the main question, he took up Nugent's simile and used it with devastating effect against Murray. Murray had been Pitt's contemporary at Oxford, where he had carried off a prize for Latin verse against Pitt's competition. Now Oxford was notorious for its Jacobite sympathies. Further, Murray's family, and especially his brother, were known to have had dealings with the Pretender, and it was likely enough that Murray himself had drunk in his youth to the King over the water—it had been a popular toast. But none of this amounted to anything, certainly not enough to outweigh the circumspection of his later life and his many services to the Crown. None the less it had all been brought vividly to mind the previous year when Murray had been mixed up in something very like a *cause célèbre*. Lord Ravensworth, an honest but impetuous man, had, on the strength of a statement by a Durham attorney, accused Murray, Stone, and the newly appointed Bishop of Gloucester of Jacobite leanings. The case had come before the Cabinet Council and had been debated at length in the House of Lords, and though all three had been honourably acquitted, the worry and anxiety must have preyed heavily on Murray's natural timidity. Pitt now recalled the case—indirectly but unmistakably. He also had known a hen, the University of Oxford, and he begged the House not to be too sure that all the chickens she hatched would ever entirely forget what she had taught them. He was little more than a voice crying in the wilderness, but he hoped that he would not live to see the day when those who ignored him now would admit, too late, that he had been in the right. Sir Roger Newdigate, the Member for Oxford, remonstrated politely, which merely had the effect of rousing Pitt further. He launched into a story of a party at the Angel Inn[1] which he had attended recently. The proceedings had terminated with God Save the King, and he had heard undergraduates beneath the windows re-echo the anthem 'with additions of the rankest treason'; then walking back along the High Street, he had noticed treasonable prints in a shop and had even been pressed to buy one. The story as Pitt told it was reminiscent of the well-known Blacow affair which had become

[1] 'A spacious old dirty Inn'—Northumberland. *The Diaries of a Duchess*, p. 2.

'the subject of general conversation throughout the Kingdom,' and had resulted in the imprisonment of two young men.[1] Quite possibly it was intended to recall it. 'Every word,' said Fox, describing the speech, 'was *Murray*; yet so managed, that neither he nor anybody else could or did take public notice of it, or in any degree reprehend him. I sate next Murray; *who suffered for an hour*.'[2] Pitt was certainly not talking out of any strong conviction, or any real belief in the treasonable activities of the Jacobites; he was giving Murray a warning, which Murray understood and accepted.

The rout of the enemy was now complete; Robinson could only look back longingly at the peaceful retrospect of the Great Wardrobe; Murray could only dream of the day when he should slide out of Parliament on to the judicial Bench; no one else counted. Newcastle's scheme had broken down, and new arrangements were imperatively demanded. Everyone recognised the fact, and in the uneasy lull George Lyttelton signalised himself by rushing in with a half-baked plan. On the 30th of November he happened to hear, at third hand, that the Duke of Bedford was inclined to make up his quarrel with the Government, and thinking this offered a solution, he promptly hurried to Newcastle to pass on the information at fourth hand and get what seemed to his heated imagination full powers to negotiate. Bursting with good intentions, he hurried to Bedford House and without any preliminaries offered *carte blanche* to its irascible owner. To his pained surprise Bedford not only rejected the offer out of hand, but immediately sent for Pitt and told him the whole story. Bedford fumed; Newcastle washed his hands of the whole affair; Pitt was superbly angry. The only effect of Lyttelton's well-meaning gaucherie was to precipitate the latent quarrel between himself and Pitt. They broke openly and the end of the 'Cousinhood' came into sight. In itself it was nothing, but in Pitt's spiritual development it was much. Hitherto, for all his leadership, he had been far too dependent on the Cousinhood; his genius had been 'cowed,' to use his own word, and, if he was ever to rise to his full height, he must first of all shake off the clog of his inferiority complex. His marriage raised him to the level of the Cousinhood; his break with Lyttelton proved his independence of them; the two together went far to resolve his inhibitions.

[1] Godley. *Oxford in the Eighteenth Century*, p. 256.
[2] Fox to Hartington, 28th November. Waldegrave, p. 152.

39

THE PARLIAMENTARY GAME

Although the attack on Murray was no doubt part of a scheme concerted with Fox, it went farther. There was always method in Pitt's campaigns, and though he may have adapted his plans to fit in with Fox, he certainly did not alter them fundamentally. On the contrary, it is probably more true to say that he absorbed Fox into them; for after all Fox was in himself an integral part. Recent events had revived Pitt's ambitions, but had not altered the basic facts around him; the King was still antagonistic, and, more important, older than he had been. Pitt was bound to play his cards with at least one eye on the future. He was still waiting for the new reign before attempting to seize power; he was still hankering after the arrangements which he had discussed with the Cousinhood in March; it would still suit him best if Fox became Leader of the House, and kept the place warm for him.

Bearing this in mind, it is easy to see why he took each particular step, and how far Fox's influence went. He had begun his campaign with threats against Newcastle which were loud-sounding indeed but actually very vague. And the object was clear: he had no hope, perhaps no desire, to drive Newcastle from office: all he wished to do was to frighten that very fearful nobleman and force him to reshuffle his Cabinet. His next step was to bully and ridicule Robinson in order to drive him from office. Up to that point he had acted alone; it was only towards the end of his attack on Robinson that Fox made overt approaches. Even if Fox had remained aloof, it is highly probable that Pitt would have taken the third step, because it was the obvious step to take. Pitt did not browbeat Murray simply because he had agreed with Fox to do it, but in order to warn him off. Murray, as all the world knew, was a man of ability, and the previous March had been in the running with Pitt and Fox for promotion to the leadership of the House. It had never been part of Pitt's plans that Murray should hold that

position. With or without Fox's support, Pitt had to make it
abundantly clear to Newcastle that he would be no better off if
he substituted Murray for Robinson, and equally clear to Murray
that he would be courting disaster if he listened to any offers
from Newcastle. By hook or by crook Newcastle must be led to
accept Fox as the only alternative. The measure of Pitt's success
is to be seen in the fact that after a bare fortnight Newcastle
gave up Robinson, in fact though not in form, and approached
Fox without making any overtures to Murray. To that extent
Pitt was entirely and brilliantly successful. But the whole position
was bristling with difficulties for all the parties concerned. It is
as well to consider them for a moment.

Newcastle's original intention had been to concentrate all
power in the hands of a triumvirate consisting of himself, Hardwicke and Carteret (now Lord Granville), of whom Newcastle
would be the resplendent head, and the other two the obedient
brains and hands. The Commons, under such a scheme, would
not require a leader but merely henchmen who would do his
bidding. He now realised that this plan had failed. He had thought
that Pitt and Fox would acquiesce because they had no option,
having been outwitted in the March manœuvres. Now he knew
that he must either conciliate or muzzle them. Here at once he
was in a quandary. He dared not conciliate both, for in conjunction they would overwhelm him. He must choose one, at the
smallest cost to himself, and then play them off against each other.
Which should he choose?

Pitt was, in a real sense, the most congenial because he had
fewer great friends, was less 'connected,' in the jargon of the day,
and owing to the King's distaste was unlikely to cut much of a
figure in the Cabinet. But Newcastle had wronged him, and now
was frightened of him. At the beginning of the session he had had
some hopes of placating him, especially as he had been given to
understand by Legge that Pitt was not insisting on office but
was merely asking to be consulted and treated with confidence.[1]
But Newcastle had since put himself entirely in the wrong by persuading Pitt to talk under a promise of secrecy and then reporting
the conversation to the King. He did not improve matters when
he attempted to justify himself by claiming that he had done so for
Pitt's benefit. Pitt had retorted indignantly: 'Fewer words, my
Lord, if you please, for your words have long lost all weight with

[1] Newcastle to Hardwicke, 17th Nov. Add. MSS. 35,414.

me.' To approach him now would be to court another stinging rebuff.

If he turned to Fox, it was obvious that his path would not be very much smoother, for Fox could hardly have forgotten or forgiven his chicanery of the previous March. But he thought Fox the more 'practicable' of the two, and incidentally the more pliable. The King did not dislike him, and he certainly had sufficient ability for the business. The real difficulty would be to persuade him to accept rather less than he had indignantly refused in March. None the less the effort had to be made.

Fox also had his problems. He might try to turn his present rather halting *rapprochement* towards Pitt into a firm alliance. Whether Pitt would respond was another matter; but, if he did, the two of them would be committed, as Waldegrave pointed out, 'to enter into all the violence of opposition, set the nation in a flame, and take the closet by storm.'[1] In any such process Pitt was bound to take the public eye and Fox fall into the background, while the results were not calculated to promote happiness in the Cabinet, or favour with the King. If, on the other hand, Fox threw in his lot with Newcastle, what substantial benefits could he expect in view of past history? Would they outweigh Pitt's resentment, which he would have to face alone, or at best with only the lukewarm and shifty backing of Newcastle? Pitt would have to be squared; it would need a great deal of finesse, and Fox might well have felt doubtful of the possibility.

If Newcastle and Fox had grounds for hesitation, so had Pitt. He had been thrown into some sort of union with Fox, certainly without his wishes, if not positively against them, and now Fox was likely to enter the Ministry. Pitt's future seemed to depend a good deal on the attitude which Fox might adopt. If he dropped Pitt altogether, he might, as Pitt owned, entrench himself very solidly in power, 'possessed as he is of the Duke [of Cumberland], pushed and supported by Lord Granville, reconciled with and assisted by Stone, favoured by Lady Yarmouth, and liked and trusted by the King.' Pitt might fulminate, but he felt that he would 'be left without a remedy,'[2] and that his only resource would be the odium on which he had banked in the previous March. However convinced he might be that Fox could not last, the outcome would be a gamble. The alternative was not much

---

[1] Waldegrave. *Memoirs*, p. 34.   [2] Chatham. *Correspondence*, I, 134.

more attractive. Fox might adopt Pitt's cause and demand satisfaction for him. Any such patronage would be humiliating in his
own eyes and in the eyes of the world: Pitt would thereby be
'reduced to a very inferior situation,' and worse still be 'entangled
inextricably by such an obligation not only for the present, but
in all appearance, for times to come.' What in the circumstances
was to be Pitt's attitude—to Fox, to Newcastle and to their
possible reconciliation?

All three, in short, were uneasy and largely bluffing. Their
methods were characteristic, and the outcome rather surprising.
Newcastle showed no little skill, as was to be expected from a
master of 'management.' He did not approach Fox directly, but
persuaded the King to have a talk with him first, in order to
prepare the ground. The King saw Fox on the 2nd of December,
mentioned no terms, but flattered him and asked him to support
the Government in the House. Then he handed the matter over to
Waldegrave whom he had very wisely chosen as the go-between
in this affair—a man who was above suspicion, a friend of Fox as
well as of Newcastle, with an insight into the characters of both
and the skill to play with tact upon their idiosyncrasies.

The negotiations were not easy because the problem was
difficult. Fox began with some hope of bouncing Newcastle into
giving him the leadership of the House, but Newcastle was not
prepared to give up Robinson entirely—to do so would be too
great a loss of face. Fox must be content with being the actual
but not the acknowledged leader; nominally he must serve under
Robinson; but what did that amount to? Just this, as Fox himself
admitted, that 'if there were a meeting of the Council, it would be
Robinson's paper and pens and his green table, and if both rose
to speak at the same time, Fox would give way.'[1] In return for a
promise of service Fox might be given some lucrative office—
say the Paymaster's job, from which Pitt could be dismissed.
That was an idea which must have appealed to Newcastle's
pettily scheming mind; it seemed to solve all problems so easily—
it would create a wide and unforgivable breach between the two
men; it would bind Fox to Newcastle, and it would effectively
muzzle Pitt. Fox, however, did not see the offer in quite the same
light; to have Pitt's office would suit his pocket, but not his
peace of mind; it would expose him to Pitt's undying wrath and
make his unacknowledged leadership of the House the merest

[1] Walpole. *Memoirs*, I, 420.

mockery. He was so obviously terrified at the idea, that the proposal was dropped forthwith—perhaps had never been very genuine—and a seat in the Cabinet Council substituted. Fox, making a virtue of necessity and with one eye on his future ease, promptly consulted Pitt, reporting the whole negotiation to him, including the offer of the Paymastership. 'What rascals they must be themselves,' he added, 'to think, as I believe they did, that I should not only accept, but be glad of it.'[1] He met Pitt privately on several occasions, and made a lot of play, for no very obvious reason, about the need for clandestine meetings.

Pitt welcomed the consultations, and not the less because they were secret. They gave him an opportunity of steering the negotiations in the direction he desired, while keeping him out of the picture. He had plenty of ground for hesitation; his own position was delicate enough and he had no wish to be finally compromised. Meanwhile there were many points to be borne in mind. Pitt was sure that Newcastle would drive as hard a bargain as possible, giving Fox the maximum amount of work with the minimum amount of recognition or power. So much the better from Pitt's point of view. But if the offer were too unattractive, Fox might easily reject it, especially if he thought Pitt would go into strong opposition. That would not suit Pitt's book; Fox must be made to accept, and consequently must somehow be satisfied on the point of opposition. How far could Pitt safely go to meet him? From another point of view Pitt as a newly married man, with all the expenses of a wife accustomed to luxury, had no desire to lose the emoluments of office and would not therefore resign of his own free will. Yet at the same time, looking to the future, he had no wish to enter into a binding alliance with Fox. To tread a safe middle course between giving too much and too little encouragement required all his finesse, but he seems to have been tolerably successful. Whilst making it plain that there could not and would not be any 'combination' between them, he managed to satisfy Fox that his neutrality would be sufficiently benevolent. In return for this concession, Fox promised to assist Pitt with the King and Newcastle, which should at least ensure his continuance in office. Having settled these preliminaries Pitt encouraged Fox, and helped him to draft his reply to the King. Pitt's amendments were aimed mostly at keeping himself out of the picture, and Fox accepted them a little reluctantly.

[1] Chatham. *Correspondence*, I, 125.

He wanted to make it absolutely clear that on no consideration would 'I venture on this weak scheme, unless strengthened by your acquiescence in it.'

The upshot was that Newcastle gained, or seemed to gain, all that he had aimed at. Fox accepted the duties of leadership without the office—a lesser position, in point of fact, than the one he had refused in March. At the same time Pitt seemed to have been isolated and gagged. Fox had not failed to let it be known that he was acting with Pitt's acquiescence—a fact which Hardwicke had already taken care to confirm: 'Could you bear to act *under* Fox,' he had asked, and to his great content Pitt had replied: 'My Lord, leave out *under*; it will never be a word between us; Mr. Fox and I shall never quarrel.'[1] What more could Newcastle want?

Fox was not so fortunate. He had obtained promotion to Cabinet rank, but it was an empty dignity. There was, as he complained to his friends, 'no pecuniary advantage,' only the satisfaction of taking what he was pleased to call the honourable course—an honour, like Lancelot's, rooted in dishonour, for he had no sooner obtained office than he 'privately forswore all connection with Pitt.'[2] For a very small mess of pottage he had sold his future prospects. 'By his admission to the Cabinet he had nominally a hand in the guidance of the ship of state. But as sole representative, for the moment, of the Cumberland Party, his voice could carry little weight. His new colleagues were either hostile, or were swayed by the tyranny of fear. His position in the House of Commons was ambiguous. Robinson, the man whom he laughed at and despised, was still his superior. He had no individual control and could be called on to support measures which he condemned.'[3] One last indignity can be added, his sole function now was to keep the post of leader warm for Pitt, the man whom he had privately disowned and imagined he had outwitted. Before long he was to confirm his mistake by losing even the appearance of friendship with Pitt, when he was to find himself standing alone, without position, without party, without policy, suspected and unpopular.

As for Pitt, he had no reason to feel disappointed. On the contrary he had won a resounding victory; he had achieved alone and in a few days all that the Cousinhood had failed to achieve

[1] Walpole. *Memoirs*, I, 418.   [2] Walpole. *Memoirs*, I, 420.
[3] Ilchester. *Henry Fox*, I, 239.

the previous March. Fox was now for practical purposes where Pitt wanted him to be, and in spite of a few natural anxieties on Pitt's part, was sinking in everyone's estimation, especially with Leicester House. Even Cumberland was a little shaken, and would have preferred him to cultivate Pitt. 'I don't know him,' he said, 'but, by what you tell me, Pitt is what is scarce, he is a man' —high praise of which Pitt was unaware. Best of all, Pitt had regained his reputation in the House; he had dominated an assembly of Newcastle's creatures still in the first flush of victory; he had routed Newcastle's chosen leader; he had cowed the one man able to meet him in debate; he had forced a reshuffle of the Cabinet and largely settled the promotion of Fox by agreeing not to oppose. Incidentally he had, by a sidewind, freed himself from the clog of the Cousinhood by breaking with Lyttelton. Beyond doubt he was the most outstanding figure in the House, and the obvious choice as Minister when the new reign began. He had every reason to be contented.

40

THE KING GOES TO HANOVER

By the middle of December Fox was a member of the Cabinet and pledged to support the Government in every way, even to the extent of answering Pitt if that should prove necessary. But Pitt gave him no trouble. However disingenuous he may have been in his advice, at least he kept his part of the bargain, and neither during the negotiations nor during the remainder of the session, which lasted till April 1755, did he make any serious attempt to harry Fox. Generally speaking, the part which he played was languid and intermittent; indeed, until the end of the year he spoke only once—on the Mutiny Bill—and then, if Walpole is to be believed, 'gently and not well.'[1]

When the House rose for the Christmas recess, he retired to Bath, leaving Hester behind in London. She stayed for a few days at the Pay Office, mostly in her 'blue dressing-room,' which seems to have been a favourite haunt, and then went to spend Christmas at West Wickham. The visit proved to be a sad one. Richard West, who in his parents' absence was her host, fell ill, grew worse and died of what Hester described as a 'bilious fever.' Meanwhile Pitt was busy at Bath recruiting his health and cheering his spirits by riding 'Poppet' over the hills, drinking the waters and speeding the building of his new house in the Circus: 'I am overwhelmed with affairs,' he wrote on the 29th of December, 'such as masons, carpenters, plaisterers, papermen etc.' The next day was not much better: 'I have lived today,' he wrote, 'in the Circus; buffeted and baited in my own arena by a N.E. wind; but able to resist. Architects, mechanicks, engineers etc. filled the place.' With such a crowd all round him, it is hardly surprising that progress was slow.

He returned about the middle of January (1755) invigorated in health, but still uninterested in politics. There was little enough to interest him, as Parliament was still occupied with election

[1] *Memoirs*, I, 421.

petitions. Only once during the remainder of the session was Pitt roused. The occasion was unpromising, but at least it was not a petition. In the turmoil following the '45, an Act had been passed under which the minor Scottish judges known as Sheriffs Depute were, for a period of seven years, to hold office during the King's pleasure instead of for life. The Act had nothing to commend it except as a precautionary measure after a rebellion, and even so was a trifle vindictive. But the lust for power is insatiable, and now that the Act was expiring and the Sheriffs Depute regaining their immunity, the Government proposed to renew the Act for a further period. Murray, whether he approved or not, felt in duty bound to support the Bill, and did so in a speech described by Walpole as 'extremely artful.' But all his skill and all his wealth of legal precedents could not conceal the fact that his sole argument was the housemaid's argument—the sin should be condoned because it was such a little one. His intervention brought up Pitt, who combined what Walpole called 'one of his best-worded and most spirited declamations for liberty' with a penetrating attack on Murray. He professed himself full of admiration for Murray's abilities, but full of contempt for the maze of distinctions and refinements in which he had displayed them. He dreaded such misuse of ability, for arbitrary power was more to be feared when dressed in the long robe than in military uniform. Definitions were dangerous when master principles were at stake; it was only too easy by excessive accuracy of distinction, by too great refinements, by too much classification, to analyse great general maxims into thin air and lose them in a cloud of detail. The Bill was a violation of liberty and was not made less so by calling the Sheriffs Depute Mr. Judge instead of My Lord Judge or by appealing to the practices of the bad old days. If he himself had to violate liberty, he would do it to support the reigning king; he would not look for his precedents in the diabolic divans of the second Charles and the second James. Not that he dated 'his principles of the liberty of this country from the Revolution: they were eternal rights, and when God said "let justice be justice," He made it independent.' But, as Walpole said, the speech 'like others of his fine orations cannot be delivered adequately without his own language,' not forgetting the conviction and grace with which it was uttered.[1] All that can be affirmed is that Pitt threw himself into the cause of a free and unfettered

[1] Walpole. *Memoirs*, II, 8.

T

judicature as being the surety for men's liberties—and perhaps he
was not the less in earnest because he was dealing with the
liberties of the Scots, for whom he had a particular sympathy.

Fox hedged; he would wait for the Committee stage and in the
meantime would merely say that he reverenced liberty, and Pitt
because he could speak better than anyone else on its behalf.
A few days later the Bill was quietly shelved after an airy speech
by Fox, which Pitt gravely rebuked. He could have wished that
Fox had omitted anything that savoured of levity in dealing with
a great question of principle. None the less he was glad that the
Ministry had shown moderation and the House zeal to strengthen
the King's hands. The admission by the Government that the
judicature should be free was a notable fact; for liberty was the
best loyalty, and the giving of extraordinary powers to the Crown
so many repeals of the Act of Settlement. So the session drew
towards its end with Pitt brooding over Parliament like a head-
master—aloof and awe-inspiring.

The House rose on the 25th of April (1755) and three days later
the impatient King left for Hanover. His going had a twofold
importance. For many months disquieting reports had been
coming from America, where there had been bickerings which
had grown into clashes not unlike pitched battles. They were in
fact the harbingers of the Seven Years War, and though at the
moment no one knew their exact significance, they created an
uneasy feeling that war was imminent, and war for most people
meant a war on the Continent. How could it be right or wise for
the King to visit Hanover at such a time? People thought, as
Walpole did, that 'the French armaments, the defenceless state of
the kingdom, the doubtful faith of the King of Prussia, and,
above all, the age of the King, and the youth of his heir at so
critical a conjuncture, everything pleaded against so rash a
journey.'[1] The feeling was so strong that Lord Poulett actually
moved in the House of Lords that an Address should be presented
to the King begging him not to visit his Electoral Dominions—
a motion which Lord Chesterfield, dismayed at the thought of
the 'absurd and improper things that would be said,' hastily
quashed by moving the adjournment of the House.[2]

The King had his way and went; but his going involved a
regency, and that at once roused all the latent antagonism
between Leicester House and the Duke of Cumberland. Whatever

[1] *Memoirs*, II, 20.   [2] Chesterfield. *Letters*, III, 1,123.

might be said against the appointment of the Duke in times of peace, no one felt inclined to ignore his claims in times of half-declared war. The Duke, strange as it may seem, was regarded generally as the great authority on military matters, and the one and only commander of British armies. If there was a war, the responsibility would fall on him, and it was unthinkable that he should have to wait on the orders of the Princess of Wales or alternatively be required to brush her on one side. A place, and a leading place, must therefore be assigned to him in the regency. And sure enough, he was left as head of the Council of Regency, and his adherent Fox was made one of the Councillors.

That was the first result of the King's determination to visit Hanover. The second result, springing out of the first, affected Pitt more directly. As already stated, when Fox entered the Cabinet he had privately forsworn all connection with Pitt, though he had studiously avoided any provocation. Whether Pitt was told of this defection or merely guessed it, he experienced a growing alienation, and when Fox was appointed to the Council of Regency the alienation took on a tinge of alarm. Fox was digging himself in too deeply, and whilst the King was abroad and Cumberland Regent must be regarded as little less than Prime Minister. That was disturbing enough, but what might happen in the event of the King's death abroad was even more disturbing because of its obscurity. To act now as Fox's ally was to accept a subordinate position; to owe anything to his favour, almost complete extinction. Policy no less than inclination drove Pitt on towards a break with Fox. The time had come to end their suspicious and half-hearted dalliance.

The decision to break was no doubt reached when Pitt heard of Fox's appointment to the Council of Regency, but the open rupture was delayed until the 9th of May, possibly because of vague feelers which Newcastle put out at about this time. Old Horace Walpole was sent to 'bring Mr. Pitt into temper,' and to hint that the Duke of Newcastle would do all in his power to serve him according to his wishes, if only he would respond and not show himself so inflexible. Pitt was a little tempted; he was still not altogether sure whether he wanted office at the moment, though his views on the point were altering, but he was certainly weary of the constant friction due to the King's animosity, which he regarded as inexplicable unless the result of

Newcastle's promptings. He was clear, therefore, that the preliminary to any negotiations must be a proof of Newcastle's sincerity, and that the proof should take the form of an end to his proscription and a promise that he should be given the seals of office as Secretary of State when a vacancy occurred; he did not ask, or expect, or perhaps wish that a vacancy should be created. His object, in short, was not office but recognition, not immediate promotion but reversionary rights. Old Horace agreed that his attitude and his demands were reasonable, but the budding promise of success was blighted when Newcastle, reacting typically, rejected Pitt's demands out of hand and blamed Walpole for exceeding his commission and discussing terms which Newcastle could not accept if he would, and would not accept if he could.[1]

[1] Dodington, p. 339.

41

STRAINING AT THE LEASH

There was nothing now left for Pitt to do but to cut himself adrift from Fox and wait on events. The break was made public on the 9th of May when the two were present at a social gathering in Lord Hillsborough's garden. Pitt, either deliberately or stirred by some sudden resentment, told Lord Hillsborough that all connection between himself and Fox was over; the ground was altered now that Fox was not only in the Cabinet but also on the Regency Council. Fox came up at that moment, and Pitt repeated his remarks, adding that even if Fox supported his claim to the post of Secretary, Pitt would not accept the seals at his hands, for that would be owning an obligation and admitting Fox's superiority; Pitt would be second to nobody and would owe nothing to anyone but himself. Fox, taken aback, asked what would put them on an equality, to which Pitt answered: 'a winter in the Cabinet and a summer's Regency'—or, in other words, nothing at all but a reversal of the past.[1]

Fox, who was obviously perturbed, made some unsuccessful attempts to placate Pitt, and at last 'early in the summer' Pitt put a final end to the matter during a formal visit to Holland House. He declared that there could be no further connection between them; time and circumstances forbad. He did not accuse Fox of having tried to rise above him; he did not even claim that they were moving on incompatible lines. If any epithet had to be used, they were on 'convergent lines' and might conceivably work together at some future date. At present Cumberland was King and Fox his Minister, and Pitt was not of their party and would owe nothing to them.[2]

The exact date of the visit is not known, though it was before the 2nd of June, when Fox referred to it in a letter to Ellis.[3] According to Walpole it took place the day after Pitt had had a

---

[1] Dodington, p. 320.   [2] Walpole. *Memoirs*, II, 37.
[3] Waldegrave. *Memoirs*, p. 157.

private audience with the Princess of Wales, and the world at large concluded that the break with Fox was the price paid for the Princess's favour. The world, however, was a little malicious and not altogether correct. There was in fact an understanding between Pitt and the Princess; there had been a meeting and it had proved mutually satisfactory; but the first move had come from the Princess, not from Pitt. As far back as the 27th of April, the day after the appointment of the Regency Council, Lord Bute, who was the Princess's favourite and was to exercise a baleful influence over public affairs in a few years time, wrote to a friend: 'Next session brings the Prince [the future George III] to age; I think 'tis likely a strong party will be formed that will set both Fox and the Cardinal [the Duke of Newcastle] at defiance, if Pitt can be induced to join, a point I have much at heart; the prospect will be pleasing, though I cannot say in the midst of such corruption my hopes can be ever sanguine.'[1]

Pitt had broken with Fox before the meeting with the Princess, and if on the following day he gave Fox the *coup de grâce*, that must not be considered as the price paid, but as a natural postscript. There were, in truth, other reasons besides his own personal fortunes which drove Pitt towards Leicester House. He did not approve Newcastle's handling of foreign affairs and the incipient war with France. He could not support the measures being taken; opposition was becoming more and more essential on the highest patriotic grounds; and the nucleus of opposition lay in Leicester House.

The course of events was rapid and followed well-worn lines. With war in the air and the King in Hanover, it was inevitable that the old round of subsidy treaties should recommence. George II began searching eagerly for allies who would defend the sacred Electorate when France and England actually came to blows. He was rebuffed by Maria Theresa and Frederick of Prussia, but had no difficulty in persuading Hesse Cassel and Russia to accept good English gold. When he sent the treaties back to England, Newcastle promised to get them ratified—they were after his own heart—but his mind misgave him. On all sides there were warnings that the treaties were unpopular. The need to bring them before Parliament emphasised the lack of powerful support on the Government benches. Who was to defend them? Who secure their ratification? Fox was unhappy,

[1] G. F. S. Elliot. *The Border Elliots*, p. 342.

Murray cowed, Robinson bewildered, and of the rest none were of sufficient weight or importance to stem the flood of Pitt's attack, if Pitt should prove antagonistic. Judging by the past, Pitt was bound to be antagonistic. It was only too likely that he would assail Newcastle in the same way and for the same reasons that he had assailed Carteret. Newcastle began to think that he must pocket his pride—if he had any—and approach Pitt once again. The fellow must be won over, and won over at no real cost to Newcastle—a little flattery, a few empty promises, and perhaps an imaginary easing of the King's dislike for him. It could be done, and it must be done; the only question was the appropriate agent. Old Horace Walpole had failed. What about young Charles Yorke, the Chancellor's second son? He had recently married and Pitt had written him a charming letter— full of felicitations and good wishes and the hope that Charles would find matrimony what Pitt himself had found it, the source of every comfort, and of every joy.[1] By all means Charles Yorke.

Yorke was at the time a promising young lawyer of thirty-three, and he readily undertook the commission. His instructions were to clear the ground for a meeting between Pitt and Newcastle. He should begin by talking of the Duke's sincere friendship for Pitt and unlimited confidence in him, and so by degrees work round to the terms which Pitt was likely to demand. If things seemed promising, the meeting should be arranged. Yorke worked it all out in his mind; he would start by referring to rumours which had come his way about the previous negotiations with Walpole, and so lead up naturally to his own mission. He saw Pitt on the 6th of July, between eleven and twelve at night, but did not get very far. Pitt brushed aside as humbug any talk of friendship and confidence; there was none between them now, whatever there might have been in the past. To talk in that strain was just waste of time. If the Duke really wanted Pitt's help, it must be on a business basis and not as a matter of senti-ment. He must state his proposals openly and clearly. What work did he want done? Who was to do it? What powers were they to have? If Newcastle cared to enlighten him on those three points, he would consult his friends and give Newcastle a considered answer. Until then, further discussion was useless.

Although Pitt's answer was so abrupt and apparently negative, it did indicate a new and positive attitude. It clearly presupposed

[1] Harris. *Hardwicke*, III, 24.

the possibility of Pitt undertaking the work, if given the necessary powers and position. The only position which would be effective was that of Secretary of State, and it must therefore be assumed that Pitt was now rapidly approaching, if he had not already reached, the point where he would delay no longer, but accept office if it was offered to him or he could force an entrance. No doubt he was influenced by two if not three factors. In the background there was the revived ambition to play a part worthy of his powers, but that was reinforced by fresh considerations. In the first place the understanding with Leicester House gave him reasonable assurance of promotion in the event of the King's death; and his immediate acceptance of the seals, if offered, could be, and perhaps had been, discussed there and agreed. In the second place events abroad were rushing to a climax, and Pitt was beginning to realise with increasing clearness the ineffectiveness of Newcastle's methods and how essential his own services were, if England was to emerge victorious from the coming war—the patriotic motive was at work. Lastly he need feel no scruples about Fox.

Whatever Pitt may have had in mind, Yorke's report could hardly have been called encouraging. But Newcastle's needs were great and his skin abnormally thick. He therefore chose to believe that it warranted him in taking further steps, and he proposed that Hardwicke should be the next to talk to Pitt; perhaps the father with his great experience and his silver tongue might succeed where the son had failed. By way of a sop, Newcastle would get authority from the King for the negotiations; that would look like the real thing. Accordingly Newcastle wrote to the King, assuring him that the only method of getting business done in the Commons was 'the engaging Mr. Pitt upon reasonable terms to support His Majesty's measures with clearness, firmness and cordiality.' The King agreed to accept Pitt's services, give him a seat in the Cabinet and 'countenance him,' whatever that might mean. Thus fortified, one of Newcastle's henchmen, with the intimidating name of Fury, wrote to invite Pitt to call on Hardwicke. Pitt, who was at Stowe with Hester, and had intended to proceed to Sunning Hill, posted up to London and on the 8th of August had a long session with Hardwicke at Powis House.

To begin with there was the usual polite sparring—Pitt could not treat an elder statesman of Hardwicke's standing quite so cavalierly as he had treated Yorke. They were both very much each other's humble servants; Pitt assured Hardwicke that he had a great regard for Newcastle, and Hardwicke assured Pitt that Newcastle had laboured to soften the King's resentments, had made some progress, and had high hopes for the future. But sooner or later they had to get down to business, when Hardwicke's finesse was brought into play, and the steel in Pitt's velvet glove began to appear.

Hardwicke hoped, but carefully avoided promising, that on a suitable opening they might procure for Pitt the seals which he so much desired. Pitt stiffened at once, and remarked coldly that he was not aware of the desire; did not remember having applied to Hardwicke for the seals and was quite sure he had never applied to Newcastle. So long as he laboured under the King's displeasure, the only use he would make of them would be to lay them at His Majesty's feet, and added—to Hardwicke's surprise but in keeping with his views up to the moment—that in the present circumstances he did not think the seals 'a desirable pillow to sleep upon.' All he had asked was the King's countenance and a public mark of favour and confidence towards himself and his friends, which would weigh far more with him than any change of office. So, if the Chancellor pleased, no more talk of the seals, and no more beating about the bush. It would be better to come to the point. What was expected of him? What was the work?

The Chancellor's answer was concise and clear; they wanted Pitt's support for the coming war both at sea and in America and for the defence of Hanover. Pitt became cautious, choosing his words carefully. The war, the national war, he would support heart and soul; as for Hanover he thought regard should be had to it, if it should be attacked on England's account. The Chancellor, hoping to take him off his balance, interrupted to express his great pleasure at finding that Pitt agreed with him in principle and thought Hanover should be defended. Pitt replied tartly that his Lordship should observe the exact word he had used, which was 'regard,' not 'defence'; and he then proceeded to develop his ideas on the subsidies, the cost of the war, and the impracticability of defending an open country like Hanover against powerful and hostile neighbours. What if it were invaded? If would become the quarters of French or Prussian troops for a season, but there was no danger of its final loss. It would be restored at the peace, which would be the appropriate time to compensate the King for any damage done to it. The Chancellor argued and Pitt replied, but all that Pitt would finally concede was that, if his friends approved, he would support the present Hessian treaty in order to save the King's face, but would have nothing to do with any further Hessian subsidy or the Russian treaty, which was extravagant and useless. In any event he must be guided by his friends. The Chancellor—a little amused—opined that Pitt's views were more likely to influence Pitt's friends than *vice versa*, and then, thinking the time opportune, suggested that as the hour was growing late and he himself was leaving town the next day, it might be as well if Pitt continued the conversation with Newcastle. Pitt saw no objection, if Newcastle cared to invite him, and Hardwicke, passing on the news, suggested that the formidable Fury should be employed once more.

Newcastle paused. It was uncomfortably plain, and Hardwicke was to make it still plainer, that negotiations were unlikely to succeed unless Newcastle was prepared to give Pitt much more power than he had intended. To give up any scrap of power was anathema to the Duke, and very possibly he would have let the matter drop if his fears had not been suddenly and sharply revived a week or two later. Towards the middle of August he presented the warrant for the Hessian subsidy to Legge for his signature as Chancellor of the Exchequer. To his consternation Legge flatly refused to have anything to do with it until the treaty had been presented to, and approved by, Parliament. This confirmation of his fears must have been a great shock and must have helped considerably in driving Newcastle to the meeting with Pitt which he obviously dreaded. It took place on the 2nd of September.

In the interval Pitt's views had hardened, possibly, as the Chancellor thought, because the news from America was depressing; perhaps because he was in closer touch and fuller agreement with Leicester House; perhaps, as some people suppose, because of Legge's refusal to sign the warrants. Whatever the reason, Pitt went to the meeting determined to demand the seals as the price of support, determined to reject all subsidies, determined to make the Duke's flesh creep by threats of open opposition.

He began, after the tedious preliminaries, by drawing a vivid picture of the disasters which must flow from a system of subsidies, and entreated the Duke not to complete the ruin which the King had begun by his ill-advised journey to Hanover—a journey which Newcastle should have allowed him to take only over his dead body—a journey at such a time and 'without one man about him that had an English heart'—a journey that had ended by his return with a pocket full of subsidy treaties!

The Duke tried to divert his attention by murmuring what a pretty figure Pitt would make as a Cabinet Councillor; what a pity it was that the King was so enamoured of Robinson and Holdernesse as his Secretaries of State; how greatly Newcastle hoped that some accident might create a vacancy, when no doubt the King would be glad of his services. Pitt brushed aside his protestations. Of course he would feel honoured if he were blessed with the King's countenance, but leaving aside the thoughts and wishes of the King, it was to be observed that Newcastle's system of running the House was impossible. There must be men of efficiency and authority to lead the Commons— at the very least a Secretary of State and a Chancellor of the Exchequer; and in order that they might carry out their duties, they must have habitual, frequent, familiar access to the King; they must be able to tell their own story and do themselves and their friends justice in the King's Closet, and not be at the mercy of Newcastle's whispering campaigns; they must have the right to advise and the power to carry out the decisions. As for Holdernesse and Robinson they were estimable men, but presumably they lacked some quality, or why had Pitt been sent for? If they could carry on the Government, let them do it; he asked nothing of them, if they asked nothing of him.

Foiled in one direction, Newcastle tried another. He turned to the subsidies. Of course he understood Pitt's dislike for a system of subsidies, but he was not pressing for a system. He only wanted two, and really no one could call two a system. Besides, the King's honour was engaged.

Pitt would have none of it; there was no difference in principle between two and two-and-twenty; and what about the other treaties which had been begun but not completed? He would agree to none, or at most one—the Hessian—and that only if it was openly admitted to be given as a mark of the affection of a ruined nation to save the honour of the King, who had entered into a rash engagement. It would really be better for everyone if the King would pay Hesse and Russia a handsome consideration out of his own private pocket to be freed from the obligations of the treaties; the King could very well afford it, considering the amount he had saved out of his Civil List. If, however, Newcastle insisted on pushing the treaties, he had better understand that the Duke of Devonshire would certainly oppose in the Lords, and Pitt would follow suit in the Commons 'as loudly and with all the powers he was able to exert.'

Newcastle was at the end of his tether; all he could do was to beg Pitt to talk it over once more with the Chancellor. It was a counsel of despair; none the less Hardwicke, who really wanted to win Pitt, did have a further meeting, without a vestige of success. Apart from the question of office, Pitt would not support the subsidies, nor would he work with Fox.

Realising that he was now committed to opposition, Pitt spent a few days collecting his forces, and then went to Bath to recruit his health and stir up the masons and architects still pursuing their leisurely course in the Circus. But he could not cease from his political labours; the times were much too serious. He was so fully occupied that one day he failed to write to Hester. The result was that her next letter had 'a certain air, as if her dear mind was overcast with discontent,' and though Pitt was charmed and touched with these marks of her sensibility and love, he entreated his sweetly unreasonable, adorable wife to tell herself the truth she knew as well as he did, that business of various kinds, of which he could not be master, must and would command his time. His excuses, for all their stilted language, had a fragrance and delicacy about them which Hester must have found abundantly consoling.[1]

Included in the business of various kinds was the news which Potter brought from London. About the time that Pitt went down to Bath, the middle of September, the King returned from Hanover. Rumour had it that he was at once told of Pitt's attitude towards the treaties, towards Fox, towards the Duke of Cumberland. The King, according to the same rumours, received the news with stolid indifference. He knew the treaties were not only right, but popular; if he had had any doubts they would have been dispelled by the acclamations of the people on his return. The defection of Pitt and five or six others could not upset so popular a measure, and the House would certainly approve. Putting various rumours together, Potter was sure that Fox would be approached to accept the full leadership of the House, and in his turn would try to obtain the support of the Bedford faction. Potter had therefore posted down to Woburn and was proud to be

[1] Pitt to Hester, Sat. 27th Sept. 1755.

able to report that he had won over Bedford, who had promised enthusiastic and wholehearted support for Pitt as 'the only man who had virtue and abilities enough to retrieve the affairs of this country.' Here was support indeed; the Opposition was growing formidable in numbers as well as talent.[1] Potter arrived in Bath with this news on the 29th of September, and he remained there with Pitt till the 6th of October, when both returned to London.

[1] Potter to Grenville. Grenville. *Correspondence*, I, 139.

42

INDEPENDENCE

The news which Potter brought was founded on fact. The King was never very perspicacious or wise where Hanover was concerned, and was still less so when war was in the offing. Besides, he had been frightened. The continental system of alliances was in a state of flux, and he had been inexplicably rebuffed by Austria and Prussia. With his two main props gone, he had toiled anxiously through the summer to ensure the safety of his Electorate, and at the end had succeeded in obtaining only two allies. The treaties with them must go through and any appointments necessary for the purpose must be made.

Newcastle had realised from the beginning that, popular or unpopular, he must get the treaties accepted. It was upon that point rather than on the question of the seals that the negotiations with Pitt had ultimately foundered. For while Newcastle loathed sharing his power and in any event would have held back as long as he could, he would probably have yielded in the end if in return he had obtained something of vital importance—not necessarily for the country, but at least for Newcastle himself. The treaties were that something of vital importance, not only because Newcastle believed in them wholeheartedly as the highest manifestation of a wise foreign policy, but also because their rejection meant the dismissal and eclipse of Newcastle. Pitt, in fact, had been two degrees removed from the seals; first, and less important, because of Newcastle's jealousy; and secondly and irretrievably because of Pitt's attitude towards the subsidies.

The failure of the talks with Pitt and the approaching return of the King made it essential for some other plan to be tried. Newcastle wrote plaintively, and quite insincerely, to Hardwicke asking whether he had not better retire in favour of Fox or Pitt. Of course he had no intention of retiring; what he was really doing was to mark time while he wondered how much power he would have to give to Fox, and whether he could bring himself to do it. He and Hardwicke were sure that Fox would make no trouble over the treaties; indeed, in the middle of August, Granville, with whom Fox was closely associated, had hinted as much, though possibly without authority. At the time, as the negotiations with Pitt were still on foot, Newcastle had listened without interest. Now he recalled the conversation, and began turning over in his own peculiar way the pros and cons of acquiring Fox. There was a respectable list of 'pros.' Fox was an able man, he was not to be browbeaten and he was a 'sticker.' His conduct during the last few months both in the Cabinet and at the Regency Council had been highly satisfactory and obliging to Newcastle. Lastly his influence with Cumberland might moderate the dislike which Cumberland and his party were supposed to feel for the subsidies. The greatest 'con' was of course the power and position which Fox was bound to demand and would have to be given. With the return of the King, Newcastle hesitated no longer. He authorised Granville to open negotiations.

If we are to believe his private letters, Fox was personally opposed to the subsidies; he saw no end to the expense and no end to the difficulties they would create at home and abroad. Obviously therefore he should have followed Pitt's example. But he was not a man to be swayed by principle when it clashed with his own interests. He found no difficulty in responding to Newcastle's approach and the two met for a long discussion on the 20th of September. Two days later, at a meeting with the King, Fox stated unblushingly that he was in favour of the treaties and would support them unwaveringly whether he were in office or out of it. If he was to be in office, it must be as Secretary of State; otherwise he would support the treaties from the Opposition benches but at the same time attack the Minister. Two days later the bargain had been struck; Fox was to be Secretary of State and Leader of the House. Robinson was to make way for him, retiring once more to the Great Wardrobe with a handsome pension for his services.

What was the immediate upshot? The King was assured of his treaties and Newcastle had been saved, for it was universally agreed that if Fox had joined the Opposition Newcastle could not have survived and the treaties would probably have been lost. As for Fox, he thought he had gained his heart's desire by means of his own diplomacy, and though he was a little scared, he was on the whole pleased with himself and his position. There were others, however, including the King, who were doubtful if he was really fitted for the post, or could last. His future was dark and uncertain, and it may well be that a sardonic smile played round Pitt's lips when he heard the news; for, after all, Fox was now exactly where not so long ago Pitt had wanted him to be— the Leader of the House, to be sure, but not very popular with the King, slightly at variance with Cumberland, disliked by Newcastle and Hardwicke and distrusted by the rank and file—an excellent stop-gap till the next reign if Pitt should be unable to oust him at an earlier date. Pitt, on his part, now knew exactly where he stood. He had broken with Fox, with Newcastle, with the Government, and though he remained in office as Paymaster for the time being, he must expect to be dismissed in the near future. In short, he was Leader of the Opposition, standing well with Leicester House and both anxious and willing to bring down the Ministry and take office himself as soon as possible.

Parliament was due to meet on the 13th of November. Fox spent the interval rallying his forces, confirming waverers and gaining recruits. His energy and push, combined with his unscrupulous methods, won a large measure of success. He even managed to badger the unstable Duke of Bedford into retracting his assurance to Potter and promising instead to support the treaties, and of course had no difficulty thereafter in winning over the Duke's followers, who were hungry for the sweets of office. Between them, they made a notable reinforcement for Newcastle's nonentities, and a woeful gap in the ranks of Opposition.

Pitt no doubt was also busy with his preparations, but was much distracted by family affairs. He was always a devoted husband and father, ready to find time for the duties and enjoyments of home life, and in this interval home made serious demands on him. On the 19th of October (1755) Hester gave birth to their first child, a daughter whom, for the confusion of posterity, they named Hester after her mother.[1] The anxieties of the confinement and especially the labour, which was long and hard, must have absorbed overmuch of his thought, and his subsequent delight in his 'little blue-eyed maid' must have proved a continual distraction. That he was otherwise busy collecting shot and shell is probable, as a little later in the year Joe Wright, a parliamentary official, told Rigby, who in turn warned Bedford, that Temple and Pitt lived in the Parliament office, demanding

[1] Climenson, II, 82.

fires to be lighted for them—at the public expense—and studying all manner of treaties for three and four hours at a time,[1] an interesting side-light on the minute attention to detail which Pitt displayed whenever he was in earnest.

Battle was joined directly the House met. The King's Speech roamed over the world, touching on the need to protect America, the defence of the West Indies, the encouragement of the colonies, the equipment of fleets, the sullenness of France, the pacific disposition of Spain. Only Hanover and the treaties were tucked unobtrusively away.

There had been some difficulty in finding anyone willing to move the Address, but Lord Hillsborough had been persuaded at the last moment. He arrived too late to hear the actual Speech, and as he had not taken the precaution of studying it beforehand, created some confusion in the ministerial ranks by emphasising, instead of veiling, the real object of the treaties. They were, he said, merely for the protection of Hanover; they must not be taken as portending a continental war; had there been any such idea, the Government would have presented the House with a far more comprehensive system of treaties. France was clearly bent on mischief, and would not only attack England but also invade Hanover; here, our safety was concerned; there, our honour; and it was to the King's credit that he had incurred great expense and made successful arrangements for the defence of Hanover, though the quarrel in which the Electorate found herself was England's and not her own.

After this indiscreet opening, the debate continued till five o'clock the next morning. The speakers were many and varied— some good, some bad—but by common consent Pitt was by far the most brilliant. He rose at about one o'clock in the morning, and his speech lasted for over an hour and a half. Its splendour has long since vanished. All that remains are bare bones, not even laid out in order, and the record of the confused emotions stirred in Walpole's breast. Pitt, according to that dazzled spectator, was 'haughty, defiant, and conscious of injuries and supreme abilities'; he 'surpassed Cicero and Demosthenes'; 'he was not abusive, yet very attacking on all sides; he ridiculed my Lord Hillsborough, crushed poor Sir George [Lyttelton], terrified the Attorney [Murray], lashed my Lord Granville, painted my Lord of Newcastle, attacked Mr. Fox, and even hinted up to the

---

[1] Bedford. *Correspondence*, II, 176.

U

Duke [of Cumberland].' As for the speech itself, 'there was more humour, wit, vivacity, finer language, more boldness, in short, more astonishing perfections than even you, who are used to him, can conceive.'[1] All his many and varied accounts have one thing in common; all of them refer in some form or another to Pitt's 'manly vivacity and dashing eloquence,'[2] the eloquence which 'like a torrent long obstructed, burst forth with more commanding impetuosity.'[3] For us of this century, the splendid loftiness and flashing spirit are reduced to one or two similes, one or two metaphors—and apart from that nothing but a heap of bare bones. What can we make of the brilliance? Little beyond two flights of fancy—one reminiscent of the Psalms when Pitt described Granville's abortive Ministry of 1746 (see p. 149): 'I saw that Ministry; in the morning it flourished; it was green at noon; by night it was cut down and forgotten'; and another when he compared the alliance of Fox and Newcastle to the junction of the Rhone and the Saône, 'the latter a gentle, feeble, languid stream, languid but not deep; the other a boisterous and overbearing torrent; but they join at last; and long may they continue united, to the comfort of each other, and to the glory, honour and happiness of this nation!'—a clear picture, perhaps great oratory, but too short to be of the highest excellence. The splendour must be conceded on hearsay evidence alone, but the content can be recovered in part from brief and scattered résumés which we must piece together as best we can.

In a sense the speech contained nothing new. It presented the policy which Pitt had always urged, and it followed a more or less familiar pattern. Where Pitt showed his skill was the way in which he seized upon the topics of the day to enforce the immutable principles which he was preaching. The previous winter he had founded his defence of Parliament's dignity on Delaval's ribaldries, and had then swept on with a fine show of logic to the evil influence of one too powerful subject. The argument hung together, each part lending weight to the whole. But if he could soar to the height of his argument from the depths of mere ribaldry, he could equally well descend like a thunderbolt from high majesty. On this occasion the King's name had been invoked to puzzle and overawe the Commons and coerce them into adopting what Pitt regarded as an un-British policy. In Pitt's

---

[1] To Conway, 15th November 1755.   [2] To Bentley, 16th Nov. 1755.
[3] *Memoirs*, II, 55.

eyes, indifference to England's need and England's honour would destroy their dignity in 1755 as completely as indifference to corruption in 1754, and subservience to the King would prove as damaging to their freedom as subservience to Newcastle. There had been altogether too much use made of the sacred name of the King. Hillsborough had made great play with the King's open-handedness and successful diplomacy. Murray had gone much farther, using all his forensic skill to draw a pathetic picture of the old King—so meritorious, so deserving of tranquillity in the evening of his life—and so resolute not to spare himself if by any means he could lift a burden from the shoulders of his successor. How hard on such a King, if the Commons abandoned the defence of his Electorate and sowed his pillow with thorns.

Pitt noted this subtle undermining of the Commons' freedom of choice, but he also noted that it cut two ways; if it placed the House in a quandary, it also exposed the King to the reproaches of the people; it loaded on to his shoulders all the odium of an unpopular measure. So, with artful eloquence, he made play at one time or another with all the facets of this subject—his solicitude at the use of the King's name so often and so unparliamentarily; the cruelty and illogicality involved—other treaties had been rejected without disgracing the King, but now he was to bear the brunt either way, disgrace if the treaties were rejected, and if they were accepted the curses of his bankrupt people. If the King were to be pitied, it was not for loss of tranquillity but because his Ministers had left him all the summer deprived of honest counsel, surrounded by panic-stricken Hanoverians and with no advocate near him to speak for England. How easy for him in such circumstances to forget that the King is not his own master but owes a supreme service to his people.

From the King he passed smoothly to the King's Ministers. After all, he, too, had received offers from the King, and he was particularly grateful for 'late condescending goodness and gracious openings'—an obscure phrase too obviously intended to suggest greater offers than Pitt had in fact received, though not perhaps greater than he could have extorted if he had been prepared to play the same part as Fox—but he had put them on one side, and he felt as yet no sensation other than gratitude to the King, unless it be pity for Fox, a tempestuous, boisterous spirit, who had taken up what he (Pitt) had rejected, and now

U*

found himself yoked unequally with the languid and ineffectual Newcastle.

Banter of the Ministers led naturally to their policies, which were dominated or clogged by Hanover according to one's point of view. The defenders of the treaties had not overlooked the British Navy; they were solicitous for it, so solicitous that they actually asked Parliament to regard the German mercenaries as a reserve in case our navy should be defeated. What an argument! What folly! If that were the real reason for the treaties, how much more sensible to follow past precedent and bargain with Scandinavia for fleets instead of with Russia for troops. But, of course, ships could not be applied to Hanover, and so common sense and the natural system of Europe were flung to the winds. The very purpose of the war looming on the horizon was in danger of being forgotten. It was undertaken for 'the long-injured, long-neglected, long-forgotten people of America.' Hanover had no lot or part in it. The Act of Limitation had excepted her as an ally, not out of prejudice but because of the logic of geography—and that disposed of any claim in justice for our assistance. There still remained the argument from gratitude. Indeed we ought to help her out of gratitude if she had done anything to draw down upon herself the resentments of France. But had she done anything? And could we really help? Even Grotius and the Law of Nations admitted that there was no need to rush to the defence of an ally where there was no hope of success. These incoherent, un-British measures were being adopted in place of our proper force— our navy; and the result would be the same as before—a general war in Europe, followed by a bad peace.

Fox, in the small hours of the morning, after a long and exhausting debate, was not unnaturally 'tired and unanimated' when he rose to reply to Pitt. He spoke shortly, and then the debate fizzled out. The voting, however, either deliberately or by chance, was manipulated in favour of the Government. There were two amendments to the Address—one for including the reference to Hanover and the other for omitting the reference to the treaties. The former was put first. Pitt and his adherents, though opposed to it, had no intention of forcing a division, as they preferred to reserve all their strength for the second question, on which they were likely to receive greater support. The Speaker, however, forced a division by the simple expedient of declaring that the 'noes' had it. The amendment was lost by 105 to

311, and Members began trooping out of the House. The crucial amendment dealing with the treaties was consequently lost by 89 to 290, though no one imagined that these figures gave a true picture of the numbers dissenting from the treaties.

But facts are facts—stubborn and inescapable. Fox had done all that was required of him, and he duly received his reward. On the 15th of November he was given the seals, and five days later, on the 20th of November 1755, as Walpole records briefly and baldly, 'Lord Holdernesse wrote to Mr. Pitt, Mr. Legge, and George Grenville, that his Majesty had no further occasion for their services.'[1]

Financially, loss of office was a serious blow to Pitt, newly married and with a family starting. The blow was somewhat softened by Temple, who with great promptitude and greater generosity offered Pitt, through Hester, an income of £1,000 a year, 'till better times.' Temple is not a sympathetic nor perhaps a very admirable character, and it is therefore only just to record that he made this handsome offer in a letter of exceptional delicacy.[2] Hester and Pitt accepted with gratitude, but it is to be feared that the gift merely tended to confirm Pitt in his habitual extravagance. When the Commons rose for the Christmas recess Pitt hurried down to Bath, partly no doubt for his health, but also to press on with the building of his house in the Circus— 'a fine house of nine windows.'[3] 'My presence here,' he assured Hester, 'is necessary in order to quicken the workmen to fit it for habitation in the spring.'[4] At the same time he was negotiating for a house in London to which he could remove from his official quarters at the Pay Office. He had heard of two which would suit so far as locality was concerned—one in Upper Brook Street and one in South Audley Street, and he wanted Hester to inspect them. Two houses in expensive neighbourhoods—one in Town and one at Bath—for a man whose income had been cut by about seventy-five per cent.!

Politically, loss of office was an undiluted blessing. Pitt was now free, his tutelage over, his apprenticeship done. He was forty-seven years of age, at the peak of his powers and abilities, mature and experienced. Pelham's death had released him from loyalty to a leader; Newcastle's trickery from the obligations of gratitude. His marriage had revived his ambitions and given him

---

[1] *Memoirs*, II, 62. [2] Grenville. *Correspondence*, I, 149.
[3] Kielmansegge's *Diary*, p. 131. [4] To Hester, 28th December 1755.

the serenity of mind which can move mountains, and the occasion which was to give him his opportunity was even then speeding across the Atlantic. He was no longer a frustrated politician striving for mastery, but the great War Minister standing at the threshold of his fame and knocking thunderously for admittance.

Bibliography

Additional MSS.	*Newcastle and Hardwicke Papers* in the British Museum.
Almon, John	*Anecdotes of the Life of William Pitt.* 3 Vols. 3rd edition, 1793.
Barrow, Sir John	*Life of George, Lord Anson.* 1839.
Bedford	*Correspondence of John, Fourth Duke of Bedford.* 3 Vols. 1842-6.
Carlisle	*Historical Manuscripts Commission.* 15th Report, Appendix VI. MSS. of the Earls of Carlisle, 1200-1820.
Charteris, Hon. Evan	*William Augustus, Duke of Cumberland. His Early Life and Times (1721-1748).* 1913.
Chatham	*Correspondence of William Pitt.* Edited by W. S. Taylor and J. H. Pringle. 4 Vols. 1840. *Speeches, The Modern Orator.* 1848.
Chatham Papers	MSS. in the Record Office.
Chesterfield	*Lord Chesterfield's Letters.* Edited by J. Bradshaw. 3 Vols. 1926.
Climenson, E. J.	*Elizabeth Montagu.* 2 Vols. 1906.
Coxe, William	*Memoirs of the Pelham Administration.* 2 Vols. 1829. *Memoirs of Lord Walpole.* 2 Vols. 2nd Edition. 1808. *Memoirs of Sir Robert Walpole.* 4 Vols. New Edition. 1816.
Dalton, Sir C. N.	*The Life of Thomas Pitt.* 1915.
Dodington, B.	*The Diary of the late George Bubb Dodington.* 1784.
Egmont, Lord	*Historical Manuscripts Commission. Diary of the 1st Earl of Egmont.* 3 Vols.
Elliot, G. F. S.	*The Border Elliots.* 1897.
Fielding, Henry	*A Clear State of the Case of Elizabeth Canning.* 1753. (2nd edition.)
Fitzmaurice, Lord	*The Life of William, Earl of Shelburne.* 2 Vols. 1875.
Fortescue	*Historical Manuscripts Commission.* 13th Report, Appendix III. MSS. of J. B. Fortescue, Esq., preserved at Dropmore.
Gentleman's Magazine	
Godley, A. D.	*Oxford in the Eighteenth Century.* 1908.
Grenville	*The Grenville Papers.* Edited by W. J. Smith. 4 Vols. 1852.

Hannay, David	*A Short History of the Royal Navy.* 2 Vols. 1909.
Hartshorne, Albert	*Memoirs of a Royal Chaplain, 1729-1763.* 1905.
Harris, George	*Life of Lord Chancellor Hardwicke.* 3 Vols. 1847.
Hastings	*Historical Manuscripts Commission.* Series 78. MSS. of Mr. Reginald Rawdon Hastings.
Hervey, Lady	*Letters of Mary Lepel, Lady Hervey.* 1821.
Ilchester, Earl of	*Henry Fox, First Lord Holland.* 2 Vols. 1920.
Kielmansegge, Count Frederick	*Diary of a Journey to England, 1761-2.* Translated by Countess Kielmansegge.
Lodge, Sir R.	*Studies in Eighteenth Century Diplomacy.* 1930.
Macaulay, Lord	*Historical Essays. William Pitt, Earl of Chatham.*
Malmesbury, Earl of	*Letters of the First Earl of Malmesbury.* 2 Vols. 1870.
Marchmont	A Selection from the Papers of the Earls of Marchmont in the possession of the Rt. Hon. Sir George Henry Rose. 3 Vols. 1831.
Northumberland, Elizabeth, Duchess of	*The Diaries of a Duchess.* Edited by James Greig. 1926.
Phillimore, Robert	*Memoirs and Correspondence of George, Lord Lyttelton.* 2 Vols. 1845.
Riker, T. W.	*Henry Fox, First Lord Holland.* 2 Vols. 1911.
Robertson, Sir C. Grant	*England Under the Hanoverians.* 2nd Edition. 1912.
Robson, R. J.	*The Oxfordshire Election of 1754.* 1949.
Rosebery, Lord	*Chatham, His Early Life and Connections.* 1910.
Ruville, A. von	*William Pitt, Earl of Chatham.* Translated by H. J. Chaytor and Mary Morrison. 3 Vols. 1907.
Suffolk, Lady	*Letters.* 2 Vols. 1824.
Treasury	*Calendar of Treasury Books and Papers, 1742-5.* 1903.
Trevor	*Historical Manuscripts Commission.* 14th Report; Appendix IX. MSS. of the Earls of Buckinghamshire and others.
Uffenbach, von	*London in 1710.* From the Travels of Zacharias Conrad von Uffenbach. Translated and edited by W. H. Quarrell and Margaret Mare. 1934.
Waldegrave, James, Earl	*Memoirs from 1754 to 1758.* 1821.
Walpole, Horace	*Letters.* *Memoirs of the Reign of George II.* 3 Vols. 2nd Edition. 1847.

Williams, Basil   *The Life of William Pitt, Earl of Chatham.*
2 Vols. 1913.

Wyndham, Maud   *Chronicles of the Eighteenth Century.* 2 Vols.
1924.

Yorke, P. C.   *Life of Lord Chancellor Hardwicke.* 3 Vols. 1913.

Index

315

DATE DUE

APR 1 5 '66			
OCT 9 1967			
MAR 1 1969			
GAYLORD			PRINTED IN U.S.A.